Evidence

The Use and Misuse of Data

Evidence

The Use and Misuse of Data

Robert M. Hauser and Adrianna Link
Editors

American Philosophical Society Press
Philadelphia

Transactions of the
American Philosophical Society
Held at Philadelphia
for Promoting Useful Knowledge
Volume 112, Part 3

ISBN: 978-1-6-618-123-2

ebook ISBN: 978-1-60618-128-7

U.S. ISSN: 0065-9746

Library of Congress Cataloging-in-Publication Data

Names: Evidence: The Use and Misuse of Data (Symposium) (2020 : American
    Philosophical Society ; Online), author. | Hauser, Robert Mason, editor. | Link,
    Adrianna, editor.
Title: Evidence : the use and misuse of data / Robert M. Hauser, Adrianna Link,
    editors.
Description: Philadelphia : American Philosophical Society Press, 2023. | Series:
    Transactions of the American Philosophical Society, 0065-9746 ; Volume 112,
    Part 3 | "Evidence: The Use and Misuse of Data, the APS symposium took
    place as scheduled, via Zoom, on June 5, 2020." | Includes bibliographical
    references and index. | Summary: "This book contains essays presented at a
    symposium on evidence and data presented by the America Philosophical
    Society. The essays discuss the role of evidence in interpreting anthropological
    fieldwork; human psychology; the mechanisms of artificial intelligence; and
    claims about the past. The natural sciences, social sciences and the
    humanities are all represented"—Provided by publisher.
Identifiers: LCCN 2023016652 (print) | LCCN 2023016653 (ebook) | ISBN
    9781606181232 (paperback) | ISBN 9781606181287 (mobi)
Subjects: LCSH: Evidence—Congresses. | Research—Moral and ethical aspects—
    Congresses. | Knowledge, Theory of—Congresses.
Classification: LCC BC173 .E97 2023 (print) | LCC BC173 (ebook) | DDC 121/
    .65—dc23/eng/20230510
LC record available at https://lccn.loc.gov/2023016652
LC ebook record available at https://lccn.loc.gov/2023016653

Cover design by Eugenia B. González.

Contents

Contributors

Nicholas Barron, PhD
Assistant Professor-in-Residence
Department of Anthropology
University of Nevada, Las Vegas

Gordon Fraser, PhD
Lecturer in American Studies
University of Manchester
Manchester, United Kingdom

Linda Greenhouse, MSL
Senior Research Scholar in Law
Yale Law School
New Haven, Connecticut
Immediate Past President
American Philosophical Society
Philadelphia, Pennsylvania

Lindsey Grubbs, PhD
Assistant Professor
Department of Bioethics
School of Medicine
Case Western Reserve University
Cleveland, Ohio

Robert M. Hauser, PhD
Executive Officer
American Philosophical Society
Philadelphia, Pennsylvania

Kathleen Hall Jamieson, PhD
Former Chair, Faculty Senate
Elizabeth Ware Packard Professor of Communication
Director, Annenberg Public Policy Center
University of Pennsylvania
Philadelphia, Pennsylvania

Jennifer Burek Pierce, PhD
Professor
School of Library and Information Science
University of Iowa
Iowa City, Iowa

Angela G. Ray, PhD
Associate Professor, Communication Studies
Associate Dean for Graduate Education
School of Communication
Northwestern University
Evanston, Illinois

Jutta Schickore, PhD
Ruth N. Halls Professor
Department of History and Philosophy of Science and Medicine
Indiana University Bloomington
Bloomington, Indiana

Andrew M. Schocket, PhD
Professor of History and American Culture Studies
Department of History
Bowling Green State University
Bowling Green, Ohio

Richard Shiffrin, PhD
Distinguished Professor
Department of Psychological and Brain Sciences
Indiana University Bloomington
Bloomington, Indiana

Joshua Sternfeld, PhD
Independent Scholar

Stephen M. Stigler, PhD
Ernest DeWitt Burton Distinguished Service Professor
Department of Statistics
University of Chicago
Chicago, Illinois

Mark Turin, PhD
Associate Professor
Institute for Critical Indigenous Studies
Department of Anthropology
The University of British Columbia
Vancouver, Canada

Introduction: Data, Knowledge, and the Space Between

Linda Greenhouse

In October 2019, the American Philosophical Society put out a call for papers for a daylong symposium exploring the nature of evidence. The symposium was to be a scholarly companion to "Dr. Franklin, Citizen Scientist," an exhibit scheduled to open shortly in the Society's Museum.

It goes without saying that no one could have imagined that a pandemic of historic dimension would soon leave APS buildings shuttered, the exhibit postponed, and Americans unable to gather in person in anything approaching substantial numbers.

At the same time, it bears saying that no one could have foreseen how relevant a symposium on the nature of evidence would prove to be as the country struggled to understand basic facts about the transmission of COVID-19. Was it safe to pick up a newspaper from one's doorstep or to open a recently delivered package? Did supermarket produce need to be not just rinsed but chemically disinfected? Fear rather than evidence drove public behavior during those early weeks of near total national lockdown. As the evidence mounted that the real danger came via airborne transmission in enclosed spaces, some members of the public did as experts advised and wore masks. Others did not, thus becoming subjects of a natural experiment that proved the experts correct.

Under the title "Evidence: The Use and Misuse of Data," the APS symposium took place as scheduled, via Zoom, during the week of June 5, 2020. It drew 1,500 viewers. As the eleven symposium papers collected here demonstrate, participants responded with liberal interpretations of the invitation tendered by Adrianna Link, head of scholarly programs, and Kyle Roberts, associate director of Library and Museum programing. The essays discuss the role of evidence in interpreting anthropological fieldwork, human psychology, the mechanisms of artificial intelligence, and claims

1

about the past. The natural sciences, social sciences, and the humanities are all represented.

In "Peculiar Blue Spots," Jutta Schickore unearths a mystery that confounded dairy farmers, government officials, and scientists for a century beginning in the 1770s: what was causing fresh milk to develop blue spots and eventually to turn completely blue? Was it something in the soil? Something the cows ate? The way milk was stored? Miasmic vapors? Even— in desperation—witchcraft? Study after study turned up empty, year after year. Even when the microscope finally brought a possible culprit into view, how could researchers tell whether this previously unknown entity was the cause of the milk's problem or simply another effect?

Schickore uses this fascinating tale to make a larger point: "by themselves, data, records, observations, and experimental results are not evidence for anything. Evidence requires a point of view as its complement—a conjecture about what to look for, whereby that conjecture structures the quest for the cause and the collection of data." Other symposium authors make a similar point. In "Isaac Ray and the Case: Narrative, Data, and Early Psychiatric Method," on the history and use of the medical case study, Lindsey Grubbs observes: "Data is the premise for argumentation—data points are not up for debate, they are for debating *with*" (emphasis in original).

And evidence neither interprets itself nor communicates itself. "Evaluating Evidence Requires Expert Judgment" is the title of the paper by Richard Shiffrin, Stephen M. Stigler, and Kathleen Hall Jamieson that opened the symposium. "Evidence is not a 'thing' or an 'object,'" they write, "but rather the beginning of a process of evaluation and interpretation, a process that is often difficult and laden with opportunities for error, and a process that requires human expertise to achieve an optimal result." Human fallibility makes all knowledge provisional; they emphasize: "there is never a single uncontestable conclusion, but rather a multitude of possibilities graded in likelihood and subject to revision." But the response to this realization need not be despair, the authors suggest, but rather a renewed commitment to norms of transparency and critique, to forging and communicating consensus.

The breadth and depth of the contributions to the symposium fulfill the hopes of its conveners for a companion to the APS Museum's "Dr. Franklin, Citizen Scientist" exhibit. Franklin founded the American Philosophical Society in 1743 for the purpose, he wrote, of "promoting useful knowledge." In her catalogue essay, the exhibit's curator, Janine Yorimoto Boldt, explains that the exhibit aims to "shed light on the production, circulation, application, and accessibility of what eighteenth-century Atlantic world intellectuals viewed as 'useful knowledge' " and to "understand the processes through which 'useful knowledge' was recognized as science (p. 1).[1]

Franklin's scientific experiments, which made him famous in his day, are well known today. Less well known is an incident that Janine Yorimoto Boldt recounts in the exhibit catalogue. Although Franklin ended his life as an abolitionist, he owned slaves for many years and displayed the deep racial prejudice of his time. But in 1759, while living in London, he supported the establishment in Philadelphia of a school for African American children, an extreme rarity. Deborah Franklin told her husband that she would send Othello, an enslaved child in the household, to the school.

When Franklin returned to Philadelphia, he visited the school, observed the children, and "examined" them on their skills. He reported back to the man who had initiated the project:

> I was on the whole much pleas'd, and from what I then saw, have conceiv'd a higher Opinion of the natural Capacities of the black Race, than I had ever before entertained. Their Apprehension seems as quick, their Memory as strong, and their Docility in every Respect equal to that of white Children. You will wonder perhaps that I should ever doubt it, and I will not undertake to justify all my Prejudices, nor to account for them. (p. 32)[2]

In other words, Benjamin Franklin, citizen scientist, looked at the evidence and drew his own conclusion.

---

[1] Janine Yorimoto Boldt, "Dr. Franklin, Citizen Scientist," in *Dr. Franklin, Citizen Scientist*, ed. American Philosophical Society (Philadelphia: American Philosophical Society Library & Museum, 2021), 10–40, at 10, https://www.amphilsoc.org/sites/default/files/2020-12/attachments/APS_DrFranklinCitizenScientist_desktop.pdf.
[2] Ibid., 32.

Chapter 1

Evaluating Evidence Requires Expert Judgment

Richard Shiffrin, Stephen M. Stigler, and
Kathleen Hall Jamieson

Practitioners in every area of inquiry, including science, art, history, music, literature, medicine, law, journalism, and business, have conventionalized their individual field's judgment of what is evidence, the ways to evaluate its quality, and the methods used to draw inferences. Various approaches notwithstanding, expert human judgment is central to each of these processes.

AGREEMENT ACROSS SCHOLARLY FIELDS ABOUT THE NATURE AND ROLE OF EVIDENCE

Although the evidence that forms the basis for argument and judgment varies both across and within fields and the methods of evaluation will always be tuned to an instance's subject matter and contextual details, they share an underlying set of realizations. All recognize not only that human ways of knowing inevitably involve uncertainty and provisional conclusions but also that they are subject to human limitations that apply to experts and others alike, although in some cases to varying degrees. At one time or another, all acknowledge that instead of uncontestable conclusions, they are dealing with a multitude of possibilities graded in likelihood and subject to revision. All accept that the inferences drawn by each evaluator are shaped by the knowledge that person brings to the task. All appreciate that the process of evaluating evidence must take into account the awareness that human bias affects the perception, gathering, analysis, and reporting of evidence. In some fields these underlying factors are tacitly acknowledged and in others explicitly so. Either way, all fields have norms of transparency and critique; tests of authenticity, inauthenticity, legitimacy, and illegitimacy; methods of assessing both the strength of evidence and the viability of the inferences drawn from it; ways to determine who has the authority and expertise to certify conclusions drawn from evidence; and methods to investigate the accuracy and validity of the suppositions and hypotheses in place at the start.

Let us take as an example the similarities between judging evidence in art and science: Consider the case of forgeries.[1] When asked to determine whether a painting is genuine or a forgery, art experts rely on a corpus of information about the purported artist and the body of paintings previously judged to have been genuine. Such judgments require sophisticated and extensive knowledge. A recent example involves authentication of a painting purportedly by Van Gogh at Norway's National Museum. When some experts raised doubts, the Norway National Museum turned to other experts at the Van Gogh Museum in Amsterdam, who, after five years of study, concluded in 2019 that the painting was genuine. Were they correct? As in all cases in which evidence is at issue there will remain some degree of uncertainty. Skilled forgers capitalize on the standards used by experts to assess authenticity. They attempt to satisfy the tests the expert will use, for example, by duplicating the artist's pigments and brush strokes. In the process, they are constrained by an asymmetry: It is easier for experts to demonstrate inauthenticity than the reverse. The expert evaluating it must consider the motivations and actions of the human who produced it.

Because the process of evaluating evidence involves a subjective element and unknowns, battles among experts are inevitable. The kinds of scientific evaluation to which the art world has increasingly turned for authentication are better at disconfirmation than confirmation and inevitably include uncertainty. A case in point is the spectrographic analysis of a sample extracted from the painting that shows use of a pigment not available when the work was purportedly painted. It might seem that this result would end the debate, but the reality is quite different. The test itself sometimes gives incorrect readings; the report of the results might be false; the humans carrying out the assessment may have been biased in the way they analyzed or interpreted the data or might have made errors; an interested party might have substituted a different sample for the one

---

[1] Noah Charney, *The Art of Forgery: The Minds, Motives and Methods of Master Forgers* (Vienna: Phaidon Press, 2015).

extracted from the painting; despite expert judgment and historical inferences to the contrary, the pigment in question might have been available
to the painter; the painting might have been exposed accidently to the
pigment in the years after the date of production; a nefarious party might
have doctored a genuine painting with pigment that was not originally used;
a human may have been bribed to submit a false laboratory finding. These
are just some of the possible factors that must be taken into account. The
expert who concludes that a painting was or was not painted by the artist
to whom it is attributed draws on knowledge and experience to judge the
likelihood of these alternative explanations.

HUMAN KNOWLEDGE IS PROVISIONAL

Some may find this conclusion surprising or even disheartening. However,
the overlap in the way science deals with evidence and the way this is
done in other fields is rooted in the observation that assertions about what
is known are always to some degree subjective—influenced by the subject
making the judgment—and provisional—they do not establish truth or fact.
Not all scientists act in ways that reflect this dictum, however. For example,
one theme underlying claims that there is a "crisis of reproducibility" is
the idea that reproducibility is the hallmark and goal of science, and that
replication studies are essential to establish what is "true." This view is
based on a serious misunderstanding of scientific evidence, namely, the
idea that scientific reports establish facts when done correctly.[2] This view
misses the idea that as time passes and new methods and knowledge
emerge, science moves forward, correcting, refining, and replacing data
and theories with new and better ones.[3]

When a summary of this essay was presented at an APS symposium
on evidence, one listener questioned the idea that objective truth is a
chimera: He asked whether it is not the case that water is H2O. One can
certainly work from such an assumption. In addition, one can deduce this
fact given a set of assumptions such as the atomic description of molecules,

---

[2] See Stuart Firestein, *Ignorance How It Drives Science* (Oxford: Oxford University Press, 2012). *See also* Stuart Firestein, *Failure: Why Science Is So Successful* (Oxford: Oxford University Press, 2016).

[3] See Bruce Alberts, Ralph J. Cicerone, Stephen E. Fienberg, Alexander Kamb, Marcia McNutt, Robert M. Nerem, Randy Schekman, Richard Shiffrin, Victoria Stodden, Subra Suresh, Maria T. Zuber, Barbara Kline Pope, and Kathleen Hall Jamieson, "Self-Correction in Science at Work: Improve Incentives to Support Research Integrity," *Science* 348, no. 6242 (2015):1420–22. See also Soren Sonnenburg, Mikio L. Braun, Cheng Soon Ong, Samy Bengio, Léon Bottou, Geoffrey Holmes, and Robert C. Williamson, "The Need for Open Source Software in Machine Learning," *Journal of Machine Learning Research* 8, (2007) 2443–66.

the rules of logic, and much more. Yet, what is deduced depends on the background: Although a simple description of water as H2O may be useful and suffice for many purposes, a physicist might need or prefer a description of a water molecule as a set of interacting quantum fields. Even more fundamental, when discussing evidence, we are discussing induction, not deduction. Deduction has a role in assessing evidence, but the assumptions necessary to support deduction are themselves always at least somewhat uncertain. If one is trying to decide whether a given sample is water, one cannot assume the sample is pure, the tests are accurate, the personnel are honest, or any of a host of similar assumptions that if made would remove uncertainty.[4]

Although a finding reproduced by an independent team has greater standing than one that fails to reproduce, the view that underlies the notion that there exists a "reproducibility crisis" treats reported evidence as if it could be indisputably verified, a view that ignores the many dimensions of human bias that affect definition, collection, and analysis of information. These dimensions increase uncertainty on the one hand and require expert human judgment on the other. In a recent *Proceedings of the National Academy of Sciences (PNAS)* article, Shiffrin, Borner, and Stigler (2018)[5] argue against the existence of a "crisis," as does Jamieson[6] in the same issue of the journal on different grounds. At one point, the former authors point out that scientists do not uncritically accept reports, even replications, regardless of what appears to be statistical support, because they are aware of the many sources of error other than variability, including experimenter error and bias.

Fields other than science would likely find these ideas obvious. Writing in *Objectivity Is Not Neutrality*, Thomas Haskell notes that "The very possibility of historical scholarship as an enterprise distinct from propaganda requires of its practitioners that they … abandon wishful thinking, assimilate bad news, discard pleasing interpretations that cannot pass elementary tests of evidence and logic, and, most important of all, suspend or bracket one's own perceptions long enough to enter sympathetically into the alien and possibly repugnant perspectives of rival thinkers."[7] He argues

---

[4] B. C. Malt, "Water Is Not H2O," *Cognitive Psychology* 27, no. 1. (1994): 41–70. https://doi.org/10.1006/cogp.1994.1011; M. Weisberg, "Water Is Not H2O," in D. Baird, E. Scerri, & L. McIntyre (Eds.), *Philosophy of Chemistry: Synthesis of a New Discipline* (Netherlands: Springer, 2006), 337–45. https://doi.org/10.1007/1-4020-3261-7_18; Hasok Chang, *Is Water H2O? Evidence, Realism and Pluralism* (New York: Springer, 2012).

[5] R. M. Shiffrin, K. Börner, and S. M. Stigler, "Scientific Progress Despite Irreproducibility: A Seeming Paradox," *Proceedings of the National Academy of Sciences* 115, no. 11, (2018): 2632–39.

[6] K. H. Jamieson, "Crisis or Self-Correction: Rethinking Media Narratives about the Well-Being of Science," *Proceedings of the National Academy of Sciences* 115, no. 11 (2018): 2620–27.

[7] Thomas L. Haskell, *Objectivity Is Not Neutrality: Explanatory Schemes in History* (Baltimore: Johns Hopkins University Press, 1998).

as well that "history is written from a perspective shaped by political and ethical values."[8]

Scholars of history, the humanities, and the arts are not uniquely subject to human bias. Its presence in science is signaled by psychological research demonstrating almost inevitable bias in selection and interpretation of results.[9] So, for example, when scholars tasked twenty-nine different research teams with answering the same research question—"are football (soccer) referees more likely to give red cards to players with dark skin than to players with light skin?"—based on evidence in the same data set their "findings varied enormously, from a slight (and nonsignificant) tendency for referees to give more red cards to light-skinned players to a strong trend of giving more red cards to dark-skinned players."[10] The reason? "Any single team's results are strongly influenced by subjective choices during the analysis phase."[11] Some protection against such biases is provided by institutional norms, but these have a downside as well, as we describe elsewhere in this essay: Norms recapitulate what is known and accepted and, in the process, inhibit discovery of the unexpected and novel.

Every field of inquiry harbors instances reminding its practitioners of the fallibility of expert judgment. Conclusions drawn in one epoch are supplanted by superior ones in a later age. Such changes occur repeatedly. The revised judgment is usually driven by new evidence or perhaps by a fresh take on long-standing evidence; sometimes the changes are produced by reevaluations of the same evidence. Just one of uncountable examples is the extent to which our view of the center of the universe we inhabit has changed, starting with the earth, then re-centering on the sun, then on the center of the galaxy, then ... (and so on). Even as these examples show how our best assessment of truth evolves, they illustrate a downside of expertise. Science, for example, relies on the idea that evidence should be considered more reliable when results can be repeated; methods and criteria have been developed to satisfy this criterion. Such is the case in *normal science*, in which the problems may be difficult but routine investigations dominate and all manner of scientific and statistical method-

[8] Thomas L. Haskell, "Objectivity: Perspective as Problem and Solution," *History and Theory* 43, no. 3 (2004): 341–59.

[9] Robert J. MacCoun, "Biases in the Interpretation and Use of Research Results," *Annual Review of Psychology* 49, no. 1 (1998): 259–87; Robert J. MacCoun, p-Hacking: A Strategic Analysis, accessed August 6, 2019, http://dx.doi.org/10.2139/ssrn.3433221; Joshua Abah, "The Quest for Statistical Significance: Ignorance, Bias and Malpractice of Research Practitioners," *International Journal of Research and Review* 5, no. 3 (2018): 112–29.

[10] Raphael Silberzahn and Eric L. Uhlmann, "Crowdsourced Research: Many Hands Make Tight Work," *Nature* 526, no. 7572 (2015): 189–91.

[11] Ibid.

ology takes over. Notwithstanding regular complaints, this is also the case in political elections, in educational accreditation, in clinical trials, and in both criminal and civil trials. In these and many other situations, institutions have implemented approaches that interlace set procedures and extensive expertise to weigh results and deal with appeals.

Ironically, this methodology works against discovery of the unexpected. To this extent expertise fails us. To elaborate, our methods and our expertise are best built upon experience under similar circumstances. However, we lack that basis in the truly novel and in social settings involving humans that form the core of social scientific inquiry. The former phenomenon was at play in some celebrated forgeries: Like everyone else, the experts confronted with the "Hitler Diaries" had never seen a Hitler Diary, and they did not do particularly well in unmasking the counterfeit ones. "Well-respected historians, including Hugh Trevor-Roper ... declared the books authentic."[12]

The history of great scientific discoveries is full of stories of initial rejection (e.g., Copernicus, Galileo, cold fusion, superconductivity). This rejection is natural, since science teaches us that entirely novel observations are generally wrong (e.g., cold fusion), and this is a reaction that serves well in normal science. We are at our best when we can, even before the observation, foresee in at least approximate terms what is likely to be observed, and map a course to assessment that allows for some variations in procedure while foreclosing others. Too much flexibility in a search (i.e., data dredging or "The Garden of Forking Paths") can remove us from our comfort zone of comparative cases.[13] When we encounter what seems to be an amazing coincidence in everyday life, we lack the grounding to rationally assess its rarity or typicality. And when the observation runs counter to received wisdom, even panels of experts may be of little use, either because they too lack the needed grounding, or more problematic, they may be heavily invested in a status quo that the observation would disrupt. So, for example, two of the historians tasked with vetting the supposed Hitler diaries "failed to notice that the history book they were using to check the diaries' facts—Max Domarus's anthology, *Hitler: Speeches and Proclamations 1932–1945—The Chronicle of a Dictatorship*—was the same one Kujau [the forger] had copied swaths of information from, word for word."[14]

---

[12] Sally McGrane, "Diary of the Hitler Diary Hoax," *The New Yorker* April 25, 2013, https://www.newyorker.com/books/page-turner/diary-of-the-hitler-diary-hoax.

[13] Jorge Luis Borges, "The Garden of Forking Paths," in *Collected Fictions*, trans. Andrew Hurley (New York: Penguin), 119–28.

[14] McGrane, "Diary of the Hitler Diary Hoax."

EXPERT JUDGMENT PLAYS AN INDISPENSABLE ROLE IN EVALUATING EVIDENCE AND INFERENCES DRAWN FROM IT

These difficulties faced by experts notwithstanding, expert judgment is the best available method of evaluation at any given time, keeping in mind that even here, uncertainty will always remain. (We are speaking of actual experts and not, for example, figures of authority who feign expertise.) That experts would favor the most likely hypotheses is understandable; it is actually useful that a complete consensus of experts is seldom reached— the way forward to new discoveries and new evaluations is often found in minority views, views that when sufficiently well-reasoned and corroborated, eventually win out. The experts who discredited the fake Hitler diaries, including those at the West German Federal Archive, based their conclusion on convergent evidence educed using dissimilar methods. Included among them were chemical tests that revealed that the paper on which the diaries were written was manufactured in the 1950s, long after Hitler's death, and that the "binding, glue, and thread, likewise, contained chemicals of postwar origin." Other tests confirmed that the stationery had been aged by dousing it in tea.[15] Moreover, historians expert in the Nazi era identified errors of fact. Specifically, under 22 June 1934, one of the diaries says, "Dr. Gurtner, was 'Reich and Prussian Minister of Justice.' This term is not correct for that date since in June 1934 Dr. Gurtner was Reichs-Minister only; he subsequently only became Acting Minister of the Prussian Ministry for Justice. The term *Reichs and Prussian Minister of Justice* was not officially used before 16 October 1934."[16]

If the evaluation of evidence requires expertise, there has to be a way to identify people with the relevant abilities. An expert is a person to whom a group defers because the person is presumed to have competence; in many cases the expert is assumed to have higher competence than the group seeking the assessment, but in some cases the issue is less the expert's competence than the expert's neutrality or fairness. In court, an expert witness is permitted to offer opinion testimony after the foundation for the claim of expertise has been laid through arguments about the expert's credentials and experience. Typically, expertise is established by years of training and often by several demonstrations of judgments that have received general acceptance as valid. Validation as an expert varies somewhat

[15] Eric Rentschler, "The Fascination of a Fake: The Hitler Diaries," *New German Critique* 90 (2003): 177–92, doi: 10.2307/3211115.

[16] Josef Henke, "Revealing the Forged Hitler Diaries," *Archivaria* 19 (1984): 21–27.

from field to field. For example, for the anthropologist, "expertise is both inherently interactional, involving the participation of objects, producers, and consumers of knowledge, and inescapably ideological, implicated in the evolving hierarchies of value that legitimate particular ways of knowing as 'expert.'"[17] Expertise is sometimes certified by a formal credential. Some credentials are awarded so broadly, such as Bachelor of Arts degrees, or even PhDs, that they are not automatically accepted as certification of expertise. Other credentials are accepted provisionally, for certain applied purposes. Thus, when confronting a problem with plumbing or electricity in one's home, a certification by an appropriate body is generally considered sufficient. In sum, formal credentialing plays a role in establishing expertise, but is just one factor in a process that emerges from the social fabric of society.

When we turn to subfields in science and fields outside of it, we see a wide array of methods designed to establish expertise: Societies and authoritative bodies develop standards to certify practitioners whose numbers are generally so large that their divergent opinions do not speak with one voice. In other instances, fields use a kind of "word of mouth" to establish expertise, relying on an informal consensus to certify that a small number of individuals are more expert than others. As attacks on the credibility of Director of the National Institute of Allergy and Infectious Diseases Dr. Anthony Fauci attested, in today's polarized society with numerous types of media and communication open to most people, and with the advent of social media, it is an open question whether such a consensus can emerge about which individuals should be considered trustworthy experts, or whether different subgroups informed by different subsets of information will rely on different ones. In both cases one might wonder whether the experts would reach a consensus on an issue of evidence, though it seems likely a consensus would be far more likely when there is an agreed-upon single group of experts.

EXPERTS PLAY AN IMPORTANT ROLE IN CERTIFYING EVIDENCE AND COMMUNICATING WHAT IS KNOWN

Although we live in an age far less deferential to experts and expertise than in decades past,[18] and deference to those with presumed expertise

---

[17] E. Summerson Carr, "Enactments of Expertise," *Annual Review of Anthropology* 39 (2010): 17–32, doi: 10.1146/annurev.anthro.012809.104948.

[18] Tom Nichols, *The Death of Expertise: The Campaign against Established Knowledge and Why It Matters* (New York: Oxford University Press, 2017).

has occasionally proven calamitous as it did when the United States invaded Iraq on the later-discredited assumption that Saddam Hussein was hiding so-called weapons of mass destruction, experts continue to play a central role in determining what qualifies as evidence, establishing the standards for assessing it, and indicating when a sufficient amount and quality exist to justify a conclusion. Experts also articulate standards by which evidence should be assessed and reported. In this process, there is often general agreement about the "big picture" (e.g., the idea in science that estimates of the sizes of effects should be accompanied by some measure of estimated accuracy, such as some form of confidence intervals) although there is often disagreement about the details (as will be seen in a later discussion of hypothesis testing). It is natural that experts will disagree about the details, because, as a statement apocryphally attributed to Albert Einstein said, "The more I learn, the more I realize how much I don't know."

Just as important as expert judgment is guidance by experts concerning general principles that should govern evaluation (e.g., absence of evidence of a difference does not constitute evidence that there is no difference, alternative explanations should be examined). For example, scholars recently argued that "In the US, the normal, oral temperature of adults is, on average, lower than the canonical 37°C established in the 19th century"; they then identified ways in which alternative explanations could be tested. "One possible reason for the lower temperature estimates today than in the past is the difference in thermometers or methods of obtaining temperature," they wrote. "To minimize these biases, we examined changes in body temperature by birth decade within each cohort under the assumption that the method of thermometry would not be biased on birth year."[19] Of course, being experts, they mentioned a variety of other factors that could be in play, such as changes in population height and weight, increased general health with reduction of low-grade fevers, air conditioning and heating in homes and offices, general use of drugs, and so on. In addition, being experts, not all agreed on the existence of a drop in average body temperature. This body temperature issue provides not just an example of using a norm for evaluation but also a microcosm of the general use of expert judgment to evaluate evidence.

It is a hallmark of expertise that experts continue to examine and contest each other's conclusions. The result is often a shift in recommendations, including redefinitions for key public metrics. For example, after

---

[19] Myroslava Protsiv, Catherine Ley, Joanna Lankester, Trevor Hastie, and Julie Parsonnet, "Decreasing Human Body Temperature in the United States since the Industrial Revolution," *eLife* 9 (2020), doi: 10.7554/eLife.49555.

economists concluded that adopting the standard used by the international community eased cross-country comparisons, in 1991 the US government relied on this expert opinion and decided that the gross national product should give way to gross domestic product as an economic indicator. The change meant that what would be reported would be changes in the value of goods and services produced by US nationals (GDP) rather than the value of those produced within the geographic boundaries of the US (GNP). Deferring to the experts, political leaders embraced the new metric in their deliberations in Congress as well as in their campaign speeches and ads.

Consider another example. After reviewing relevant scholarly findings, in 2017 the American Heart Association, the American College of Cardiology, and nine other health professional organizations changed the US guidelines for high blood pressure. "High blood pressure, previously defined as 140/90 mm Hg, is now defined as 130/80 mm Hg," they declared. Their rationale presupposed that because these expert organizations were speaking in concert, physicians and the public would accept their assertion that, "This change reflects the latest research that shows health problems can occur at those lower levels. Risk for heart attack, stroke and other consequences begins anywhere above 120 mm Hg (systolic), and risk doubles at 130 mm Hg compared to levels below 120."[20] The importance of the power to define is evident in the fact that as a result of this change the percentage of the US adult population 20 years of age and older with high blood pressure, and hence subject to appeals to treat a medical condition, increased from 32 percent to 46 percent.[21]

As these examples suggest, experts evolve their consensus concerning what constitutes quality evidence, what interpretations should be drawn from it, and what practices society should adopt. They also identify and police threats to the current consensus. An example particularly relevant for the health sciences and education is a current consensus that a well-done randomized placebo-controlled, double-blinded clinical trial provides a higher quality evidence than does a well-done observational study. In 2020, the emergence of such evidence led the Food and Drug Administration (FDA) to stop distributing the anti-malaria drug hydroxychloroquine from the federal supply for emergency use in hospitals as a COVID-19 treatment.

Of course such simple conclusions are useful for public consumption but often omit a host of conditions that experts know should apply. For

---

[20] John Warner, "New Hypertension Guideline Updates How We Measure and Treat High Blood Pressure," *American Heart Association Center for Health Metrics and Evaluation* November 13, 2017, https://health metrics.heart.org/new-hypertension-guideline-updates-how-we-measure-and-treat-high-blood-pressure/.
[21] Ibid.

example, another consensus holds that the results of a meta-analysis constitute stronger evidence than those drawn from a single study. Yet meta-analyses often assume the separate pieces of evidence are independent. This assumption is violated when several studies are published by the same person or group. Thus, experts often provide additional information about the conditions that should hold if the conclusions are to be valid. Accordingly, it is said that "Well-established limitations of randomized trials include failure to conceal allocation, failure to blind, loss to follow-up, and failure to appropriately consider the intention-to-treat principle ... stopping early for apparent benefit and selective reporting of outcomes according to the results."[22] An unfortunate consequence of expert advice occurs when experts feel compelled to outline in detail all the conditions that ought to hold, and in the process of recounting this complex story obscure their own findings. Worrying that exposure to a cascade of possible side effects of a medication was obscuring the ones of greatest public concern, in 2015 the FDA changed its guidelines on the disclosures required in televised pharmaceutical ads. "In general, FDA believes that exhaustive lists that include even minor risks distract from, and make it difficult for, consumers to comprehend and retain information about the important risks," the agency noted at the time.[23]

At times, groups, organizations, and outlets adopt the changing expert recommendations even when they are still quite controversial, and do not yet reflect a clear expert consensus (not that a clear consensus is necessarily correct). A recent example is found in the adoption by some journals of requirements or recommendations that studies be preregistered, a controversial recommendation still being debated.[24] At other times, expert consensus is called into question and needed action forestalled by those who find it ideologically inconvenient. Scholarly journals are themselves a voice of authority and their policies considered to represent the best current expert judgment. As a result, journals have hastened to establish standards designed to uncover the effects of human bias in the evidence-gathering and presentation process. For example, it is increasingly the case that submitters are required to disclose conflicts of interest, to disclose those who contrib-

---

[22] Gordon H. Guyatt et al., "GRADE Guidelines: 4. Rating the Quality of Evidence—Study Limitations (Risk of Bias)," *Journal of Clinical Epidemiology* 64, no. 4 (2011): 407–15, doi: 0.1016/j.jclinepi.2010.07.017.

[23] John Russell, "Drug Ads Include a Lot of Warnings—Probably Too Many, FDA says," *HeraldNet* September 14, 2015, https://www.heraldnet.com/business/drug-ads-include-a-lot-of-warnings-probably-too-many-fda-says/.

[24] For a pro-preregistration argument, see Brian A. Nosek et al., "Preregistration Is Hard and Worthwhile," *Trends in Cognitive Science* 23, no. 10 (2019): 815–18; for an argument against preregistration, see Aba Szollosi, David Kellen, Danielle J. Navarro, Richard Shiffrin, Iris van Rooij, Trisha Van Zandt, and Chris Donkin, "Is Preregistration Worthwhile?" *Trends in Cognitive Science* 24, no. 2 (2020): 94–95.

uted to the process and their roles in doing so, and to ensure that data are available for scrutiny by reviewers and investigators not involved in the study.

HOW THE EXPERT COMMUNITY DEALS WITH UNCERTAINTY AND COMMUNICATES CONSENSUS

It is particularly important that expert communities be consulted when evidence is shrouded in uncertainty, and interpretation is controversial. In a number of important cases, such communities are granted and exercise their authority by carrying out systematic reviews. Notable examples include reports by the National Academy of Sciences, the Cochrane, which reviews scholarship in the health care area, the Campbell Collaboration, which focuses on social policy, and the United Nations' Inter-Governmental Panel on Climate Change (IPCC). Although recent years have seen some erosion of trust in expertise, of these four examples, only the expertise of the IPCC has been subject to sustained attack, and even in this case public attitudes have moved in the direction of the consensus position: In April 2019, a Pew survey found that "Compared with a decade ago, more Americans today say protecting the environment and dealing with global climate change should be top priorities for the president and Congress."[25] It must be admitted that the changing views of society could also be due in part to environmental changes that even nonexperts can see, but it is vitally important that society continues to place trust in the advice of the best experts.

GENERALITY AND DIVERSITY

Experts are often asked for advice that applies generally, across many contexts, to most people. The FDA is asked for example to determine whether use of a particular drug for a particular purpose at a specified dose is safe and beneficial, and whether a vaccine is safe and effective enough to justify distribution to a specified population. At other times very specific advice is sought. For example, experts may be asked whether a painting is a forgery. When giving advice meant to apply generally there

---

[25] Cary Funk and Brian Kennedy, "How Americans See Climate Change in 5 Charts," *Pew Research Center*, April 19, 2019, https://www.pewresearch.org/fact-tank/2019/04/19/how-americans-see-climate-change-in-5-charts/.

is a tension between two dangers: saying too little and failing to recognize the numerous exceptions, special circumstances, and unique conditions, and saying too much, confusing the issue, and giving the impression that there is no generally applicable conclusion. The same tension causes difficulties when experts try to communicate their advice in ways that are effective and productive. This tension admits of no easy resolution, because almost all general issues have important exceptions and conditions or caveats that should hold for the advice to be put into practice.

It is one thing to point out that the evaluation of evidence requires expert judgment, but even granting that this is the case, the benefit of reliance upon experts is lost if the evaluations are not communicated properly. Experts as a group are, unsurprisingly, expert at communicating what they know to other experts in the same domain. However, relatively few have the art and the skill to communicate effectively to experts in other domains, let alone the lay public. Experts often have the impression that nonexperts are only willing to tolerate sound bites, with the result that communications are too brief, distorted, and oversimplified. Certainly, the nonexpert does not want to hear the entire background and analysis that often makes evaluation complex and difficult. It makes sense that those receiving the expert evaluations prefer them in summary form—the underlying reason for not wanting to hear all the complexities is not only that the recipient cannot follow the threads, but rather that every thread is itself an excursion into uncertainty—each part of the complex context of the issue is something uncertain and something experts might well argue about. Unraveling all these threads does not help nonexperts. Instead, they need an expert to evaluate these different uncertain threads and come up with a best available assessment. Accordingly, it is rational for the nonexpert to prefer a simple story without the messy details. Yet the story must be compelling and provide enough of the relevant basis for the final judgments to be convincing and cover the main possibilities and the reasons for favoring them.

CHALLENGES TO A MODEL RELIANT ON EXPERT JUDGMENT

To this point we have argued that the evaluation of evidence entails expert human judgment, and that this is the case in every field of inquiry. However, that theme leaves open a host of critical questions, a few of which we have flagged already and others that will be discussed later in this essay: How should experts be chosen, and how can agreement with those choices be established? What is to be done, as is often the case, when experts disagree? Should the proportion of experts who disagree matter? Should the minority view ever be preferred? How should degree of trust in various subgroups of experts be established? Are there ways to evaluate the reliability of the sources of evidence? How should multiple sources of evidence be combined? As our computational society continues to evolve and it becomes ever easier to fabricate convincing but false evidence, how can any system of evidence evaluation continue to operate effectively? As social media act to partition groups into selective evidentiary enclaves, how can any field hope to reach accepted conclusions? After an evaluation of evidence has been made, what are the ways to test and validate the inferences that have been drawn? How might it be possible for those not expert in the subject matter to make informed judgments and decisions? Which groups in society need to make informed evaluations? What can be done when the evidence evaluation system breaks down? (We are certain this list of difficult issues is incomplete.)

EXPERTS DISAGREE

Mindful that we can take up only a few of these issues here, let us consider disagreements among experts. There are many reasons why different experts might draw different conclusions from the same evidence. Although it is possible that a resolution lies in a consensus among them, that solution leads to many additional questions. Because experts may have differing degrees of expertise, the extent of expertise itself is open to debate. There may be many alternative assessments available in different proportions in different expert groups. It is not unknown for experts to disagree. In addition, disagreements are sometimes not about the evidence per se, but instead reflect differing goals about the societal consequences of the conclusions. This has been seen in debates about climate change that focus not on the existence of change, or its cause, but rather on the costs and benefits of proposed actions. Finally, as mentioned earlier, expert disagreement is sometimes healthy, as is the case when a minority view challenges an entrenched paradigm by championing a position that is novel, unexpected, and invites the scholarly community to rethink hoary presuppositions. When expert disagreement is encountered it is an open question about the optimal ways to proceed.

     An interesting and informative case arises in science when one asks for the best way to evaluate quantitative evidence. This example highlights yet other problems that arise when experts disagree. It is typical in science to have multiple observations that differ in nominally identical conditions. The differences are presumed to be caused by unknown factors but this variability must be considered when evaluating the evidence and reaching conclusions. Statisticians have developed methods to do so. These methods do not take into account all sources of variability, such as human error, bias, and distortion, but rather model the observed variability seen in the data as inevitable probabilistic distortion that is not explained by other factors. One not familiar with statistical methodology might assume this a straightforward matter, with methods that experts would agree are appropriate. This is far from the case: The debate among statisticians provides a case study of a situation in which experts have not been able to reach a consensus.

One debate among expert statisticians arose from a series of challenges to one of the oldest and most frequently employed (and best understood) statistical procedures, tests of significance. In the simplest versions these involve comparing a statistic calculated from experimental data with a hypothesized value specified by some theory and concluding from variation within the data that either the difference was so great the chance of such a difference if the theory held was very small, raising questions about the theory, or the difference was not large enough to reach such a conclusion. In the parlance of the field, either the difference was "statistically significant" or one would "accept the hypothesis at (say) the .05 or 5% level." Statisticians—or at least well-educated statisticians—have known for over a century that such decisions were always subject to several caveats: The difference may be accurately termed "statistically significant" and still be so small as to be of no practical interest, or the measurements may be of such great variability that such deviations were just about as likely whether or not the hypothesis was correct, and so the test was of no use (the test "had low (discriminatory) power"). Experts also generally recognize that most scientific questions require much more than a simple yes/no. To this extent, experts do agree. They do not, however, agree on whether tests of significance are the best way to draw inferences.

Part of the disagreement is based on the limitations just expressed. Scientists using significance tests often draw stronger conclusions than these limitations would allow. Statisticians who use and sometimes favor significance tests have worked hard to instill these considerations in students, with mixed success. The spread of computer packages reporting statistical results confers such a veneer of artificial expertise that users too often accept the results as inferences not subject to considered thought and debate. Attempts to counter these tendencies with classroom instruction tend to fail because students learn better from failures of personal action than even excellent teaching. Because many fields have come to accept inferences drawn from such statistical packages, the users do not experience the personal failure that would lead both to learning and valuable caution. Numerous examples can be found throughout science. In some instances, an underpowered test has led to a striking conclusion that evaporated under further testing (the result was "irreproducible"), and in others the investigator was led to proclaim a difference when no practical one existed. For these reasons, a few journals have threatened to ban papers using a test of significance, and opinion pieces in *Nature* and *Science* have proclaimed a "crisis" in statistics.

To deal with this situation, in 2016 the editors of a magazine published by the American Statistical Association (ASA) sought to correct what was thought to be a troublesome public relations problem. Their solicitation of expert opinion resulted in twenty-one short articles written by a range of scholars. Because that number was too many to publish, the editors sought to summarize the general consensus, placing the pieces themselves on a seldom-visited website. But the attempt to summarize the work faced a problem: There was very little common ground among the twenty-one. Most were excellent pieces that were more like inventive research summaries in different areas of specialization. This was a fire in which everyone had an iron, and the lack of commonality was not so much a disagreement but rather offered different perspectives on the best ways to go deeper and inform analyses. The short, cautious summary the editors published gave a broader readership the impression significance tests were not being seriously endorsed, emphasizing caveats over utility. Several of the participants, who felt the summary was wrong, revised their pieces to be effectively minority reports that were consigned to the website.

The cries about a crisis grew even louder. The editors doubled down and in early 2019 produced a special issue of more than 400 pages, this time with forty-three additional contributions and a longer summary editorial titled "Moving to a World Beyond $p < 0.05$" that was even more dismissive of significance tests and even more emphatic about caveats. Although that entire issue appeared only as a website posting, unlike other issues that were given printed publication, the blow back was swift. There were soon signs that many people in fields, such as medicine and social science, that made frequent use of these tests took this as license to dismiss them entirely. The goal of the enterprise had been more careful use of statistical methods in common use; the outcome of the diversity of voices of expertise and negative summaries threatened not to be better use of significance tests but an abandonment of them. The ASA president tried to engage in damage control, including emphasizing in several columns that the editorials should not be interpreted as speaking for the Association, but the overall message heard by the user community and the public was not nuanced, but rather a condemnation of all use of significance testing.

The problem here was not that the 21 + 43 = 64 pieces by a large list of authors were divided about the utility of significance testing if used judiciously. Many—even most—of the authors of the pieces would continue to use them as one part of the evaluation of evidence, as thoughtful statisticians have done for over a century. The articles reflected an understanding that significance testing was a well-understood technique that answered a specific question quite well, even though the question was quite limited in scope and the conclusions needed to keep those limitations in mind. Whether significance testing is the best approach is another matter, as recent years especially have seen increasing advocacy of Bayesian methodology. But even many or most of those who favor Bayesian approaches would not want to conclude that significance tests properly applied and evaluated lead to invalid inferences. One example is a recent controversial publication signed by more than seventy methodologists of various stripes advocating a guarded form of significance testing even though many preferred Bayesian approaches.[26]

This example illustrates a fundamental problem of reliance on a consensus of experts: Serious issues are usually complex, and experts appropriately acknowledge and publicize those complexities. Nonexperts, both users and practitioners and the general public, are often unable to ferret out a core message embedded in the complexities that might represent a consensus. This is a general problem and is exacerbated when, as is often the case, the loudest voices fail to take a nuanced position and instead offer a simpler one.

STATISTICAL ANALYSES NEED TO BE COUPLED WITH EXPERT JUDGMENT

Statisticians debate endlessly about the best and most appropriate tests for different goals of inference. However, knowing what test is appropriate for a given problem setting, and what inference can be drawn from the

[26] D. J. Benjamin et al., "Redefine Statistical Significance," *Nature Human Behaviour* 2, no. 1 (2018): 6–10. doi: 10.1038/s41562-017-0189-z. PMID: 30980045.

results of the test require statistical and scientific judgment and expertise. Every scientist and every researcher has seen numerous examples of applications of a statistical package, perhaps used because of the convenience of doing so, with claimed results that clearly do not match the data analyzed. This point is elaborated in the next section.

It is thus a given that, when using statistics, expert knowledge must be combined with statistical analyses. Statisticians have sometimes suggested introducing expert knowledge into statistical inference with the use of Bayesian analysis. The inferences about some hypotheses are then based on two factors, one based on the likelihood of the data given the hypothesis, and the other based on the background knowledge about the likelihood of the hypothesis. This latter factor is known as the *prior*, representing prior knowledge before the data are observed. Of course, experts have different kinds of personal knowledge and also disagree about the evaluation of shared prior knowledge. The inevitable disagreements about prior knowledge have led some Bayesians to advocate the use of a prior that is somewhat deceptively termed *uninformative*, or in mathematical terms that is a uniform or transformation invariant. By contrast we are arguing that drawing inferences from a formal statistical analysis that assumes no background knowledge is seriously flawed. The best way to take such knowledge into account, whether with Bayesian analysis or a skeptical and considered approach to certain statistical procedures, is unclear and a subject of current debate.

CAN EXPERTISE BE AUTOMATED?

If experts disagree, why not disregard them? With new computing technology, often described by terms such as *machine learning* and *artificial intelligence (AI)*, there is a strong temptation to replace human experts with computational or algorithmic alternatives. Recent advances, particularly ones using *deep learning*,[27] have produced AI systems that in limited and well-defined situations may be capable of evaluating evidence quite well. In some cases they may be better than an average human (or will be soon), as in the case of self-driving automobiles on well-marked freeways.[28] In some limited domains they may even be better than human experts, as in some domains of medical diagnosis.[29] Even so, there is considerable

---

[27] V. Minh et al., "Human-Level Control Through Deep Reinforcement Learning," *Nature* (25 February 2015): 518, 529–33. https://doi.org/10.1038/nature14236.

[28] L. P. Robert, "Are Automated Vehicles Safer than Manually Driven Cars?" *AI & Society* (2019): 34. doi: 10.1007/s00146-019-00894-y.

[29] S. M. McKinney et al., "International Evaluation of an AI System for Breast Cancer Screening," *Nature* 577 (2020): 89–94. https://doi.org/10.1038/s41586-019-1799-6.

resistance to giving complete control of evidence evaluation, decision-making, and action to AI systems.[30] There are good reasons for this hesitancy. First, it is necessary that the relevant evidence be quantified in terms that can be submitted to the algorithm; these conditions hold particularly well in well-defined games such as Chess and Go,[31] in which programs are now considerably superior to the best humans. Second, granting control to an AI system requires that the situation be routine, so that the algorithm does not face inputs that are unexpected: An algorithm designed for highway driving may fare poorly if the car is forced to deviate onto natural terrain without pavement. Third, it is almost impossible to design complex AI systems that are "bug-free," something we all experience when we receive annoying updates to our computer operating systems. Fourth, It is possible for "bad actors" to take advantage of an algorithmic system,[32] as we experience when "holes" in our computer operating systems are used to gain access to our computers, hijack them, and steal information.[33] Fifth, it is now well recognized that AI systems carry with them the biases and prejudices of the programmers, and of the society that provides the data.[34] Experts share such societal biases, but can try to compensate for them, and some do. Sixth, it is dangerous to trust so-called expert systems when even the developers and other experts do not understand how and why they work; lack of understanding has led to the recent development of a field termed *explainable AI*.[35] Beyond such rational bases for distrust of complex AI systems, humanity seems to regard an error made by an AI system as more serious than the same error made by a human.[36] As AI systems continue to improve, it is probably inevitable that they will be given more and more control of evaluation, decision-making, and action

---

[30] L. Petersen, L. Robert, X. Yang, and D. Tilbury, "Situational Awareness, Driver's Trust in Automated Driving Systems and Secondary Task Performance," *SAE International Journal of Connected and Automated Vehicles*2, no. 2 (2019): 129–41. https://doi.org/10.4271/12-02-02-0009.

[31] D. Silver et al., "A General Reinforcement Learning Algorithm that Masters Chess, Sogi, and Go through Self-Play, *Science* 362, no. 6419 (2018): 1140–44. doi: 10.1126/science.aar6404. PMID: 30523106.

[32] M. Comiter, "Attacking Artificial Intelligence: AI's Security Vulnerability and What Policymakers Can Do About It," (Belfer Center for Science and International Affairs, August 2019). https://www.belfercenter.org/publication/AttackingAI.

[33] Peter Warren Singer, *Cybersecurity and Cyberwar: What Everyone Needs to Know* (New York: Oxford University Press, 2014).

[34] Z. Obermeyer, B. Powers, C. Vogeli, and S. Mullainathan, "Dissecting Racial Bias in an Algorithm Used to Manage the Health of Populations,"*Science* 366 (2019): 447–53.

[35] Filip Dosilovic, Mario Brcic, and Nikica Hlupic, (2018-05-25). "Explainable Artificial Intelligence: A Survey," Paper presented at the 41st International Convention Proceedings, MIPRO (Opatija, Croatia, May 2018), 214–15. doi:10.23919/MIPRO.2018.8400040.

[36] N. Kallioinen et al., "Moral Judgements on the Actions of Self-Driving Cars and Human Drivers in Dilemma Situations from Different Perspectives," *Frontiers in Psychology* 1, no. 10 (2019): 2415. https://doi.org/10.3389/fpsyg.2019.02415.

in various domains, particularly ones in which human reaction time is too slow to foster effective action, and ones in which humans are known to make errors causing serious harm. An example of the latter: When there are 40,000 deaths each year in automobile accidents it is hard to argue that well-designed AI systems cannot improve matters.

Because humans, especially human experts, are capable of imagination, synthesizing important but distant-seeming information from superficially irrelevant knowledge and dealing with novel and unexpected situations, a good case can be made that the output of AI systems ought to be treated as another form of evidence, evidence to be considered by human experts when they consider it appropriate to do so. This idea is seen in the development of hybrid systems attempting to combine the best elements of AI and human judgment.[37] Universities have, for example, put together various metrics by which faculty productivity is measured, and it might be possible to develop an expert system to evaluate whether a given case satisfies those metrics. Nonetheless, notwithstanding error-prone human judgment, most academics would be unlikely to turn over to an expert system the final decision on their tenure and promotion. They might, however, accept the output of an expert system as one of the many pieces of evidence that are used in reaching a decision.

These large issues in society are seen also in narrower domains, such as evaluation of statistical evidence. With the computerization of analyses, the statistical methods themselves have often come to be viewed as the essence of any quantitative investigation, no matter who is operating the computer. Who can argue with computer output that delivers the welcome news that you have just done something "significant"? In public discourse, it is not uncommon for even major newspapers to run a front-page story with a headline that begins "Data Suggest" to describe the results of an unrefereed preprint, for which not even one of the authors is named "data."

For well over a century, statisticians have been warning mostly unreceptive scholars that statistics is an essential but potentially fraught tool. Statistical analysis requires expert choices involving decisions about how to frame the question, proceed in a sequential investigation, and determine how much of the analysis should be reported. The answer will almost never be "show everything." Such total transparency would be more likely to obscure than focus attention on methods, measures, inferences, and results. Any investigation requires that choices be made. As early as 1885, Alfred Marshall, the major British economist of that era noted: "The most reckless

---

[37] Upol Ehsan and Mark O. Riedl, "On Design and Evaluation of Human-centered Explainable AI Systems," Proceedings of the 2019 CHI Workshop on Human-Centered Machine Learning, 2019.

and treacherous of all theorists is he who professes to let facts and figures speak for themselves, who keeps in the background the part he has played, perhaps unconsciously, in selecting and grouping them." As desirable as such automation would be, it cannot now be done responsibly. Some modern methods can perform marvelously in limited situations, yet they may fail without notice in others. Although fallible, experts remain essential.

EXPERTS ARE FALLIBLE

The example of art forgery leads us to turn next to instances in which evidence has been crafted to lead experts to reach false conclusions. Historically, examples have been identified in every field from the forgery of the supposed "Donation of Constantine" that purported to grant the royal insignia to Saints Peter and Paul[38] and the forged sculpture that helped jumpstart Michelangelo's career, to the "lost" Shakespearean drama *Vortigern*,[39] to the supposed twentieth-century missing link between ape and man that turned out to be a human skull appended to an orangutan's jawbone (i.e., *The Piltdown Man*).[40] In science such cases of outright fraud are thought to occur with low probability, but in every field, including science, the actual proportion of cases in which false evidence is constructed is unknown. Until recently the costs to society of fraudulent evidence construction seem to have been low enough to be manageable. This situation is changing rapidly because the ability to produce false evidence in the form of convincing auditory and visual episodes is rapidly evolving. AI software that transposes the image of one individual's face onto the image of another's body has created deep-fake pornography.[41] Using easily available programs, Jordan Peele and *BuzzFeed* warned about the uses of deep-fakes in politics by creating a public service announcement in which actor and comedian Peele ventriloquizes Barack Obama, having the forty-fourth US president voice opinions he had not expressed.[42] This problem is perhaps most pressing for journalists because that profession often has played the

---

[38] Johannes Fried and Wolfram Brandes, *"Donation of Constantine" and "Constitutum Constantini": The Misinterpretation of a Fiction and Its Original Meaning* (Berlin: Walter de Gruyter, 2007).

[39] Jeffrey Kahan, *Reforging Shakespeare: The Story of a Theatrical Scandal* (Bethlehem: Lehigh University Press, 1998).

[40] Miles Russell, *Piltdown Man: The Secret Life of Charles Dawson & the World's Greatest Archaeological Hoax* (Stroud: Tempus Publishing, 2003).

[41] Douglas Harris, "Deepfakes: False Pornography Is Here and the Law Cannot Protect You," *Duke Law & Technology Review* 17 (2019): 99–127.

[42] James Vincent, "Watch Jordan Peele Use AI to Make Barack Obama Deliver a PSA about Fake News," *The Verge* (April 17, 2018). https://www.theverge.com/tldr/2018/4/17/17247334/ai-fake-news-video-barack-obama-jordan-peele-buzzfeed.

role of society's watchdog. For example, factcheckers unmasked "A doctored video of an interview with House Speaker Nancy Pelosi [that] portrays her speech as being slowed and slurred, and has been used to advance a false claim that she was 'drunk,'"[43] as well as "a fake photo of former President Barack Obama shaking hands with the Iranian president."[44] They also disconfirmed viral allegations that "Fox News posted a "fake picture" of U.S. soldiers cheering President Donald Trump during his recent visit to Afghanistan."[45]

AN EXPERT CONSENSUS CAN BE WRONG

An expert consensus represents the best current evaluation of the evidence, but it can be wrong. Anyone relying on a consensus view should entertain the possibility of error when planning action. If the consensus is widely embraced, it is easy to forget this possibility. When there are evidence-based minority views that are not cogent enough or do not occur in numbers that seem great enough to call a consensus into question, those planning to use the expert assessment should at least consider the merits of the alternative judgments, even though many may in the end dismiss them in favor of the dominant view. It is wise for both experts and those relying on expert judgment to retain a healthy dose of skepticism about their own conclusions, given the many sources of uncertainty that make induction so difficult.

However, uncertainty does not necessarily justify inaction. The answer to the question, "When does one know enough to act?" is shaped by one's philosophical assumptions. In the decision to phase out chlorofluorocarbons through the international treaty known as the 1987 Montreal Protocol, for example, the nations of the world were guided by two assumptions: The risks associated with the continued use of a chemical that destroyed the ozone layer were greater than the economic benefits of its continued manufacture and use, and preventive action was warranted despite the existing uncertainties in the science.

---

[43] Angelo Fichera, "Manipulated Video Targeting Pelosi Goes Viral," FactCheck.org (May 24, 2019). https://www.factcheck.org/2019/05/manipulated-video-targeting-pelosi-goes-viral/.
[44] Veronica Stracqualursi, "GOP Congressman Shares Fake Image of Obama with Iranian President," (January 7, 2020). https://www.cnn.com/2020/01/07/politics/paul-gosar-fake-photo-obama-iran/index.html.
[45] Angelo Fichera, "Photos of Soldiers during Trump Visit Not 'Fake'," FactCheck.org (December 3, 2019). https://www.factcheck.org/2019/12/photo-of-soldiers-during-trump-visit-not-fake/.

EXPERTS ARE TASKED WITH FORGING AND COMMUNICATING CONSENSUS

Consider next the identification and acceptance of experts. For thousands of years, societies have adopted informal and ad hoc solutions. An example of note for the American Philosophical Society arose during the eighteenth century when doubts emerged about the validity of what would now be thought of as hypnotism as a treatment for hysteria. Such treatments were being promulgated by Franz Mesmer and his colleague Charles d'Eslon. Mesmer was an eighteenth-century physician and astronomer (interestingly, a patron of the arts and of Mozart who was rewarded with mention in the opera *Così fan tutte*). In their medical practices, he and d'Eslon proposed and used a then influential theory of **animal magnetism**. The supposed mechanisms underlying this theory were wrong, but some of the ideas were surprisingly forward thinking. Mesmer and d'Eslon were likely not charlatans: They believed in the efficacy of their mesmerism treatments and saw marked responses in their patients (likely due to what we now ascribe to placebo effects). Indeed, it is possible that mesmerism helped initiate the field of psychiatry.

What was the treatment and who was being treated? In Mesmer's role as physician, he began treating "hysterical" women. *Hysterical* did not then have its present meaning (i.e., extreme, uncontrolled emotion)[46] and stood for supposed ailments particular to women. First identified by Hippocrates, *hysteria* draws its name from the Greek word for *uterus*.[47]

Mesmer's treatments, initially done with magnets and based on his theory, proved successful by standards of the day. They involved what we now know as *hypnotism* but for quite some time was known as *mesmerism*. The treatments were so "successful" that Mesmer and d'Eslon soon came to have more patients than they could handle. They branched out by magnetizing bottles of water and trees, allowing treatment of multiple women at once. Many members of society, including a number of prominent scientists, raised an outcry, believing the treatments a scam, and the theory behind them ludicrous.

In 1782, the king of France, Louis XVI, appointed two commissions to investigate Mesmer's claims. One was led by Benjamin Franklin, the

---

[46] Helen King, *Hysteria beyond Freud: Once upon a text: Hysteria from Hippocrates* (Berkeley: University of California Press, 1993), 3–30.

[47] Kathleen Hall Jamieson, *Beyond the Double Bind: Women and Leadership* (New York: Oxford University Press, 1995), 89.

US ambassador to France at the time, and eight eminent scientists, including Antoine-Laurent Lavoisier, the father of modern chemistry. Testing was done at Franklin's estate due to his then health problems. What may have been the first controlled psychology studies were used, showing no difference in results for objects patients believed to have been magnetized, whether or not they actually were. It is interesting to note that the effects in both the treatment and the control conditions were very strong, as the commissioners noted, and treatments based on the effects of mind upon body, and "placebo effects" have continued in various forms to the present day. To return to the main point, realizing that the issues required a consensus of experts, Louis XVI appointed a group whose expertise and authority he believed would be beyond question and whose conclusions would therefore be accepted generally.

Because Abraham Lincoln too recognized the need for our country to rely on valid scientific advice, in 1863 the sixteenth president signed into law the incorporation of the National Academy of Sciences, whose members were tasked with giving the government the best possible advice on scientific matters. For the most part the Academy has provided good advice, and the government has accepted it and acted upon it, sometimes taking actions that took into account political considerations in addition to the expert advice. Although even a consensus of experts can be wrong, such agreement is usually the best evaluation of evidence that is available at a given time. Because this is the case, it is usually wisest to plan action based on such a consensus. Unfortunately, throughout history, the best expert advice has often been ignored, with immediate or potential unfortunate consequences. It is not uncommon for a public decision-maker's personal beliefs to differ from an expert consensus, and it is a difficult matter to communicate that consensus view in a way that will change entrenched beliefs.[48]

THE PRECISION OF EVIDENCE VARIES

The examples we have mentioned and the ones we all have encountered suggest that the accuracy and quality of evidence vary enormously. At the less precise end of the spectrum, we have lie detection, a fragment of

---

[48] Stephan Lewandowsky, Giles E. Gignac, ad Samuel Vaughan, "The Pivotal Role of Perceived Scientific Consensus in Acceptance of Science," *Nature Climate Change* 3, no. 4 (2013): 399–404. https://doi.org/10.1038/nclimate1720; Stephan Lewandowsky, John Cook, Nicholas Fay, and Giles E. Gignac, "Science by Social Media: Attitudes towards Climate Change Are Mediated by Perceived Social Consensus," *Memory & Cognition* 47, no. 8 (2019): 1445–56, https://doi.org/10.3758/s13421-019-00965-x.

an ancient manuscript, a part of a fossil, testimony concerning an event experienced thirty years in the past, a possible observation of a neutrino collision, and much more in this vein. At the more precise end of the spectrum, we have DNA analysis, massive destruction occasioned by explosion of a bomb, a bullet found lodged in a body, and so on. However, as we have tried to demonstrate, whatever the precision, human expert judgment is essential.

CONCLUSIONS

Evidence is not a thing or an object, but rather the beginning of a process of evaluation and interpretation, a process that is often difficult and laden with opportunities for error, and a process that requires human expertise to achieve an optimal result. This story is an old one. At the dawn of history in ancient Mesopotamia there were seven kingdoms in seven cities, founded on principles formulated by seven wise men who advised the kings. These seven sages were, according to recent scholarship, the source of the "seven pillars of wisdom" referred to in Proverbs 9:1, and in the title of Lawrence of Arabia's memoir.[49] The practice of institutionalized expertise is then as old as writing, has persisted in both formal and informal incarnations to the present day, and overall has managed to guide progress in human society.

---

[49] Stephen Stigler, *The Seven Pillars of Statistical Wisdom* (Cambridge, MA: Harvard University Press, 2016), 11–12.

Chapter 2

Peculiar Blue Spots: Evidence and Causes around 1800

Jutta Schickore

In 1778, the journal *Hannoverisches Magazin* published the following query: "For several years, I have experienced the misfortune that my fresh milk develops blue spots, which gradually spread across the surface and eventually color the cream blue. The consequence is that either the milk has to be thrown out or it has to be skimmed early, which means that only half of the cream is obtained. Various measures have been taken, the jars were boiled and cleaned, but to no avail. Anyone who knows of a well-proven means against this evil is requested to announce it in this journal."[1]

Several late eighteenth-century journals and magazines reported that blue spots sometimes appeared on fresh milk, eventually turning it completely blue. Blue milk tastes bad, it cannot easily be turned into butter or cream, and some observers even reported that people and animals who consumed it would get sick.[2] The phenomenon posed a significant threat to the prosperity of farmers. What was it? What caused it? What could be done about it? Who could say? Many people weighed in: those with training in pathology (veterinary and human), organic and agricultural chemistry,

---

[1] Anon., "Anfragen," *Hannoverisches Magazin, worin kleine Abhandlungen, einzelne Gedanken, Nachrichten, Vorschläge und Erfahrungen, so die Verbesserung des Nahrungs-Standes, die Land- und Stadt-Wirthschaft, Handlung, Manufacturen und Künste, die Physik, die Sittenlehre und angenehmen Wissenschaften betreffen, gesamlet und aufbewahret sind* 16, 73tes Stück (1778): 1165–67.

[2] There was red and yellow milk as well, but blue milk was the focus of inquiry until the late nineteenth century. The problem went away around 1900 with increased attention to hygiene and the reorganization and regulation of dairy farming as part of consumer protection. See K. Smith-Howard, *Pure and Modern Milk* (Oxford: Oxford University Press, 2014). In the eighteenth and nineteenth centuries no systematic inspections were performed; sanitation officers mostly only got involved when a problem appeared.

natural history, and hygiene, as well as farmers and even parish priests. Around 1800, the phenomenon was considered so bad for the economy that government officials were called in to help. The inquirers suggested possible causes and various remedies for blue milk and reported successful and unsuccessful attempts to prevent milk from turning blue.

Blue milk research illustrates several aspects of evidence collection and assessment in the search for its causes. It exemplifies how inquirers dealt with and thought about the difficult problem of establishing causes for something in situations when not much is known about a phenomenon of interest. In the late eighteenth century, many empirical strategies for distinguishing between causation and correlation were well established. Yet it was by no means easy to apply them to the problem of blue milk because it was not even clear where and how to start the inquiry. Inquirers needed to determine what factors *could* potentially be relevant for the occurrence of blue milk. To do that, they needed to adopt an interpretation of the phenomenon (however preliminary) that could guide their search for putative causes and subsequent testing of the suspected cause–effect relationship. The initial reports on blue milk suggest that these were not easy tasks, even though accepted strategies for establishing cause–effect relations were in place. Eighteenth-century practitioners mobilized everyday experiences and various available medical and scientific theories to chart the inquiry space and to guide their search for causes, slowly turning observations and empirical trials into evidence for and against their nascent conjectures about the nature of blue milk, its origin, and its prevention.

Blue milk continued to puzzle practitioners and researchers until the early twentieth century. In this chapter, I concentrate on investigations in the late eighteenth century, the time when discussions about blue milk began to appear in print. I take only a brief look at mid-nineteenth-century research on blue milk to consider diachronic changes in practices of evidence collection. The general understanding of causation and of how to examine cause–effect relationships did not change, but as invisible agents became serious candidate causes for blue milk, new kinds of evidence became significant in the debate. For the purposes of this chapter, I limit myself to inquirers in the German lands, although blue milk was not just a German problem.

FOOD, DIRT, WITCHCRAFT, AND DISEASE

In the late eighteenth century, the occurrence of blue milk was reported in cameralist and agricultural journals, in magazines for general audiences, and even in philosophical journals and magazines for juvenile readers. All authors agreed that the blue spots on milk were undesirable. Everything else was in flux: There was no agreed-upon description of blue milk and of how it developed, it was unclear what might cause it, there was not even an agreement on how dangerous it was to consume blue milk: Was it safe for humans? For animals?[3]

It appears that the problem had been long-standing but had rarely been reported. The editor of the agricultural journal *Landwirthschaftliches Magazin* Sebastian Georg Friedrich Mund noted in 1788 that the problem was far more common than previously assumed. Various periodicals— specialist journals and nonspecialist magazines—published queries, asking all readers for input on how to treat the problem. Farmers, professors, naturalists, doctors, veterinarians, and government officials offered observations, small trials, and good advice on treatments, but nothing very definite. It was not even clear how to categorize or interpret the phenomenon—was it a sign of disease? A result of contamination? A product of a physiological process? If one does not even know what the problem is, then it is very hard to investigate it and look for possible causes. If the cause was in the milk, the milk needed to be handled differently. But perhaps it was something in the soil or the air of the stables or the dairy? Where to start?

In hindsight, we notice that the trials and treatments that were proposed were colored, as it were, by the inquirers' assumptions about the nature of the phenomenon. Some of these assumptions mobilized everyday experiences, others were informed by contemporaneous science and medicine. The section on blue milk in the synoptic article on cattle husbandry in Johann Georg Krünitz's economic encyclopedia of 1782, for instance, recommended storing the milk in a clean place, not in the living room where the farmhands would smoke tobacco. The storage room should be well aired; milk should not be stored with sauerkraut or meat. Vats should be clean. Glass vats would be better than wooden ones because they could so easily be cleaned.[4] Krünitz—or the practitioners the article drew upon— evidently assumed that blue milk could be understood against the background of miasmatic theories of disease. In this view, diseases were caused by polluted vapors or dirty, filthy environments.[5] Blue coloration could be prevented if no contaminated air reached the milk.

---

[3] The considerations reflect the social hierarchies of the period. The question really was whether the milk was safe to consume for farmhands and maid servants (and pigs).

[4] Krünitz, Johann Georg, *Oekonomische Encyklopädie, oder Allgemeines System der Staats- Stadt-Haus- u. Landwirthschaft, in Alphabetischer Ordnung*, vol. 124 (Berlin: Pauli, 1817), 527.

[5] On the classification and cultural significance of "dirt," see Mary Douglas's classic, *Purity and Danger: An Analysis of Concepts of Pollution and Taboo* (London: Routledge & K. Paul, 1966).

Krünitz's encyclopedia article contains a second section that deals with blue milk, about 200 pages later. This section assumes that an actual cow disease caused blue milk. In it, Krünitz reported that some people had successfully used "1 spoonful of ground caraway with half a quart of water. Herr Gerike recommends stinkstone [anthraconite—a mineral], Herr Sander *Buchaschenlauge* [lye made by lixiviating hornbeam ashes], red Bolus [curative earth] and linseed oil."[6] He did not indicate how the success was determined, nor did he report whether the treatment had helped once or repeatedly.

Other inquirers suggested different remedies to give to the animals, depending on what kind of disease they suspected. For instance, those who thought that the cows' digestive system was affected recommended Glauber's Salt, as it was known to regulate the digestive system. Belladonna was recommended because of its generally known purifying powers. Occasionally, but not always, the short notices recommending these drugs reported a case of successful treatment of the suspected disease—a piece of evidence that the proposed remedy worked.

A nameless author for *Hannoversches Magazin* (a nonspecialist journal for the educated public) who self-identified as "careful physician" considered two possible causes of blue milk: miasmatic vapors and bad feed. He settled for the first, drawing on previous experience with cattle farming, dirt, and cleaning and supported by observations. He excluded contaminated storage vats as causes for blue milk because those were clean. He excluded bad feed because the grazing land was good; it was as it had always been and sheep and goats grazing on it did not produce blue milk. He then observed the milk itself "very closely," finding that some surfaces had small spots, others big spots; some spots remained on the surface, others had spread to the bottom of the container. "Naturally," he put it, the cause must be external to the milk and in the vapors of the cellar. As it "occurred" to him that fire had cleansing powers, he carried out a quick trial: He burned a wood fire for several hours, thus removing the suspected cause. Indeed, the evil "disappeared immediately," Concluding with a warning about making fire in a cellar with wooden beams, the author asked that other people communicate their experiences.[7] This author thought of the blue coloration of milk in analogy to a disease-like defect of milk,

---

[6] Krünitz, *Encyklopädie*, 766.

[7] Anon., "Mittel wider das Blauwerden der Milch," *Hannoverisches Magazin, worin kleine Abhandlungen, einzelne Gedanken, Nachrichten, Vorschläge und Erfahrungen, so die Verbesserung des Nahrungs-Standes, die Land- und Stadt-Wirthschaft, Handlung, Manufacturen und Künste, die Physik, die Sittenlehre und angenehmen Wissenschaften betreffen, gesamlet und aufbewahret sind* 17, 30tes Stück (1779): 475–80.

produced by unclean and impure environments. Blue milk could thus be prevented by removing dirt, as his observations affirmed.

Some people suspected that certain plants might be the cause of the evil and thus changed the cattle food. In 1799, an agricultural handbook reported a small trial: One farmer, who had suspected blueweed, which grew in his field of clover, fed grass for two days, thus removing the suspected cause. The blue color disappeared. Then he again fed clover and blueweed for three days, and the milk turned blue again. The report concluded that those plants were thus the cause of blue milk—not witchcraft, as the author added.

These examples show several things: First, there was a general sense that the observations of the circumstances in which blue milk appeared could give clues to its nature. Second, for the search for potential causes among these circumstances, some guiding assumptions about the nature of the phenomenon had to be in place. As long as the investigators did not quite know what they were looking for, their findings were not evidence. Third, inquirers' trials tested for putative causes by removing certain factors to see whether that prevented the phenomenon from appearing, or they observed carefully to see whether the phenomenon occurred when these factors happened to be present. Fourth, even if someone did have a conjecture about a putative cause, testing the conjecture may not be straightforward. How does one clean the air in a cellar, for example? Fifth, quick trials (just done once or without the complementary trial)[8] were tolerated and deemed useful enough for publication by both journal editors and authors.

Only one interpretation of the phenomenon was explicitly excluded from the outset, namely, an explanation by a supernatural cause. Mund noted that "self-interest and superstition" had been the reason why so many people wished to keep the problem secret.[9] I think what he was referring to was the farmers' economic interests and widespread belief in supernatural forces. Afflicted farmers wanted to avoid the impression that their farms were under a bad spell, as it would of course keep itinerant workers from stopping by. Moreover, farmers feared that farmhands and

---

[8] The farmer trying blueweed conducted complementary trials. He first removed blueweed from the cows' food and then introduced it again, comparing the results.

[9] [Georg Heinrich] Borowsky, "Bericht und Gutachten über das Blauwerden der Milch in der Molkerey des Königlichen Amts Frauendorf bei Frankfurt an der Oder," *Landwirthschaftliches Magazin* 4. Quartal (1788): 22–58, 22.

servants would refuse to eat their food if they had reason to assume that it was prepared with blue milk.[10]

A number of authors brought up witchcraft or Satan's evil machinations as a possible cause of blue milk, but only to dismiss them outright and to contrast superstition unfavorably with proper scientific inquiry. This criticism went both against the ordinary people and against the authority of churchmen. Several authors expressed concern about the level of superstition among farmhands, servants, and the occasional clergyman. The Enlightenment magazine *Deutsche Zeitung für die Jugend und ihre Freunde* of 1789 lamented that the local pastor, his wife, and the maid believed blue milk to be a sign of Satan's influence in our daily lives and had turned to a "wise woman" to get rid of the evil. The stable was smoked out (while making the sign of the cross), little bags with chamomile were placed in it, herbs mixed with hairs from the affected cows were boiled slowly to cause pain to the witch, and so forth. The writer (likely the editor of the journal, Rudolph Zacharias Becker) concluded, with indignation: "such a superstitious man is supposed to teach wisdom and virtue to the common people!"[11] The naturalist and pastor Johann Ephraim Goeze reported, with exasperation, "various silly applications," such as "holy water, holy salt, and three square little pieces of bread" added to the milk along with a prayer.[12] Goeze complained that although he had demonstrated the effectiveness of certain rational [*vernünftige*] measures—such as the addition of a spoonful of buttermilk to the fresh milk or the use of new storage vats—farmhands, maids, and even his wife were not to be convinced. From their point of view, it seems, Goeze's demonstration was not sufficient evidence that blue milk was a natural occurrence and could be dealt with systematically.[13]

Occasionally, an inquirer took a more systematic approach to the problem. In 1788, Mund's *Landwirthschaftliches Magazin* carried a long

---

[10] One contributor to the debate, the public health inspector Borowsky, noted that it was common to give the butter from blue milk to servants—he thought that it should not be done, as it was probably unhealthy. However, on the farm he had inspected, the servants had become used to it and were able to overcome their disgust (Borowsky, "Bericht," 26).

[11] Anon. [Becker], "Crossen in der Neumark," *Deutsche Zeitung für die Jugend und ihre Freunde; oder, Moralische Schilderungen der Menschen, Sitten und Staaten unsrer Zeit* 6 (1789): 361–62, 362; see also Johann August Ephraim Goeze, "Von der blauen Milch; ingleichen von der Blutmilch der Kühe," *Nützliches Allerley aus der Natur und dem gemeinen Leben für allerley Leser*, vol. III (Leipzig: Weidmann, 1786), 103–15.

[12] Johann August Ephraim Goeze, "Mittel wider die blaue Milch," *Eine pure Dorfreise: zum Unterricht und Vergnügen der Jugend* (Leipzig: Weidmann, 1788), 245–49, especially 247.

[13] It would be most interesting to have more detailed records of Goeze's demonstrations and the people's reactions to it—what exactly was Goeze's evidence against the supernatural? Why did his audience continue to believe in witchcraft? Why did they consider blue milk to be evidence of supernatural powers, and what would have convinced them otherwise?

article by one Dr. Lichtenstein, a "doctor and professor" at the local university of Helmstädt. The academic title did not automatically mark an expert: Lichtenstein felt compelled to point out that while he was not a farmer himself, he had the necessary expertise to conduct the investigation, having cooperated with local farmers. Lichtenstein called for "close exami-nation" [*genaue Prüfung*] of the causes of blue milk. He had an interpreta-tion: His idea was that blue milk was a product of putrefaction. But defending this view was not the point of his article. His interests were practical. He wanted a treatment and expressed the hope that he would be able to move the search for treatments beyond what he described as the haphazard trial of this or that putative remedy. At the same time, he surmised that the phenomenon could be produced by different causes, which would presumably require different means of prevention.

Lichtenstein presented his article as a "proposal" to the "economic public." It is in fact a call for empirical data, an invitation to everyone to contact him if they had encountered the evil and to describe in detail in what circumstances it had occurred. He offered some guidelines: To give "the thinking farmer's attention a direction for observation,"[14] Lichtenstein suggested some things to which the farmers might pay attention. On ten pages, Lichtenstein listed a total of twenty-six "special circumstances" [*specielle Umstände*]; circumstances ranging from the quality of the feed to the age of the cows to the process of churning while making butter—and he thought that his list was nowhere near completion.

The proposal illustrates the extent of the task everyone faced: Where does one begin the search for a remedy for a disease or defect when one is not even sure about the nature of the phenomenon itself? What circumstances might possibly be relevant and should be closely examined? Which ones could be ignored? As Lichtenstein's list shows, there were endless possibilities—vapors, dirty stables and dairies, the constitution of the animals, feed, soil, the seasons, and so on. By themselves, the descrip-tions of these circumstances were not evidence for or against anything. They became significant relative to a point of view, but what was the appropriate point of view?[15]

Lichtenstein was not the only one who expressed dissatisfaction with quick superficial observations and trials. In 1788, Theodor Pyl's pharma-ceutical and forensic journal *Neues Magazin für die gerichtliche Arzney-*

---

[14] [Anton] Lichtenstein, "Anfrage. Ueber die blaue Milch der Kühe," *Landwirthschaftliches Magazin* 1. Quartal (1788): 48–66, especially 65.

[15] I am using the broad notion "point of view" because I want to set aside the question of whether these conjectures can be properly considered scientific theories. This question is not relevant for the present discussion.

kunde und medicinische Polizey published the detailed report of an official investigation. Government officials instructed Professor Borowsky, naturalist from Frankfurt/Oder, to investigate the problem, as blue milk had appeared in the dairy in Frauendorf near Frankfurt. The journal *Landwirthschaftliches Magazin*, which was more accessible to farmers, reprinted the report in the same volume as Lichtenstein's piece. Introducing the article, the editor, Mund, voiced some concerns about the abundance of notices, scattered observations, and reports on quick trials, favorably contrasting Borowsky's painstaking inquiry with the available "separate, superficial remarks and thoughts," which were more "suggestions for treatments and promotion of certain quite absurd remedies" than thorough investigations of the problem and its causes.[16]

Borowsky himself began his meticulous official report with some remarks about proper methods of inquiry. His goal had been "to observe as carefully and exactly as possible all relevant circumstances and phenomena as well as to make his own observations [*Bemerkungen*], experiences, and investigations in this respect, and especially to examine the state of their fields [*Hütung*] in all conditions and purposefully, in order to establish the reason [*Grund*] and proximate causes [*veranlassende Ursachen*] of such a strange physical-economic occurrence."[17] His report shows that the account of the phenomenon itself had become much more complex. Borowsky's is one of the first detailed descriptions of blue milk—its changing appearance, its taste, and its behavior in the dairy. Borowsky tells us that the phenomenon alternately appeared and disappeared for a few days. The weather was dry and warm, with some rainy days. The milk is first white but somewhat bitter; after two or three days, light blue spots appear; the spots get bigger and turn darker blue; then the spots extend to the bottom of the vessel. If there is cream, it is slimy, it is very difficult to make butter, which is also slimy and "extremely disgusting [*höchst ekelhaft*]."[18]

Borowsky's report also shows, once again, that without a point of view the possibilities for observing potentially relevant circumstances of a phenomenon are virtually endless. In his own trials, Borowsky examined the impact of various circumstances on fresh milk, such as whether different storage vats, storage places, and types of feed made a difference to it. He

---

[16] Borowsky, "Bericht," 21.

[17] Borowsky, "Bericht," 23.

[18] Borowsky, "Bericht" 26. Borowsky outsourced the chemical analysis of blue milk to a local expert, apothecary Graf, but did not get very helpful information back. Graf performed a comparative chemical analysis of white and blue milk and found nothing remarkable except a lack of oily parts in blue milk, to which he ascribed the blue color (Graf, "Versuche mit der Frauendorfer sogenannten blauen Milch," *Landwirthschaftliches Magazin* 4. Quartal (1788): 58–60).

considered numerous small details that might affect the milk, even the cleaning techniques for the storage vats. Reading through the report, one finds many descriptions of trials done to establish what happened when a specific circumstance, a putative cause, was removed. However, one can again appreciate how difficult it must have been to determine just what the candidate factors were when one does not quite know what one is looking for, and how laborious it was to try them all systematically.

For example, different types of containers were tried—wooden and clay, old and newly purchased. They were boiled with various herbs—wormwood, hops. Sometimes, the problem disappeared—perhaps by accident, as Borowsky noted.[19] Borowsky had some Frauendorf dairy milk transported to his home and put in clay pots to see whether the blue color would appear in a different location. He observed it carefully, and it did not turn blue. Why not? What was different? Perhaps shaking and moving the milk during transport had an influence on the behavior of the milk?[20] Perhaps this sample would not have turned blue had it remained in Frauendorf? One can easily think of many other factors that he did not mention and that could have had an impact on the behavior of the milk—the temperature in the storage rooms? The season? The location of the farm? And so on. These and many other factors would have to be tested one by one to see whether they had anything to do with blue milk.

Overall, the results of Borowsky's trials were confusing to him, even though he tried his best to proceed systematically and to keep everything fixed except the factors to be tested. For instance, sometimes two samples of the same milk turned blue in some containers, not in others; and when the same containers were used again with fresh milk, the milk sometimes stayed white even though it had turned blue previously in the very same container. In addition, his own findings occasionally contradicted other reports. Rinsing the containers with buttermilk did not help in Frauendorf—although it did elsewhere, according to a report published in *Beckmann's physikalisch-ökonomischer Bibliothek*; and it worked on a nearby farm as well.[21] Borowsky did not follow up on this point, even though it would have been straightforward to design a trial to test the effects of buttermilk.

Nevertheless, this was an official report, so a concluding statement was called for. Borowsky ended with a recommendation, but he also indicated

---

[19] Borowsky, "Bericht," 31.
[20] Borowsky, "Bericht," 28.
[21] Borowsky, "Bericht," 27–28.

that numerous questions remained open.[22] In the end, he blamed the land. He reiterated that neither the dairy, nor the containers, nor air, nor water were to blame. He believed the cause was, indeed, the state of the fields. He was convinced that it was the extremely bad location and constitution of the grazing grounds—specifically, the plants that grew on the wet and bad soil—that was "the only efficient cause" of the blue coloration.[23]

In contrast to the previous authors, who did not go into much detail about their observations and trials, Borowsky argued his view by pointing to trials and observations as evidence for it. There was evidence from trials—when he had a couple of cows brought to a different farm with better land, they gave white and good milk. There was observational evidence and evidence from analogy as well. The soil was wet, the ground uneven, some plants were rotted. Farming expertise suggested that these conditions were not ideal for cattle. It was known that certain plants—hard, coarse, rough grass—was not good for cattle, and it was exactly this sort of grass that was growing on the land at Frauendorf. This was a consequence of flooding that had occurred twice in the recent past. Other farms with similar land, which had also been affected by flooding, also had blue milk. Moreover, in the winter, when the cows were fed dried plants, milk never turned blue. Borowsky included four pages listing the names of plants he had found on the land but was unable to identify which of the plants had the evil effect—probably a combination of several, he surmised, but he was not able to test them all.

Last, he offered an explanation as to how the effect might be produced in the milk, assuming that certain plants were to blame. In the article, the hypothesis (Borowsky's term) appears almost as an afterthought, not at the beginning, as in Lichtenstein's piece. Borowsky suspected that pungent, coarse, and corrosive plant ingredients in the alimentary fluid would injure interior vessels. Blood globules would get into the milk, and a chemical reaction (generation of volatile alkali [ammonia]) took place and caused the milk to turn blue. He did not offer much evidential support for his hypothesis. It informed the choice of the drug he had given the cows, but

---

[22] For an attempt to be comprehensive and to answer *all* the questions arising from investigating any and all of these circumstances, see Christoph Hoffmann's account of Jean-André Deluc's treatise on barometers and thermometers. Hoffmann concludes: "Every solved problem led simultaneously to another unsolved one: the correction of the influence of temperature on the mercury column involved the analysis of the thermometer; the right method to take the reading lead to the investigation of the tube; the effect of temperature on the air-pressure called for the study of its humidity, and so on" (Hoffmann, Christoph, "The Ruin of a Book: Jean Andre De Luc's *Recherches sur les modifications de l'atmosphère* [1772]," *Modern Language Notes* 118 (2003): 568–602, especially 601). Hoffmann describes the remaining tome, and the entire project, as *the ruin of a book*.

[23] Borowsky, "Bericht," 50.

no decisive evidence was forthcoming. He had made the drug himself from "strengthening and astringent" ingredients—the recipe is provided. He gave it to two of the cows. He professed to be mystified by the results: a few days after the treatment ended, they gave milk that sometimes stayed white, sometimes turned blue, a little blue, completely blue ... the other cows gave milk that would always turn blue.[24]

Unlike some of the farmers and veterinarians who only had time for a quick trial, Borowsky carried out a series of trials and formulated a position that he supported with a variety of findings that provided evidence for his position. It was not conclusive evidence, as he himself admitted. It convinced the officials only to an extent, as the tortuous addendum shows. Perhaps alarmed by the prospect of having to invest in new draining systems, the sanitation office added its own assessment to the report. While praising Borowsky for his thoroughness, the officials argued that there were *two* causes for blue milk; one being a kind of mold "due to dirt and bad air in the dairy."[25] As Borowsky had shown that the Frauenhofer dairy was clean, this cause could be excluded there. Borowsky's trials showed, the officials found, that the other cause obtained, the plants growing on the bad soil. This cause needed to be removed, otherwise the seeds of the inferior plants would spread to the surrounding farms. That, however, was a task for "economic experts and surveyors" who knew more about drainage than the sanitation office, yet it would be "not unuseful" [*nicht unnützlich*] to call in Borowsky, who had demonstrated all the required expertise.[26]

OBSERVATION AND DISSECTION OF ACCOMPANYING CIRCUMSTANCES

I have noted that several late eighteenth-century reports of blue milk appeared rather quickly and were superficial and some trials were found to be unsatisfying even by people at the time. Borowsky and Lichtenstein both raised concerns about the quality of available information. At the time, quite elaborate methodologies of experimentation had been advanced by several luminaries, including Alexander von Humboldt, Felice Fontana, Jean Senebier, and Albrecht von Haller. Enlightenment educators offered similar advice in their books on practical logic. They all emphasized how

---

[24] However, Borowsky added, even if that drug were successful, it would not do anything to remove the primary cause, and it would be too expensive to use these drugs permanently anyway.

[25] K. P. O. C. S., "Gutachten des Königl. Obercollegii Sanitatis, über vorstehenden Bericht," *Landwirthschaftliches Magazin* 4. Quartal (1788): 60–62, especially 61.

[26] K. P. O. C. S., "Gutachten," 62.

important it was in a search for putative causes for effects to record carefully and test all the circumstances in which the phenomena of interest would appear or not appear.[27] This was the first step, and once a putative cause had been identified, the hypothesis could be tested. Borowsky's and Lichtenstein's methodological remarks echo these more elaborate ideas, and their projects turn them into practice—thus inadvertently illustrating how difficult this was.

Encyclopedias and books on logic explained that careful observation of all circumstances was the first step, but only the first step, in establishing cause–effect relationships. Merely observing an association between two phenomena could lead to error. Notably, in books about practical logic, the "correct method" is contrasted with superstition. As Peter Villaume explained in his book, the superstitious would hear the cry of an owl while someone was dying and would conclude from this experience that owls announce death, failing to consider that owls fly and cry every night and that many people die without an owl announcing their death. It was, therefore, prudent to check carefully whether there was indeed a connection between the putative cause and effect. And once a connection was "visible, or probable," it was still necessary to observe many instances to make sure that there really was a cause–effect relation, not just a connection. An experimental trial [*Versuch*] could do this better than repeated observation because in it, "one places a thing in different circumstances to observe its effects; one separates in one trial those things which were connected in another trial.[28]

In 1787, the *Berlinische Monatsschrift* printed a delightful illustration of some methodological ideals of the period, authored by one Philozoos (a lover of animals). The journal, a favorite of Immanuel Kant's, published Enlightenment philosophy and scientific reports. Philozoos set out to ridicule animal magnetism—the idea that magnetic powers could be used to influence human and animal bodies and to cure diseases—using the phenomenon of blue milk.[29] The fact that research on blue milk served to

---

[27] For details, see Jutta Schickore, *About Method: Experimenters, Snake Venom, and the History of Writing Scientifically* (Chicago: University of Chicago Press, 2017), chapters 5 and 6.

[28] Peter Villaume, *Practische Logik für junge Leute die nicht studieren wollen* (Berlin: Lagarde & Friedrich, 1787), 120. For similar distinctions between the goals of observations and experiments, see the contemporaneous encyclopedia articles on experiment by Gehler (Johann Samuel Traugott Gehler, "Versuch," in *Physikalisches Wörterbuch oder Versuch einer Erklärung der vornehmsten Begriffe und Kunstwörter der Naturlehre* [Leipzig: Schwickert, 1791]) and Fischer (Johann Karl Fischer, "Versuch," in *Physikalisches Wörterbuch; oder, Erklärung der vornehmsten zur Physik gehörigen Begriffe und Kunstwörter* [Göttingen: Dieterich, 1804]).

[29] According to the Brockhaus encyclopedia, this could be done by influencing the iron in the animal's body (F. A. Brockhaus, "Der Magnetismus," in *Brockhaus Conversations-Lexikon*, vol. 3. [Amsterdam: Kunst- und Industrie-Comptoir, 1809], 18–22).

illustrate the principles of good experimental science tells us how momentous the topic had become. Philozoos first lavished the advocates of animal magnetism with mock praise: They wrote with "sublime abstractness" and could divine diseases and future events out of one-hundred observed facts (Philozoos 1787, 45). Of course, he added, such a kind of writing would be "obscure to the eyes of the benighted, who demand cold, dry statements of accurately observed facts, dissection [*Zergliederung*] of all accompanying circumstances, dissociation of all preconceived opinions, careful separation of the observed fact from speculation."[30]

Philozoos then described how he used animal magnetism, this "wonderful means," to deal with blue milk. Typically, a treatment involved "manipulations" [*Manipulationen*]—touching and rubbing the patient—to allow the flow of magnetic powers. Philozoos reported that it was very difficult to "manipulate" the cows and apply the means of "disorganization," not only because cows are not used to this treatment but especially because they do not read. Their recovery is thus not improved by the powers of hope and imagination, as a human patient's recovery would be. At long last, Philozoos did succeed in hypnotizing one cow. The animal was in magnetic raptures, raised its head and named the herbs that could remove the problem. Its sensibilities and powers of perception were vastly increased, not to mention its sudden sexual prowess.

The audience of *Berlinische Monatsschrift* was probably well read and aware that the description of the treatment was copied out from a much-discussed letter on Lavater's animal magnetism, published in the journal *Hannoverisches Magazin* earlier that year.[31] In the episode recounted in that letter it was a young woman who had been manipulated and hypnotized, and who performed the exact same acts as Philozoos's enchanted cow.

The article is frivolous, and it is of course not about blue milk, its causes and treatment. It is about the hallmarks of good science and the principles of sound inquiry, although the fact that the phenomenon of blue milk serves as an illustration does indicate how much attention blue milk was getting at the time. The remark about the benighted researchers and what they failed to do tells us something about the methodological goals of the period: It is, in fact, the benighted researcher who fails to separate

---

[30] "Philozoos," "Auszug eines Schreibens, über eine neue sehr merkwürdige Entdeckung, den Magnetismus betreffend," *Berlinische Monatsschrift* 10 (1787): 44–56, 46–47.

[31] Bicker, "Herrn Doctor Bickers zu Bremen Brief an den Herrn Hofrath Baldiner, über Lavaters Magnetismus," *Hannoverisches Magazin, worin kleine Abhandlungen, einzelne Gedanken, Nachrichten, Vorschläge und Erfahrungen, so die Verbesserung des Nahrungs-Standes, die Land- und Stadt-Wirthschaft, Handlung, Manufacturen und Künste, die Physik, die Sittenlehre und angenehmen Wissenschaften betreffen, gesamlet und aufbewahret sind* 15, 3tes Stück (1787): 33–48.

observed fact and speculation, and who does not do what a good, diligent inquirer must do—dissect all accompanying circumstances of the thing under study.

As we have seen, several late eighteenth-century inquirers did their best to "dissect the circumstances" while investigating blue milk. Some investigators, such as Borowsky, outlined quite elaborate ideas about how to conduct the trials that were needed to identify causes. Borowsky's expressed plan echoes contemporaneous views on good science—careful observation, meticulous recording of circumstances, and trials conducted to establish causal relations. At the same time, his own trials fell short of his ideals. Moreover, there were plenty of less sophisticated trials that did not provide very strong evidence for the causal associations that inquirers had in mind. Some made little effort to dissect fully the circumstances, and many did not perform repeated or comparative trials, checking whether a putative factor really did make a difference.

It is likely that some practitioner-authors simply lacked the time and the means for systematic investigations. More important, however, "dissection of all accompanying circumstances" is not an easy task. It is one thing to insist that all circumstances of certain phenomena be examined; it is quite another thing to determine what the accompanying circumstances *are* in a given situation. Besides, how can one be sure that one has identified everything that is relevant to the task at hand? That is only possible against the background of a hypothesis, however preliminary, that helps separate the relevant from the irrelevant and to decide which circumstance is worthy of dissection and observation, and which is just an unimportant background condition. And even then, one may miss something of importance.

The philosopher of science Carl Gustav Hempel once remarked: "what particular sorts of data it is reasonable to collect is not determined by the problem under study, but by a tentative answer to it that the investigator entertains in the form of a conjecture or hypothesis."[32] Together, Lichtenstein's and Borowsky's reports and all the other small notices and records exemplify the hard work that goes into that task. Methodological ideas about how to establish a causal nexus were in place in the late eighteenth century. General strategies for distinguishing the spurious correlation from the cause–effect relation were available and widely accepted. Yet there were so many tentative answers for the inquirers to entertain, whereby each came with its own set of data that would be reasonable to collect. Testing for an unhealthy plant, for instance, would require specimen collection,

---

[32] Carl G. Hempel, *Philosophy of Natural Science* (Upper Saddle River, NJ: Prentice-Hall, 1966), 12.

classification, and feeding varying quantities of the plant, perhaps in in different combinations with other plants. Removing dirt from the surroundings would require—what, exactly? How can one remove contaminations that may be invisible? *Even if* one has a conjecture, or two, about a probable cause, it may not be immediately obvious how to test it or how to put the test in practice. Each mode of collecting evidence posed technical and logistic problems that needed to be solved. Evidently, a research methodology is not sufficient for doing good science.

ACADEMIC MILK

The story of blue milk does not end here. In the mid-nineteenth century, blue milk was still a frequent nuisance. By the 1850s, it was usually treated as one of many "milk defects" [*Milchfehler*], yet it was more damaging to the farm economy than red, yellow, or bitter milk. Practitioners—mostly veterinarians—continued to observe the phenomenon on farms and in dairies and tried to deal with it there. They continued to report that it occurred often and was very difficult to treat. In 1850, the veterinarian G. Wieners commended William Löbe for devoting more than three pages of his treatise on dairy farming to blue milk, given the "frequent occurrence and stubborn persistence" of this phenomenon.[33] In 1856, the veterinarian Gielen noted that the question of blue milk was "one of the most important" for "our housewives."[34]

Meanwhile, the broader institutional contexts for biomedical research had changed quite dramatically. An increasing number of anatomists and physiologists pursued experiments at universities and medical schools and in designated lab spaces with specialized instruments and equipment. Researchers within these professionalized, academic institutions aligned themselves with different programmatic ideas as they debated fundamental questions about life and health, such as the nature of ferments (chemical vs. organismic?), the nature of disease (miasmatic, contagious, or both?), spontaneous generation, chemical elements, and vital forces.

In the 1840s, investigations of blue milk had also become academic research, and professors of veterinary medicine, anatomists, and physiologists as well as chemists pursued sometimes extensive projects on the topic

---

[33] G. Wieners, "Die Milchwirthschaft u. s. w., besonderer Abdruck aus der Encyclopädie der gesammten Landwirtschaft, herausgegeben v. William Löbe" Leipzig 1851, Verlag von Otto Wiegand," *Repertorium der Thierheilkunde* (Leipzig: Verlag von Otto Wigand, 1851), 197–203, especially 202.

[34] W. Gielen, "Von der blauen Milch der Kühe,"*Magazin für die gesammte Thierheilkunde* 31 (1865): 203–4, especially 204.

in their labs. During the nineteenth century, the conjectures about blue milk gradually solidified into well-defined, distinct positions, in line with the larger programmatic issues under discussion. Some academic inquirers interpreted blue milk as a result of a chemical process of fermentation,[35] others as caused by infusoria or mold.[36] I do not have the space here to discuss the nineteenth-century developments in depth, but I do want to sketch what difference the changes in the research contexts and interests made for the ways in which empirical information was collected, interpreted, and assessed.

In 1842, the veterinarian scientist Christian Joseph Fuchs in Berlin published an extensive study of healthy and defective milk in a major academic journal of veterinary medicine, incorporating microscopic obser-vations. His findings spoke to the larger programmatic questions about the nature of the cause. He supported the organismic explanation of diseased or defective milk, according to which these defects were due to organic causes, to tiny organisms.

Fuchs worked with Christian Ehrenberg, the renowned naturalist and microscopist. At the time, Ehrenberg was widely known for his work on infusoria.[37] Among other things, Ehrenberg's research had shown that infusoria could produce coloration of water and soil.[38] Fuchs seized on the analogy with blue milk and looked for minute organisms in this liquid. The blue spots grew in size and were irregular, which was additional evidence that they were probably organic.[39] Together with Ehrenberg, Fuchs finally found and was able to isolate infusoria in the blue liquid, which were not present in normal milk. Ehrenberg identified these as "vibrion," and Fuchs named them, quite appropriately, "Vibrio cyano-genus." (We still find references to the bacteria cyanogenus in early twenti-eth-century handbooks of hygiene.)

Now Fuchs had identified—even named—a putative material cause for blue milk. But was it really the causal agent? Maybe the defective blue

---

[35] See Gottlieb Carl Haubner, "Ueber die fehlerhafte Beschaffenheit der Kuhmilch im Allgemeinen und über die blaue Milch insbesondere," *Magazin für die gesammte Thierheilkunde* 18 (1852): 1–84,129–202.

[36] Christian Joseph Fuchs, "Beiträge zur nähern Kenntniss der gesunden und fehlerfreien Milch der Hausthiere," *Magazin für die gesammte Thierheilkunde* 7 (1841): 133–96; Carl Lehmann, *Lehrbuch der physiologischen Chemie* (Leipzig: Engelmann, 1853).

[37] Christian Ehrenberg, *Die Infusionsthierchen als vollkommene Organismen. Ein Blick in das tiefere organische Leben der Natur* (Leipzig: Voss, 1838).

[38] For a synoptic, recent overview of Ehrenberg's work at the time, see Mathias Grote, "Aus dem Kleinen bauen sich die Welten—Christian Gottfried Ehrenberg's ökologische Mikrobiologie avant la lettre," in *HiN: Alexander von Humboldt im Netz, XXII*, eds. Ottmar Ette, Eberhard Knobloch, and Ulrich Päßler (Potsdam: Universitätsverlag Potsdam, 2021), 19–32. https://doi.org/10.18443/318.

[39] Fuchs, "Beiträge," 189.

milk generated vibrions?[40] These questions were inspired and enabled by new technical tools (the microscope, especially), but direct evidence of causal agency was hard to come by. It was not so easy to establish what microscopic organisms "really" looked like, let alone what their agency was.[41] On the other hand, there were the familiar problems of dissecting the circumstances and establishing agency, now more difficult because the dissection and manipulation had to be done on the micro level: the blue stuff, the microorganisms, and the surrounding fluid had to be tested separately to see what effects they produced in the milk (if any).

Fuchs found an ingenious solution to his problem of testing for causal efficacy, which mobilized a new kind of evidence. He produced blue milk by indirectly manipulating the invisible agent. He put a trace of blue milk in different fluids (water, sugared water, solution of gum Arabic, blood serum, and marshmallow root solution) and he found that vibrions died in all of them except the last, and no blue color appeared except in marshmallow root. In this medium, they proliferated, coloring the entire sample blue. Transferring a drop of this liquid to healthy milk turned that milk blue.[42] As Fuchs had transferred vibrions from blue milk to marshmallow root solution at a time when no other infusoria were present in the milk, this was (to him, at least) an "evident proof" that they had to be the cause of the blue color in the marshmallow root solution.[43] He could keep vibrio alive in a solution of marshmallow root. Fuchs was thus able to produce blue milk reliably at will, something that other researchers before him had not been able to do. Other liquids, such as water, sugared water, and blood serum, would not turn blue.[44]

Other investigators, however, did not find the evidence as conclusive as Fuchs did. On the contrary, Fuchs's work stimulated intense investigation, not least because Fuchs aligned himself so explicitly with an *organismic* theory of milk defects. Gottlieb Carl Haubner, for instance, interpreted his own experiments on blue milk as evidence for a *chemical* theory of

---

[40] Fuchs, "Beiträge," 191.

[41] The microscopist Focke found them "too small" for meaningful discussions of their features, as Carl Siebold reported (C.T. Siebold, "Bericht über die Leistungen im Gebiete der Anatomie und Physiologie der wirbellosen Tiere," *Archiv für Anatomie, Physiologie und wissenschaftliche Medicin* (1843): I–LXXXVII, especially LXXXV.

[42] Fuchs, "Beiträge," 191.

[43] Fuchs, "Beiträge," 192.

[44] Fuchs was not the first to ever surmise that living organisms might be responsible for blue milk. Other inquirers had already proposed that it was caused by fungus, mold, or infusoria. He was also not the first who solved the practical problem of establishing causal agency by transferring an invisible cause to a new environment (see Jutta Schickore, "Parasites, Pepsin, Pus, and Postulates: Jakob Henle's Essay on Miasma, Contagium, and Miasmatic-Contagious Diseases in Its Original Context, *Bulletin of the History of Medicine* 96 (2022): 612–38.

fermentation.[45] Yet, regardless of the interpretation, the task was, and remained, also for Haubner, the identification of all the factors that could potentially generate the phenomenon, of those background conditions that did not have an impact, and of any factors that interfered with the trial and had to be prevented from having an impact on the situation.[46]

While these investigators were debating the nature of the phenomenon, practitioners—mostly veterinarians—continued to observe blue milk on farms and in dairies and tried to deal with it there.[47] They continued to make their own observations, carried out trials with various drugs, and explored preventive measures, occasionally supplementing their trials with chemical or microscopical investigations or asking experts to do certain analyses for them.[48]

Their main goal was to find a treatment for the still frequent and persistent problem of milk defects. The treatment they hoped to find would prevent the occurrence of blue milk by removing its cause. For them, it was not so important whether the cause of blue milk was living or nonliving, organic or nonorganic. For them it was important to figure out the measures by which this causal agent could be made ineffective or removed. That way, the milk stayed fresh and ready for consumption or processing. The relevant evidence, for them, was not the successful production of blue milk in experiments but the successful prevention of its occurrence.

Academic researchers published their findings in the new, specialized physiological, pharmaceutical, veterinary, and chemical journals. Practitioners published their findings either in new journals for veterinary medicine or in journals whose scope was similar to the eighteenth-century cameralist or "economic" journals, which covered agricultural and home economics, forestry, and hunting. They were attuned to the bigger issues that drove their colleagues in academia and sometimes mentioned the question of spontaneous generation, for instance,[49] but rarely engaged

---

[45] Haubner, "Beschaffenheit."

[46] This task is the same as the task Jakob Henle described in the oft-quoted passage from his essay on miasma, contagion, and miasmatic-contagious diseases (Jakob Henle, "Von den Miasmen und Contagien und von den miasmatisch-contagiösen Krankheiten," in *Pathologische Untersuchungen* [Berlin: Hirschwald, 1840], 1–82.). Henle has often been understood as envisioning a "hypothetical" experiment, and Robert Koch is credited for developing the necessary techniques for experimental demonstration of disease causation through germs. In light of Fuchs's work, however, we can appreciate that Henle referred to common *practical* problems arising from well-established methodological ideas (see Schickore, "Parasites").

[47] These practitioners typically also had academic training, but they did not work in academic environments.

[48] G. Wieners, "Beobachtungen über blaue Flecken auf dem Rahme saurer Milch," *Landwirthschaftliche Zeitung für Kurhessen. Im Auftrag des Kurfürstlichen Ministeriums des Innern verfasst* 20 (1842): 276–84, especially 278.

[49] Rust, "Über die blaue Milch der Kühe," *Ökonomische Neuigkeiten und Verhandlungen* 5 (1844): 39–40, especially 40.

actively in these broader discussions.[50] They did not treat the scientific questions as settled. Yet, from their perspective, the task was to prevent infusoria—or ferment—from getting into the milk or from doing their work in the milk. The conditions of action for infusoria or ferment were quite similar, that was the important point—never mind their real nature.

A few notices regarding blue milk can be found in popular magazines, although we may surmise that the readers of these journals did not have to deal with the phenomenon themselves. What those magazines report is typically old news. In 1854, *Gartenlaube* briefly noted that blue cow's milk was due to "infusoria or mold,"[51] a suggestion that had been widely considered in the 1830s. In the 1863 issue of *Illustrirtes Hausbuch* we even find a late echo of eighteenth-century conjectures—blue milk was due to indigo-containing plants, the *Hausbuch* stated, or else to "bad storage," or weak cows with digestive or respiratory issues, or airless stables, or perhaps the atmosphere.[52] The eighteenth-century notion that blue milk might be resulting from witchcraft was now reported as a fanciful myth in magazines on German legends and folktales.

CONCLUSIONS

In the late eighteenth century, naturalists, medical and veterinary doctors, and public health officials published on blue milk in journals alongside farmers and chemists. They responded to queries, occasionally mentioned someone else's work, and called for reports of experiences and detailed descriptions of the circumstances of the occurrence of blue milk. We saw that these requests made sense given the accepted notions of correlation, causation, and how to study them correctly.

When the late eighteenth-century inquirers were confronted with the riddle of blue milk, strategies for securing causal relations were in place. Proper evidence for causal relations had to be experimental. Encyclopedia authors, writers of scientific treatises, and even satirists reminded their readers of the difference between observing combinations of things and

---

[50] In 1855, the Wetterauer Verein announced a lecture by "Dr. Rohde" on "blue milk from stables in a nearby village together with multiple explanations concerning this interesting and not yet scientifically ascertained phenomenon" (Roeder, "Bericht über Stand und Gang des Vereinslebens in der Wetterauer Gesellschaft für die Gesammte Naturkunde," in *Jahresberichte der Wetterauischen Gesellschaft für die gesammte Naturkunde zu Hanau über die Gesellschaftsjahre von August 1855 bis dahin 1857* (Hanau: Druck der Waisenhaus-Buchdruckerei, 1858), iii–xxv. Unfortunately, the content of the lecture is not reported.

[51] Anon. Milch! Milch! Milch! *Die Gartenlaube* (1854), 131–32.

[52] E. Brecher, "Die Milch als Nahrungsmittel," in *Illustrirtes Haus- und Familien-Buch* (Wien: C. Dittmarsch, 1863), 276–79.

experimenting on them to test for causal relations. To figure out the cause of an effect—and how the effect could be prevented—inquirers tried to establish what happened if the putative cause was introduced in one experimental situation but not in another, similar one, or else what happened if certain factors were removed from the setting. But to begin these experiments, potential causes had to be found by "dissecting" the circumstances of the phenomenon of interest.

Encyclopedias offered summary reports of experiences. In hindsight, the publication of multiple short reports proved beneficial for blue milk research. Authors recorded observations of blue milk and quick trials to check for potential causes and for the success of certain treatments. As inquirers accepted as credible and valid the reports from farmers and investigators without formal academic training, it became clear that the problem was widespread, appeared in various situations and environments, and was difficult to treat. Conjectures about the nature and treatment of blue milk and the evidence to support them were worked out collectively through a network of contributions, both substantial and modest. Candidate factors emerged from the works of better known researchers *and* from reports by unknown farmers and country doctors who sent little notes describing observations and small trials to farmers' magazines. Both the editorial attitude vis-à-vis smaller trials and the fact that research on blue milk was a collective effort turned out to be advantageous because more varied descriptions of accompanying circumstances were published. If nothing else, they had heuristic value. All types of contributions—except the ones involving witchcraft—were considered significant. Arguably, in the late eighteenth century, increased impatience with superstition allowed the widespread phenomenon to become visible in the first place.

Following the eighteenth-century inquirers through their trials and tribulations, some readers may have been reminded of John Stuart Mill's famous four methods of experimental inquiry—especially of the first two, the method of agreement, "comparing together different instances in which the phenomenon occurs" and the method of difference, "comparing instances in which the phenomenon does occur, with instances in other respects similar in which it does not."[53] If Borowsky concluded that bad grazing land was the cause of blue milk because blue milk occurred on two farms whose farmland had been affected by flooding, would this not be an application of the method of agreement? If a farmer who suspected blueweed as the cause of blue milk did not feed blueweed for several days

---

[53] John S. Mill, *System of Logic* (London: John W. Parker, 1843), 450.

to see if the milk did not turn blue, would this not be the method of difference? Indeed, the strategies of inquiry prescribed in late eighteenth-century encyclopedia articles and practical logic books and described in the inquirers' reports sound very much like the first two of Mill's methods.

We have already seen that Mill was by no means the first commentator who drew attention to the strategies encapsulated in the methods of agreement and difference. His comments were more systematic and comprehensive than the discussions we find in encyclopedia articles and Methods sections in experimental reports, but the underlying strategies are the same. What is nice about Mill's discussion is that it also accounts for the major challenge that inquirers into blue milk had to meet as they were dealing with blue milk: The crucial step that made the experimental search for causes possible in the first place, namely, "the resolution of a complex whole into the component elements," as Mill called it. The "analytical operation" required for this resolution was both mental and practical: "The order of nature, as perceived at a first glance, presents at every instant a chaos followed by another chaos. We must decompose each chaos into single facts. We must learn to see in the chaotic antecedent a multitude of distinct antecedents, in the chaotic consequent a multitude of distinct consequents. This, supposing it done, will not of itself tell us on which of the antecedents each consequent is invariably attendant. To determine that point, we must endeavour to effect a separation of the facts from one another, not in our minds only, but in nature."[54]

The study of blue milk exemplifies how the eighteenth-century inquirers "decomposed the chaos." We saw how putative antecedents and consequences, or, in Hempel's terms, conjectures and tentative answers emerged together, as researchers mobilized everyday experiences and available scientific concepts and theories. Studies of blue milk illustrate how challenging this task can be when not much is known about the phenomenon under study. They also illustrate that this task is both a mental and a practical one. In addition to the analytical operation of parsing the "chaotic" space of inquiry into potentially significant and likely irrelevant factors, inquirers also had to deal with the logistics of finding appropriate techniques to separate, monitor, and manipulate these factors in the field, in the dairy, or in the lab. How does one clean the air in a dairy? Making a fire is an option, but, as the eighteenth-century author pointed out, it has its limitations, especially in a building constructed of wood.

Can we say that the practices of collecting evidence changed as blue milk moved into the academic lab? Yes, and no. No, because the

---

[54] Mill, *Logic*, 379.

methodological ideas about how to establish cause–effect relations had long been in place and continued to inform the laboratory researchers. Moving the investigation from the dairy or home to the university laboratory just made it easier to carry out more tightly controlled tests, and the feuds about broader programs offered points of view on which potential causes and circumstances for the occurrence of blue milk could be identified. Then again, the application of the methodological ideas forever posed new practical challenges, especially as the relevant causal nexus was moved to the micro-level. The identification of vibrions immediately led to new practical problems. How could *their* causal efficacy be determined? And, because veterinarian-practitioners and academic researchers had different goals, they favored different kinds of evidence: academic researchers sought to establish causation by reproducing the phenomenon of interest; for practitioners, the successful prevention of an effect was evidence that their assumptions had been correct.

There is no "vast store of evidence" out there to which we can go to validate our hypotheses or conjectures. It is also not the case, however, that we simply construct our evidence in such a way that any and all new conjectures will be supported by it. Evidence for causal agency is often hard to come by, and sometimes it needs expertise (such as competence with the microscope) to produce or evaluate it. Sometimes we entirely lack the logistics and infrastructure to get the evidence we need to warrant our hypotheses, even though we have a good idea about the kind of evidence we need.

ACKNOWLEDGMENTS

I thank the organizers of the American Philosophical Society symposium "Evidence: Use and Abuse of Data" in June 2020 for inviting me to present, and to the audience for their questions and suggestions. I am grateful to Jordi Cat, Klodian Coko, Yves Gingras, and Christoph Hoffmann for their helpful comments on earlier drafts of this chapter. I also received very useful feedback from the audience at the history of science colloquium series at the Deutsche Akademie der Naturforscher Leopoldina, where I presented a version of this chapter. I began the research on which this chapter is based while I was a member of the Institute for Advanced Study at Princeton (NJ) and gratefully acknowledge the IAS's support.

REFERENCES

Anon. "Anfragen." *Hannoverisches Magazin, worin kleine Abhandlungen, einzelne Gedanken, Nachrichten, Vorschläge und Erfahrungen, so die*

Verbesserung des Nahrungs-Standes, die Land- und Stadt-Wirthschaft, Handlung, Manufacturen und Künste, die Physik, die Sittenlehre und angenehmen Wissenschaften betreffen, gesamlet und aufbewahret sind 16, 73tes Stück (1778): 1165–67.

Anon. [Becker]. "Crossen in der Neumark." *Deutsche Zeitung für die Jugend und ihre Freunde; oder, Moralische Schilderungen der Menschen, Sitten und Staaten unsrer Zeit* 6 (1789): 361–62.

Anon. "Milch! Milch! Milch!" *Die Gartenlaube* (1854): 131–32.

Anon. "Mittel wider das Blauwerden der Milch." *Hannoverisches Magazin, worin kleine Abhandlungen, einzelne Gedanken, Nachrichten, Vorschläge und Erfahrungen, so die Verbesserung des Nahrungs-Standes, die Land- und Stadt-Wirthschaft, Handlung, Manufacturen und Künste, die Physik, die Sittenlehre und angenehmen Wissenschaften betreffen, gesamlet und aufbewahret sind* 17, 30tes Stück (1779): 475–80.

Bicker. "Herrn Doctor Bickers zu Bremen Brief an den Herrn Hofrath Baldiner, über Lavaters Magnetismus." *Hannoverisches Magazin, worin kleine Abhandlungen, einzelne Gedanken, Nachrichten, Vorschläge und Erfahrungen, so die Verbesserung des Nahrungs-Standes, die Land- und Stadt-Wirthschaft, Handlung, Manufacturen und Künste, die Physik, die Sittenlehre und angenehmen Wissenschaften betreffen, gesamlet und aufbewahret sind* 15, 3tes Stück (1787): 33–48.

Borowsky [Georg Heinrich]. "Bericht und Gutachten über das Blauwerden der Milch in der Molkerey des Königlichen Amts Frauendorf bei Frankfurt an der Oder." *Landwirthschaftliches Magazin* 4. Quartal (1788): 22–58.

Brecher, E. "Die Milch als Nahrungsmittel." In *Illustrirtes Haus- und Familien-Buch*, 276–79. Wien: C. Dittmarsch, 1863.

Brockhaus, F. A. "Der Magnetismus." In *Brockhaus Conversations-Lexikon*, vol. 3, 18–22. Amsterdam: Kunst-und Industrie-Comptoir, 1809.

Douglas, Mary, *Purity and Danger: An Analysis of Concepts of Pollution and Taboo*. London: Routledge & K. Paul, 1966.

Ehrenberg, Christian. *Die Infusionsthierchen als vollkommene Organismen. Ein Blick in das tiefere organische Leben der Natur*. Leipzig: Voss, 1838.

Fuchs, Christopher Joseph. "Beitrage zur nähern Kenntniss der gesunden und fehlerfreien Milch der Hausthiere." *Magazin für die gesammte Thierheilkunde* 7 (1841): 133–96

Gielen, W. "Von der blauen Milch der Kühe." *Magazin für die gesammte Thierheilkunde* 31 (1865): 234–37.

Goeze, Johann August Ephraim. "Von der blauen Milch; ingleichen von der Blutmilch der Kühe." In *Nützliches Allerley aus der Natur und dem gemeinen Leben für allerley Leser*, vol. III, 103–15. Leipzig: Weidmann, 1786.

———. "Mittel wider die blaue Milch." In *Eine pure Dorfreise: zum Unterricht und Vergnügen der Jugend*, 245–49. Leipzig: Weidmann, 1788.

Graf. "Versuche mit der Frauendorfer sogenannten blauen Milch." *Landwirthschaftliches Magazin* 4. Quartal (1788): 58–60.

Grote, Mathias. "'Aus dem Kleinen bauen sich die Welten' – Christian Gottfried Ehrenbergs ökologische Mikrobiologie avant la lettre." In *HiN: Alexander von Humboldt im Netz, XXII*, edited by Ottmar Ette, Eberhard Knobloch, and Ulrich Päßler, 19–32, 42. Potsdam: Universitätsverlag Potsdam, 2021. https://doi.org/10.18443/318.

Haubner, Gottlieb Carl. "Ueber die fehlerhafte Beschaffenheit der Kuhmilch im Allgemeinen und über die blaue Milch insbesondere." *Magazin für die gesammte Thierheilkunde* 18 (1852): 1–84, 129–202.

Henle, Jakob. "Von den Miasmen und Contagien und von den miasmatisch-contagiösen Krankheiten." In *Pathologische Untersuchungen*, 1–82. Berlin: Hirschwald, 1840.

Hoffmann, Christoph. "The Ruin of a Book: Jean André De Luc's *Recherches sur les modifications de l'atmosphère* (1772)." *Modern Language Notes* 118 (2003): 568–602.

K. P. O. C. S. "Gutachten des Königl. Obercollegii Sanitatis, über vorstehenden Bericht." *Landwirthschaftliches Magazin* 4. Quartal (1788): 60–62.

Krünitz, Johann Georg. *Oekonomische Encyklopädie, oder Allgemeines System der Staats- Stadt-Haus- u. Landwirthschaft, in Alphabetischer Ordnung*, vol. 124. Berlin: Pauli, 1817, 520–32, 766–67.

Lehmann, Carl. *Lehrbuch der physiologischen Chemie*. Leipzig: Engelmann, 1853.

Lichtenstein, [Anton]. "Ueber die blaue Milch der Kühe." *Landwirthschaftliches Magazin* 1. Quartal (1788): 48–66.

Mill, John S. *System of Logic*. London: John W. Parker, 1843.

"Philozoos." "Auszug eines Schreibens, über eine neue sehr merkwürdige Entdeckung, den Magnetismus betreffend." *Berlinische Monatsschrift* 10 (1787): 44–56.

Roeder. "Bericht über Stand und Gang des Vereinslebens in der Wetterauer Gesellschaft für die Gesammte Naturkunde." In *Jahresberichte der Wetterauischen Gesellschaft für die gesamte Naturkunde zu Hanau über die Gesellschaftsjahre von August 1855 bis dahin 1857*, iii–xxv. Hanau: Druck der Waisenhaus-Buchdruckerei, 1858.

Rust. "Über die blaue Milch der Kühe." *Ökonomische Neuigkeiten und Verhandlungen* 5 (1844): 39–40.

Schickore, Jutta. *About Method: Experimenters, Snake Venom, and the History of Writing Scientifically*. Chicago: University of Chicago Press, 2017.

———. "Parasites, Pepsin, Pus, and Postulates: Jakob Henle's Essay on Miasma, Contagium, and Miasmatic-Contagious Diseases in its Original Context." *Bulletin of the History of Medicine* 96 (2022): 612–38.

Siebold C. T. v. "Bericht über die Leistungen im Gebiete der Anatomie und Physiologie der wirbellosen Thiere." *Archiv für Anatomie, Physiologie und wissenschaftliche Medicin* (1843): 1–87.

Smith-Howard, K. *Pure and Modern Milk*. Oxford: Oxford University Press, 2014.

Wieners, G. "Beobachtungen über blaue Flecken auf dem Rahme saurer Milch." *Landwirthschaftliche Zeitung für Kurhessen. Im Auftrag des Kurfürstlichen Ministeriums des Innern verfasst* 20 (1842): 276–84.

———. "Die Milchwirthschaft u. s. w., besonderer Abdruck aus der Encyclopädie der gesammten Landwirtschaft, herausgegeben v. William Löbe. Leipzig 1851. Verlag von Otto Wigand." *Repertorium der Thierheilkunde* (1852): 197–203.

Chapter 3

Bunk History and the Standards of Historical Interpretation

Andrew M. Schocket

History, we have a problem. The high overall quality of academic historical inquiry has not precluded the proliferation of poor historical claims. As with mathematics, the social sciences, or the sciences, the trappings and rhetoric of history lend a veneer of objectivity. But less than those disciplines' practitioners, historians, whose assertions are primarily qualitative, do not require measures for what constitute levels of certitude. Furthermore, despite its nature as an inherently ideological endeavor, history has erected weak guardrails against historians being influenced by our preconceived notions. Indeed, the American Historical Association—the professional organization of practicing historians in the United States—while giving nods to scholarly integrity in its code of ethics, advises us to be aware of our biases, but offers no suggestion that we reveal them.[1] This essay first offers two examples of bunk history: the American Civil Rights Union's white paper "The Truth about Jim Crow," and Michael Bellesiles's award-winning 1996 article, "The Origins of Gun Culture in the United States, 1760–1865." It then considers a long-running controversy in the study of early America: the validity of the "Iroquois influence thesis." I argue that a lack of standards of proof combined with confirmation bias inhibits historians' capacity to assess the validity of our assertions, and

---

[1] American Historical Association, "Statement on Standards of Professional Conduct (Updated 2019)" (Washington, DC: American Historical Association, 2019), 4, https://www.historians.org/jobs-and-professional-development/statements-standards-and-guidelines-of-the-discipline/statement-on-standards-of-professional-conduct#Scholarship.

I offer a pair of modest suggestions that might mitigate against these deficiencies.[2]

Sometimes, looking at failures can help us to understand systemic problems. In July 2014, the American Civil Rights Union (ACRU)—according to its website, a nonpartisan advocacy organization—released "The Truth about Jim Crow," a 41-page white paper packed with evidence and quotations, documented by 72 footnotes.[3] Pundits touted it as revealing a fundamental historical insight, and the ACRU presented an executive summary to a major congressional caucus.[4] The more attention Americans pay to understanding Jim Crow's horrors and legacy, the better. But not this way. The report exhorted readers to "come away understanding the three most important facts about Jim Crow: Jim Crow was Dehumanizing; Jim Crow was Deadly; and Jim Crow was Democratic."[5] As the piece accurately indicates, the South's Jim Crow regime was perpetrated by late nineteenth-century Democratic-voting Whites. However, the ACLU publication extends its chronological scope into the 1960s, professing to prove that Republicans single-handedly ended Jim Crow. It stakes this claim based on congressional Republicans having voted in the affirmative at a slightly higher rate than Democrats for the twenty-fourth Amendment (banning poll taxes, which were wielded in Southern states to prevent Black people from voting) and the 1965 Civil Rights Act. However, as one can easily discern from the source the report cites for those tallies—despite the report's contention that "a partisan breakdown of the [Senate] vote is not available"—party affiliation was a poor predictor of 1960s civil rights legislative behavior. Instead, congressional resistance to civil rights legislation was highly correlated with whether a legislator hailed from a Confederate state, regardless of party.[6] Because of these and other easy-to-spot

---

[2] Interpretive reflexivity statement: As a liberal Democrat, and disagreeing with the ACRU on many issues, I am inclined to be hostile to "The Truth about Jim Crow"; as someone in favor of gun control, and susceptible to arguments that historicize contemporary societal problems, I was liable to be hospitable to Bellesiles's ideas; I initially agreed completely with critiques of the Iroquois influence thesis, and one of its published critics and I are friends from graduate school.

[3] American Civil Rights Union, "The Truth about Jim Crow" (Alexandria, VA: American Civil Rights Union, 2014). http://www.theacru.org/jimcrow/.

[4] John Fund, "Setting the Record Straight on Jim Crow," *National Review Online* (July 22, 2014). http://www.nationalreview.com/corner/383357/setting-record-straight-jim-crow-john-fund; "#Truth Campaign Exposes the Truth About Jim Crow," *The American Civil Rights Union* blog entry), June 23, 2014. http://www.theacru.org/truth_campaign_exposes_the_truth_about_jim_crow/.

[5] American Civil Rights Union, "The Truth about Jim Crow," 1.

[6] American Civil Liberties Union, "The Truth about Jim Crow," 32; "S.j. Res. 29. Constitutional Amendment to Ban the Use of ... -- House Vote #193—Aug 27, 1962," GovTrack.us, accessed February 25, 2018, https://www.govtrack.us/congress/votes/87-1962/h193; "S.j. Res. 29. Approval of Resolution Banning the Poll Tax ... —Senate Vote #226—Mar 27, 1962," GovTrack.us, accessed March 7, 2018, https://www.govtrack.us/congress/votes/87-1962/s226; Harry J. Enten, "Were Republicans Really the Party of Civil Rights in the 1960s?" *The Guardian*, August 28, 2013, http://www.theguardian.com/commentisfree/2013/aug/28/republicans-party-of-civil-rights.

errors, "The Truth about Jim Crow" reads less as an exploration of Jim Crow than as a poorly reasoned screed drawing unsupportable distinctions between one political party's virtue and another's perfidy.

Lest we be quick to attribute debacles in historical practice only to laypeople eager to grind partisan battle-axes, let us consider a broad failure of the academic historical community: Michael Bellesiles's 1996 article, "The Origins of Gun Culture in the United States: 1760–1865."[7] Some readers may remember the brouhaha over the award-winning book evolving from that article, *Arming America: The Origins of a National Gun Culture,* later revealed to have a host of documentary deficiencies.[8] The article argued that gun ownership in early America was much less widespread than earlier assumed, and that American "gun culture" arose after the Civil War. Bellesiles's article exhibited numerous flaws as inexcusable in an upper-level undergraduate research paper as they should have been in any work published in one of the discipline's most highly selective professional journals.

As far as I can tell, no one during the review process flagged shocking lapses in two of the article's tables, that, had they been interrogated, would have put the main premise of the piece in question. Table 1 relates the proportion of probates that included guns, separated by region.[9] Its first column, "1765–1790," reports that nationally, 14.7% of all probate records mentioned one or more guns as part of the decedent's estate. However, the only region of the four listed in that column whose percentage falls below 14.7% is "frontier," which, for the table to be mathematically correct, would mean that more probates (usually roughly proportional to the overall free population) were recorded in the less densely populated frontier region than the rest of the nation combined. This anomaly alone should have raised concerns. Then, for each sample from 1765 through 1821, Table 1 lists a higher proportion of gun ownership in "Northern coast, urban" counties than in frontier counties. The article's text, though, argues that rural people had more use for guns than did city-dwellers. If Table 1 is correct, it undermines the article's thesis that there was no "gun culture," because it appears to indicate that people living in areas where they had a lesser need for guns were more likely to own firearms than were people in areas where they were more likely to need them.

---

[7] Michael A. Bellesiles, "The Origins of Gun Culture in the United States, 1760–1865," *The Journal of American History* 83, no. 2 (September 1996): 425–55.

[8] Michael A. Bellesiles, *Arming America: The Origins of a National Gun Culture,* (New York: Alfred A. Knopf, 2000); Stanley N. Katz, Hanna H. Gray, and Laurel Thatcher Ulrich, "Report of the Investigative Committee in the Matter of Professor Michael Bellesiles" (Atlanta: Emory University, July 10, 2002), http://www.emory.edu/news/Releases//Final_Report.pdf.

[9] Bellesiles, "The Origins of Gun Culture," 427.

Similarly suspect, Table 3 indicates the population of Massachusetts rising from 524,946 people in 1795 to 675,509 in 1808—and then, in 1812, dropping to 482,289, a 27% decrease.[10] A charitable interpretation for this change, without access to the sources Bellesiles cites, could be that Massachusetts took Maine's population off its books during this time frame—notwithstanding that Maine was not carved from Massachusetts into a state until 1820. The article does not explain why, during the same interval, Table 3's Massachusetts gun total decreased from an estimated 50,000 to 49,000, a mere 2% loss. But Table 1 indicated that "frontier" residents, which described most Mainers at the time, were more likely to have guns than their more urban Massachusetts cousins. If the excising of Maine from Massachusetts's count does explain the population drop, then one would have expected a much higher loss in the gun count than 2%. If that is not the explanation for the decreased population, then we are left with the question of where those nearly 200,000 Massachusetts residents disappeared to during a time of considerable demographic growth. In other words, a quick examination of two of the article's first three tables presents contradictions that render the entire piece questionable.

Many historians solely blamed the authors for the ACLU's and Bellesiles's poor reasoning and blindness to their own data, some implying bad faith.[11] I suggest, however, that these fiascoes did not stem from historians gone bad. As in any discipline, historians make poorly reasoned arguments all the time. The difference between most lousy arguments and these two was that the former usually get rejected or ignored, whereas the latter were published and celebrated. The fault here lies less with the authors, I argue, and more with the wider communities, neither stupid nor fraudulent, that elevated these works despite their appallingly poor quality. The ACRU's board as of 2014 featured a former US attorney general, two former assistant US attorneys general, a senior consultant on Central America to the Under Secretary of Defense, the holder of an endowed professorship of economics, and a former Supreme Court litigator.[12] Bellesiles listed eight colleagues in his acknowledgments as having seen the manuscript, which was vetted by at least three blind, outside reviewers chosen by the *Journal of American*

---

[10] Bellesiles, "The Origins of Gun Culture," 433.

[11] For a full evaluation of the Bellesiles case and reactions to it, see Peter Charles Hoffer, *Past Imperfect: Facts, Fictions, and Fraud: American History from Bancroft and Parkman to Ambrose, Bellesiles, Ellis, and Goodwin* (New York: PublicAffairs, 2007), 141–71; James Lindgren, "Fall from Grace: Arming America and the Bellesiles Scandal," *Yale Law Journal* 111 (2002): 2195–249.

[12] The ACRU site, imaged by the Internet archive as of February 27, 2014, "Policy Board," American Civil Rights Union, February 27, 2014, https://web.archive.org/web/20140227142534/http://www.theacru.org/about-policy-board.html.

History (JAH); the published result was recognized with the Binkley-Stephenson Award as the best 1996 *JAH* article.[13] Highly accomplished scholars touted the piece as "pathbreaking," providing "excellent new insights" that "explod[e] the myth of near universal gun ownership."[14] The essay was republished, with identical tables, in two edited anthologies.[15] That article's publication, celebration, and republication did not result from poor procedure. Nor did it suffer from a lack of review by expert eyes. How could no fewer than a dozen pairs of them miss such colossal deficiencies? The ethical-lapse theory might explain the missteps of the original authors, but it does not account for the seemingly skepticism-free acceptance of their work by broader communities with the demonstrated capacity for critical examination of complex arguments.

These cases, I argue, represent extreme examples of routine, long-standing historical practice in the United States. To make an analogy, if a person ran up to someone and violently threw them to the ground, inflicting bodily pain, we would assume the assailant meant harm. Under certain conditions, though, thousands of people would cheer: if the takedown occurred during an American football game, in accordance with its rules. Regardless of the tackler's feelings toward ballcarrier, the act of aggression followed the game's norms, sanctioned by players, coaches, referees, and the league. Similarly, I suggest, the ACRU report and the Bellesiles article were celebrated by their respective communities. And, just as with football injuries, these essays' faults are the nearly inevitable collateral damage resulting not from people who necessarily intended to do harm or flout norms, but from adherence to broadly accepted ways of doing things.

Two norms of historical disciplinary practice, in combination with each other, render such results rare but likely to occur. First, historians do not employ explicit or rigorous standards for evaluating our contentions. Second, history is especially prone to confirmation bias. Either one of these would pose problems; in tandem, they invite the kind of bunk history these two cases represent, exposing the historical profession to many more, less-well-known but equally pernicious contentions. Worse, this compounding of faults can render entire lines of inquiry nearly impossible to evaluate.

---

[13] Bellesiles, "The Origins of Gun Culture," 425; "Announcements," *Journal of American History* 84, no. 1 (1997): 329.

[14] Don Higginbotham, "The Second Amendment in Historical Context," *Constitutional Commentary* 16, no. 2 (Summer 1999): 263; Robert E. Shalhope, "To Keep and Bear Arms in the Early Republic," *Constitutional Commentary* 16, no. 2 (Summer 1999): 269.

[15] Jan E. Dizard, Robert Muth, and Stephen P. Andrews, eds., *Guns in America: A Historical Reader* (New York: NYU Press, 1999); Saul Cornell, ed., *Whose Right to Bear Arms Did the Second Amendment Protect?* Historians at Work (Boston, MA: Bedford/St. Martin's, 2000).

History lacks explicit, accepted standards for the interpretation of arguments. This should not be confused with methodological torpor: for almost any type of source, from nearly every period of human history, specialists have debated and, to some extent, established consensus on how to extract meaning from artifact. Interpretations based on oral history provide a good example. Oral history guides in general offer extended advice on how to parse an interview; specifically, we have much discussed protocols concerning how to interpret 1930s Works Progress Administration interviews of slavery survivors.[16] However, we have no standards for how to evaluate a scholarly claim, based upon those interviews, concerning, say, why and how different people experienced enslavement differently.

The charge that historical argumentation has the potential for slack logic is no news flash. Peter Charles Hoffer, writing in 2007, examined several recent debacles, including that of Bellesiles's scholarship, and found similar problems stretching to the dawn of the American historical profession.[17] The prevailing work on historian's argumentative faults, however, dates much further back than Hoffer's fine book: 2020 marked the fiftieth anniversary of David Hackett Fischer's *The Historians' Fallacies: Toward a Logic of Historical Thought*.[18] Running the tonal gamut from caustic to cranky, Fischer accused his fellow historians of "misology," that is, despising logic.[19] The book delivers a taxonomy of thought-process-related deficiencies in some of the field's most prominent works, cataloging them into three families, eleven genuses, and over 100 species.[20] As Fischer and others have noted, these problems result partly from the kinds of arguments that historians make, given our subject matter. Historians have no possibility of running multiple experiments so as to reproduce our results (not that science has solved that particular dilemma).[21] Few historical contentions, no matter how likely to be valid or clearly dubious, can be expressed in such a way that, should they be wrong, they could be definitely

---

[16] See, for example, Norman R. Yetman, "Ex-Slave Interviews and the Historiography of Slavery." *American Quarterly* 36, no. 2 (1984): 181–210; Donna J. Spindel, "Assessing Memory: Twentieth-Century Slave Narratives Reconsidered," *The Journal of Interdisciplinary History* 27, no. 2 (1996): 247–61.

[17] Hoffer, *Past Imperfect*. Ironically, one prominent reviewer accused Hoffer of similar biases: David Grimsted, "Review: Past Imperfect: Facts, Fictions, Fraud: American History from Bancroft and Parkman to Ambrose, Bellisles, Ellis and Goodwin," *History: Reviews of New Books* 33, no. 2 (Winter 2005): 80, https://doi.org/10.1080/03612759.2005.10526524.

[18] David Hackett Fischer, *Historians Fallacies: Toward a Logic of Historical Thought:* (New York: Harper & Row, 1970).

[19] Fischer, *Historians Fallacies*, xi.

[20] Fischer, *Historians Fallacies*, 337–38.

[21] Kelsey Piper, "Science Has Been in a 'Replication Crisis' for a Decade. Have We Learned Anything?" *Vox*, October 14, 2020, https://www.vox.com/future-perfect/21504366/science-replication-crisis-peer-review-statistics.

refuted. That is how charlatans like David Barton, who is not an historian but credibly plays one on various cable television networks, can defend his otherwise indefensible theories concerning American Philosophical Society founder Benjamin Franklin and his founding-generation colleagues.[22] Worse, we employ no explicit methods of evaluating assertions, either in terms of burden of proof or certainty compared to other explanations. Although many historians do use quantitative methods, most historical work is qualitative. Most historical assertions are thus impervious to quantitative methods of correlation and certainty (which is not to say that these are infallible, either, as others in the volume attest). As a matter of habit, we historians do not require statements of how probable we think an interpretation is, much less how confident we are in gauging its likelihood.

At the same time, the ideological nature of history combined with our nonreflexive rhetorical stance, and, no less, the very fact that we are human render us especially prone to "confirmation bias," defined by cognitive psychologist Raymond S. Nickerson as "the seeking or interpreting of evidence in ways that are partial to existing beliefs, expectations, or a hypothesis in hand."[23] As Nickerson noted in 1998, and as even a cursory search of *confirmation bias* in various databases of scholarly activity will show, cognitive scientists and others have demonstrated, time and time again, in a great range of contexts, that human beings are not very good at setting aside our prior assumptions when looking at data or evaluating others' contentions.[24] Those results apply to the highly educated, and, counterintuitively, the more we know about a subject, the more our confirmation bias kicks in. College students have been found to be not only overly skeptical toward arguments with which they disagree, but also, after encountering information challenging their beliefs, to have become more entrenched in their position.[25] We might like to think that, professional

---

[22] Julie Ingersoll, "Meet the Tea Party's Evangelical Quack: David Barton Is Glenn Beck's Favorite 'Historian,'" *Salon*, accessed April 12, 2016, http://www.salon.com/2015/08/23/meet_the_tea_partys_evangelical_quack_david_barton_is_glenn_becks_favorite_historian/; Jennifer Schuessler, "Hard Truth for Author: Publisher Pulls 'The Jefferson Lies,'" *New York Times ArtsBeat*, blog entry, 1344949458, // artsbeat.blogs.nytimes.com/2012/08/14/hard-truth-for-author-publisher-pulls-the-jefferson-lies/; Warren Throckmorton and Michael L. Coulter, *Getting Jefferson Right: Fact Checking Claims about Our Third President* (Grove City, PA: Salem Grove Press, 2012).

[23] Raymond S. Nickerson, "Confirmation Bias: A Ubiquitous Phenomenon in Many Guises," *Review of General Psychology* 2, no. 2 (1998): 175. See also P. E. Lehner et al., "Confirmation Bias in Complex Analyses," *IEEE Transactions on Systems, Man, and Cybernetics—Part A: Systems and Humans* 38, no. 3 (May 2008): 584–92.

[24] Nickerson, "Confirmation Bias."

[25] Charles G. Lord, Lee Ross, and Mark R. Lepper, "Biased Assimilation and Attitude Polarization: The Effects of Prior Theories on Subsequently Considered Evidence," *Journal of Personality and Social Psychology* 37, no. 11 (1979): 2098–109, https://doi.org/10.1037/0022-3514.37.11.2098.

thinkers as we are, we may be more resistant to this flaw, or we might suppose that this bias does not affect us when we have time to reflect. However, research indicates that professionals are no less susceptible to a range of cognitive biases, confirmation bias among them. Psychologists have found confirmation bias in studies involving doctors and nurses, defense analysts, psychiatrists, and software engineers.[26] And, unlike what historians do, none of the interpretive tasks asked of participants in these studies of experts involved the necessarily ideological work that historians do. I would like to think that we historians are somehow better able to weed out our conceptual crabgrass than such folk. But my reading of the scholarship at the intersection of the practice of history and cognitive bias—and, indeed, that of psychologist-historian Nancy Digdon, who, examining the work of her colleagues, came to conclusions that mine echo—tells me that for me to believe that historians are somehow better thinkers than the rest of humanity is just my confirmation bias talking.[27]

Perhaps this dangerous intersection of resistance to logic and lack of reflexivity results from our ambivalence concerning the extent to which history is one of the humanities or a social science. In the West, one could trace this fault line as far back as the ancient Greeks. Both Herodotus and Thucydides used interviews and weighed sources in their efforts to interpret the human past for future consumption. Herodotus aimed through his *Histories* to limn what it meant to be a true Greek, and was willing to include the apocryphal and outlandish, though discounting the veracity of some of those accounts. Thucydides showed more discernment, explaining his methodology and thought process in analyzing causation in his *History of the Peloponnesian War*. We should understand this distinction as an intramural difference of emphasis: Herodotus tended to use the past as a way to understand the human condition, whereas Thucydides sometimes leaned on a theory of human nature to better illuminate the past for its own sake. That tension continues to be manifested in myriad ways, some of them institutionalized. In US K-12 education, history gets grouped in "social studies" with economics and political science; for federal research funding, historians compete with philosophers and literary scholars under

---

[26] Annie Y. S. Lau and Enrico W. Coiera, "Do People Experience Cognitive Biases While Searching for Information," *Journal of the American Medical Informatics Association* 14, no. 5 (2007): 599–608, https://doi.org/10.1197/jamia.M2411; Lehner et al., "Confirmation Bias in Complex Analyses"; R. Mendel et al., "Confirmation Bias: Why Psychiatrists Stick to Wrong Preliminary Diagnoses," *Psychological Medicine* 41, no. 12 (December 2011): 2651–59, https://doi.org/10.1017/S0033291711000808; Gul Calikli and Ayse Bener, "Empirical Analysis of Factors Affecting Confirmation Bias Levels of Software Engineers," *Software Quality Journal* 23, no. 4 (December 1, 2015): 695–722, https://doi.org/10.1007/s11219-014-9250-6.
[27] Nancy Digdon, "The Little Albert Controversy: Intuition, Confirmation Bias, and Logic," *History of Psychology* 23, no. 2 (January 26, 2017): 122, https://doi.org/10.1037/hop0000055.

the bailiwick of the National Endowment for the Humanities. Across American higher education, some history departments are classified with the humanities, others with social sciences (as my department happens to be), a few as both. Most relevant here, this double heritage contributes to our difficulties in meeting the challenge of more rigorous argumentation.

Our humanities heritage leads us to resist formulaic considerations of proof. As one of the humanities, history aims to provide contemporary meaning about what it is to be human; to find lessons not just about the past but also about the present is central to its DNA. Historians understand our work as necessarily a cultural, political, and ideological act. We put this ethos into practice: The learning outcomes for nearly every US undergraduate history program include some expression of applicability of understanding of the past to contemporary issues, an objective enshrined in the "Tuning Project," a recent effort of the American Historical Association (the discipline's US professional organization) to provide resources for undergraduate instruction.[28] With the exception of a few areas of historical inquiry in which scholars used sophisticated statistical methods, one would be hard-pressed to find strict measures of certainty in a work of, say, literary analysis or cultural studies, also commonly accepted as subjective exercises in the finding of meaning.[29] The resurgence of the use of the narrative form among historians—including by Fischer himself, later in his career—and other kinds of creative rhetorical structures tends to lead us further away from this kind of language, and in some ways, is refreshing.[30] Which is not to say that measuring certitude, even in a narrative, in the face of limited information, cannot be done. For example, Annette Gordon-Reed's open speculation concerning Sally Hemings's motivations while in Paris, where Hemings could have remained free, to return with Thomas Jefferson to enslavement in Virginia, invokes the elements of uncertainty and doubt in its qualified assertions.[31]

Nonetheless, the authoritative voice in which we historians were taught to write, and, in turn, that we teach our students to employ resembles that

---

[28] "AHA History Tuning Project: 2016 History Discipline Core," American Historical Association, 2016, https://www.historians.org/teaching-and-learning/tuning-the-history-discipline/2016-history-discipline-core.

[29] Though of course there are always counterexamples; see, Matthew Lee Jockers, *Macroanalysis: Digital Methods and Literary History*, Topics in the Digital Humanities (Urbana: University of Illinois Press, 2013).

[30] David Hackett Fischer, *Washington's Crossing*, Pivotal Moments in American History (Oxford: Oxford University Press, 2004). For example, the *American Historical Review* has recently inaugurated a series titled "History Unclassified" that publishes pieces that can appear in more exploratory forms: *American Historical Review*, "What Form Can History Take Today?" accessed July 2, 2021, http://academic.oup.com/ahr/pages/history_unclassified.

[31] Perhaps Gordon-Reed's training as a lawyer inspired this passage. Annette Gordon-Reed, *The Hemingses of Monticello: An American Family* (New York: W.W. Norton, 2008), 326–75.

of economics or political science: history, as written, is nearly entirely unreflexive. This seemingly "objective," scientific, dispassionate affect constituted a central pillar of the professionalization of the various social science disciplines in the United States in the late nineteenth century, of which historians were eager participants.[32] For history, the internalized imperative of the carved-in-stone tablets, third-person voice entrenches our resistance to even the mildest self-reflection, notwithstanding the necessarily ideological terrain that our inquiries purport to map. The irony here is thicker than a print edition of the entire run of *Poor Richard's Almanac.* History majors are required to be acquainted with "historiography," that is, the scholarly conversation over time concerning a particular historical event or process. Historiography, with a broad brush, explicitly considers the social, cultural, and institutional contexts in which historians work. We emphasize how such factors necessarily drive the questions we pose, the ways that we design our research to answer them, and the answers we are likely to provide. Nonetheless, we teach future historians to write scholarly pieces always in the third person, rather than the first, thus absolving them of explicitly examining their own assumptions. Our acculturation deepens this contradiction: At faculty meetings and conferences, we rail against the presumption many of our undergraduates hold, that because people in the past lacked our understandings, they were not as smart as people today. We then return to our keyboards and write as if older historical interpretations were framed by benighted historians' quaint cultural assumptions, remaining bizarrely silent about our own. Because of this almost aggressive repression of our own biases, we become especially susceptible to seeing evidence that reinforces our unstated ideological commitments while discounting that which challenges our unspoken assumptions.

So, you ask, dear reader, how certain am I that historians do not invoke measures of certitude in our work? I contend that the vast majority of historians' published work does not include such measures, perhaps 90% or higher. I am not particularly confident in that nine-of-ten ratio. On the one hand, I suspect that the actual proportion is higher; on the other hand, I want to extend my colleagues (and me) the benefit of the doubt, as well as admitting that there can be ways of expressing nuance that can imply levels of certitude without putting it into those exact terms. Furthermore, my evidence is anecdotal, in that it draws from my impressions based on my own consumption, but that I have not quantified. Most of the hundreds (thousands?) of articles and books written by professional

---

[32] Peter Novick, *That Noble Dream: The "Objectivity Question" and the American Historical Profession,* Ideas in Context (Cambridge, UK: Cambridge University Press, 1988), 47–85.

historians that I have read do not express these measures. Then again, like anyone's, my reading choices are idiosyncratic. In all, I am fairly sure that few scholarly historical pieces consider a probability that their thesis is the best explanation or offer a level of confidence in that estimation.

Either of these problems—history's lax approach to logic or its vulnerability to confirmation bias—might be surmountable on its own; together they form a challenge deeply entrenched in historical instruction and practice. Academic journals act as the primary gatekeepers in the discipline. Double-blind reviewing is the norm, with the more selective journals subjecting submissions to the evaluation of three or more referees. However, editors' guidance to referees concerning how to evaluate those submissions remains sparse. I queried the editors of three of the field's most revered and selective journals concerning their instructions to referees. Only two of those journals offer explicit review criteria, and, in terms of arguments, solely ask whether the piece's "conclusions [are] justified."[33] None required referees to consider their own positionality regarding the subject matter or thesis. Such inattention to these issues begins early in historians' training: My informal survey of several better selling textbook guides to undergraduate history research found hundreds of combined pages on the selection, documentation, and interpretation of sources and on the rhetorical performance that is a research paper, but only one of them gave a brief wave to the construction of arguments. Although several noted that students might be on the lookout for implicit bias that can lead to confirmation bias, none exhorted students to be explicit about what those biases might be.[34]

To be fair, history's gatekeepers do largely make up for the dearth of explicit standards through exactly what the consensus of authors of this volume have emphasized, their use of sharpened judgment. Editors rely upon the expertise and wisdom that their scholarly communities identified in them when they were tapped for this crucial task.[35] The system balances between prevailing theories and more challenging ones. On the one hand, journals want to publish scholarship that moves the field forward; doing

---

[33] David Waldstreicher to Andrew M. Schocket, "Re-JER Manuscript Reviewer Instructions/Guidelines," in discussion with the author regarding *Journal of the Early Republic*, April 27, 2020; Benjamin H. Irvin to Andrew M. Schocket, "JAH Manuscript Reviewer Instructions," in discussion with the author regarding *Journal of American History*, May 5, 2020; David Waldstreicher to Andrew M. Schocket, "JER Author Guidelines," October 5, 2020; Joshua Piker to Andrew M. Schocket, "MS Reviewer Instructions," May 20, 2020. Quotation from Irvin.

[34] See, for example, Jules R. Benjamin, *A Student's Guide to History*, 14th ed. (Boston: Bedford/St. Martin's, 2018); Anthony Brundage, *Going to the Sources: A Guide to Historical Research and Writing*, 6th ed. (Malden, MA: Wiley-Blackwell, 2017). Mary Lynn Rampolla, *A Pocket Guide to Writing in History*, 9th ed. (Bedford/St. Martin's, 2017).

[35] David Waldstreicher, in discussion with the author concerning journal editing, June 10, 2020.

so necessarily means revising or overturning previous arguments. On the other hand, editors must select referees who have demonstrated their expertise by already having successfully made the run through the reviewing gauntlet. Wise editors combat tilts toward the status quo by avoiding soliciting reviewers whose interpretations might be threatened by new work. They pore over reviewers' reports, discounting hostile or overgenerous ones, while valuing those that home in on submissions' logical validity, methodological soundness, and evidentiary solidity. Furthermore, editors possess latitude to publish work challenging prevailing opinions, sometimes overruling what they might see as unreasonably negative reviews. Doing so might be a good reason to publish a provocative piece that may not be as strongly researched as one that is safer as a way to stimulate constructive discussion in the field. Then again, maybe sometimes editors subject potentially controversial work to more exacting standards than safer submissions, either out of undue skepticism, or so as to ensure that its contentions are more likely to be accepted because of the accompanying mounds of evidence.[36] My experience with editors is, perforce, anecdotal, and that experience has been that journal editors have been selected for their judgment, and, between that and extended practice may be less susceptible to cognitive bias than the rest of us benighted humans (me included). Nonetheless, I submit that, as humans, even expert ones, they are not immune from it.

This combination of a dearth of evidentiary standards and a lack of reflection can render some historiographic debates intractable. To illustrate these challenges, let us look at the controversy over a particular set of historical contentions that, for over forty years, like a Franklin stove, has generated more combustion than illumination. In 1977, Donald A. Grindé's monograph, *The Iroquois and the Founding of the American Nation* was released; Bruce Johansen's *Forgotten Founders: Benjamin Franklin, the Iroquois, and the Rationale for the American Revolution.*[37] came out five years later. Grindé and Johansen coauthored the 1991 *Exemplar of Liberty: Native America and the Evolution of Democracy.*[38] These and works by

---

[36] Perhaps the most illustrative example from early American history is Jesse Lemisch's groundbreaking—but, at the time, controversial—1968 article whose footnotes far exceed its text, "Jack Tar in the Streets: Merchant Seamen in the Politics of Revolutionary America," *The William and Mary Quarterly* 25, no. 3 (July 1968): 371–407.

[37] Donald A. Grindé, *The Iroquois and the Founding of the American Nation* (San Francisco: Indian Historian Press, 1977); Bruce E. Johansen, *Forgotten Founders: Benjamin Franklin, the Iroquois, and the Rationale for the American Revolution* (Ipswich, MA: Gambit, 1982).

[38] Donald A. Grindé and Bruce E. Johansen, *Exemplar of Liberty: Native America and the Evolution of Democracy*, Native American Politics Series, no. 3 (Los Angeles: American Indian Studies Center, University of California, Los Angeles, 1991).

other authors argue that the men who wrote the nation's founding documents wittingly and unwittingly borrowed ideas from Native American political practice. At their most expansive, proponents contend that North American Indigenous political praxis permeated the English political thought that inspired the American Revolution and that it continued to influence the United States, from John Locke's conjectures of society in "a state of nature" through the establishment of women's suffrage. However, the most specific usage inspired its label. Grindé and Johansen assert that what Colonial British Americans referred to as the *Iroquois Confederacy* (the Haudenosaunee Six Nations of the Cayuga, Mohawk, Onondaga, Oneida, Seneca, and Tuscarora) provided the inspiration for Benjamin Franklin's outline of the failed 1754 Albany Plan of Union, a stillborn precursor to the Continental Congress and thus an early step toward American federalism.[39] Historians refer to this set of claims as the *Iroquois influence thesis.*

This chapter does not pass judgment on the veracity of the Iroquois influence thesis, nor am I here to flog the historians who have pronounced previously on it for or against; quite the opposite.[40] They were practicing the way they had been taught, and more crucially, their published work was subjected to revision and review, thus passing muster with disciplinary gatekeepers. The central idea seems not far-fetched. Mid-eighteenth-century British settlers faced the dilemma of coordinating defense and diplomacy across colonies. Each of the Haudenosaunee Six Nations administered its own internal affairs and executed war, but together they conducted diplomacy. The Albany Plan of Union, composed by colonists at a 1754 set of meetings while they were also trying to come to terms with Haudenosaunee in Albany for peace talks, bears resemblances to how the Six Nations' Great League of Peace operated. The Albany Plan of Union, although never adopted, called for each colony to maintain authority within its borders while a representative central body would take collective responsibility for defense and diplomacy.[41] To put the matter abstractly, this highly contentious historical debate hinges on whether one group of people with a particular problem, in proposing a solution with similarities to that of another group that had addressed an analogous dilemma with considerable

---

[39] "The Albany Plan of Union," 1754, https://founders.archives.gov/documents/Franklin/01-05-02-0104, *Founders Online*, National Archives.

[40] For an evaluation that does note some of the deficiencies on all sides, see Jerry D. Stubben, "The Indigenous Influence Theory of American Democracy," *Social Science Quarterly* 81, no. 3 (September 2000): 716–31.

[41] "The Albany Plan of Union"; For a discussion of the Great League of Peace, see Daniel K. Richter, *The Ordeal of the Longhouse: The Peoples of the Iroquois League in the Era of European Colonization* (Chapel Hill: University of North Carolina Press for the Institute of Early American History and Culture, 1992), 39–46.

success, and was meeting with that second group at the time, may have borrowed some of its ideas from that second group.[42]

However, as with most historical controversies, the debate over the Iroquois influence thesis is not an abstract one. It bears deep contemporary cultural significance, especially for its proponents, and maybe therein lay the pitfalls for all participants. Perhaps to be provocative—and who can blame the authors, as US historians have a long, shameful record of chronically underestimating at best and, at worst, deeply denigrating Native Americans and Indigenous culture—pro-Iroquois influence thesis works have been encyclopedic in their efforts to find any sort of evidence bolstering their contentions, but reticent about its merits compared to other explanations that might be equally or more likely. For example, they tend not to mention that many of the Albany Plan's elements resembling those of the Great League of Peace, such as a deliberative body of approximately fifty representatives, also had long Colonial precedent predating settlers' knowledge of Haudenosaunee politics. Nonetheless, critics appear at least as attuned to the collective chip on proponents' shoulders as to the question itself. Furthermore, critics, in their other work, often acknowledge Native American influence upon settlers' dress, agriculture, transportation technology, and military tactics, among other things, yet dismiss the idea of the borrowing of political ideas out of hand. They also tend to pick nits off of the larger animal rather than considering it in toto, and have mostly aimed to find fault rather than meaning.[43] Partisans on both sides, citing in their work ample evidence that their interlocutors appear not even to acknowledge, imply the worst of their antagonists—as intentionally ignoring what should be incontrovertible evidence—and engage in ad hominem attacks.[44] The acrimony has resulted in a few scholars, often those most sympathetic to current Native American concerns, accepting the proposition

---

[42] For one of the few judicious, more extended discussions of this debate, see Alan Gibson, *Interpreting the Founding: Guide to the Enduring Debates over the Origins and Foundations of the American Republic*, American Political Thought (Lawrence: University Press of Kansas, 2006), 72–78.

[43] Among these are William A. Starna and George R. Hamell, "History and the Burden of Proof: The Case of Iroquois Influence on the U.S. Constitution," *New York History* 77, no. 4 (October 1996): 427–52; Samuel B. Payne, "The Iroquois League, the Articles of Confederation, and the Constitution," *The William and Mary Quarterly* 53, no. 3 (1996): 605–20; Philip A. Levy, "Exemplars of Taking Liberties: The Iroquois Influence Thesis and the Problem of Evidence," *The William and Mary Quarterly* 53, no. 3 (1996): 588–604. Although taking a more measured stance, anthropologist Elisabeth Tooker leaps over the Articles of Confederation in Elisabeth Tooker, "The United States Constitution and the Iroquois League," *Ethnohistory* 35, no. 4 (October 1988): 305–36.

[44] See, for example, Donald A. Grindé, "Iroquoian Political Concept and the Genesis of American Government," in *Indian Roots of American Democracy* (Ithaca, NY: Akwe:kon Press, Cornell University, 1992), 57; Donald A. Grindé and Bruce E. Johansen, "Sauce for the Goose: Demand and Definitions for 'Proof' Regarding the Iroquois and Democracy," *The William and Mary Quarterly* 53, no. 3 (1996): 636; and even the title of Levy, "Exemplars of Taking Liberties."

without qualification, while the entire idea goes largely unmentioned in mainstream historical scholarship, whether of the Constitution specifically or of American history generally. Historians are supposed to synthesize and refine. Instead, an outside observer could conclude that we have stubbornly decided to inhabit two different conceptual universes, each with its own logic and evidence.

If we historians are to fortify our logical rigor to avoid such impasses, two basic improvements come to mind, working like the bifocals Franklin invented, to better our historical vision. First would be to require student papers and scholarly manuscripts to consider our theses in their relation to previously proposed interpretations of the same or similar phenomena. This could be a simple declaration of the validity of the author's claim compared to those explanations. To apply this technique to the Iroquois influence thesis, we could ask what parts of the Albany Plan show the heaviest Haudenosaunee intellectual fingerprints, based on what evidence, and, crucially, compared to previous interpretations that have emphasized Colonial and European precedent. One might also ask to what extent were similar solutions to the Haudenosaunees' and colonists' challenges probable regardless, much like the biological process of convergent evolution, in which different organisms evolve similar functional structures, and to what extent were the two plans unique in ways that their comparable situations would not account for. This may be a lot to demand, and the current requirement of placing an argument in previous scholarly conversations partly achieves this task, though not directly.

A second improvement would be to apply levels of confidence to our assertions. Here we might look to another arena in which people are asked to weigh to what extent they believe a particular interpretation of the past: policing and civil and criminal legal proceedings. Although we would not want to mimic the American legal system's adversarial heuristics, it does provide no fewer than nine escalating levels of certitude in the evaluation of contentions. These escalate from "some evidence" to "proof beyond a reasonable doubt." How confident are we historians, based upon the available evidence, that particular elements of the Albany Plan of Union not only resemble, but were inspired by Haudenosaunee custom? Here, if we were to borrow from the American law regime, then, depending upon what evidence we bring to bear and the context, we might suggest that there is somewhere between "reasonable indications" at the second level, but not, say, as much as "clear and convincing evidence," several levels above. No such system of scaled degrees of confidence is perfect, of course, and, as recent legal authors have noted, each one can be subjected to levels of nuance that neither humans nor artificial intelligence can definitively determine.[45] Nonetheless, including these two measures would force historians to be more precise in making our own arguments, and evaluating each other's.

In terms of combatting confirmation bias, we historians have no need to reinvent the lightning rod. Although there are no sure-fire fixes, one place to start would be to adopt a bit of self-reflexivity. A variety of social science disciplines, such as ethnography and sociology, have long debated and adopted models for how scholars should consider their social position and ideological commitments before they leap into their research, much less interpret their findings.[46] Here, too, easy-to-make adjustments might go a long way. One could be to encourage our asking more open-ended questions, rather than beginning with hypotheses, so as to keep our minds awake to all sorts of evidence, not only that which would be likely to support our conjectures. Another would be to include, pro forma as an element of all scholarly work, some form of short personal statement as the first footnote in any project, one that might be specific enough for the task at hand while masking the author's identity for the purpose of keeping reviews double blind. In terms of gatekeeping, reviewers' instructions could ask them to read the abstract first, and to consider the extent to which they find the argument plausible; then, to be generous in their reading if their first instinct was skepticism, but to read with a more jaundiced eye if their initial assessment was positive.[47] Perhaps such injunctions might have led reviewers of work regarding the Iroquois influence thesis to be more judicious. To be sure, engaging in reflexivity is neither easy nor simple, nor does doing so provide magic inoculation against human fallibility. Reflection has its inherent flaws. As philosopher Hilary Kornblith notes, we apply the same resistant brain to our reflection that we do to our research material. She points out that, logically, we must then examine the assumptions we bring to our reflection, and then those assumptions in turn, engaging in a fractal-like, endless exercise of ever-more precise, and absurd, navel-gazing.[48] That said, cognitive psychology indicates that self-knowledge may be our least bad defense against confirmation bias.

[45] See, for example, C. M. A. McCauliff, "Burdens of Proof: Degrees of Belief, Quanta of Evidence, or Constitutional Guarantees?" *Vanderbilt Law Review* 35, no. 1293 (November 1982): 34; Floris Bex and Douglas Walton, "Burdens and Standards of Proof for Inference to the Best Explanation," *SSRN Electronic Journal* (2010), https://doi.org/10.2139/ssrn.2038431.
[46] For the roots of this movement across a number of fields, see Steve Woolgar, ed., *Knowledge and Reflexivity: New Frontiers in the Sociology of Knowledge* (London: Sage, 1988).
[47] See Paul Lichterman, "Interpretive Reflexivity in Ethnography," *Ethnography* 18, no. 1 (March 1, 2017): 35–45.
[48] Hilary Kornblith, *On Reflection* (New York: Oxford University Press, 2012), 9–14.

Please do not take this essay to imply that history, as a discipline, is a wild arcade of unsubstantiated claims and wishful thinking. Maybe my interpretation that "The Truth about Jim Crow," the Bellesiles case, and the Iroquois influence thesis fall at the end of a spectrum is wrong. Maybe they are qualitatively distinct. Maybe I am prey to my own cognitive bias, primed to see them as indicative of a pattern rather than outliers, the proverbial exceptions proving the rule. As a longtime editor and keen observer of these controversies, David Waldstreicher has noted to me that these controversies invoked particularly politicized dynamics far more intense than most historical research, ones that perhaps warped these discussions in ways that generally do not affect most research.[49] Furthermore, the practice of history possesses strengths to be envied by many fields. History's emphasis on clear writing results in major journals including articles that could be read and appreciated by a lay audience. That clarity directly contrasts many other academic lines of endeavor, much of whose scholarship's impenetrability to all but specialists shields them from scrutiny by the wider public. Such accessibility, including to sources, especially online ones (unlike science requiring access to labs or heavily mathematical pursuits), helps with self-correction: indeed, it was a layperson who most effectively identified the faults in Michael Bellesiles's work.[50] Although we historians lament our comparatively piddly federal grants and small nonprofit fellowships, and the lack of for-profit monetary support for our efforts, that dearth of outside money frees us from the financial intellectual dependence that permeates some fields, dictating paths of research. Despite a general hostility to theory, we historians are voracious in our incorporation of methods and evidence from a range of categories of inquiry, not limiting our explanations to those only available through our own discipline-driven heuristics. For example, the introductory textbook that I have been assigning, more cutting-edge than most but not outside the mainstream, offers conclusions drawing on scholarship that has gleaned insights from a score of scientific, social scientific, and humanities disciplines and interdisciplinary fields.[51] Historical research remains an endeavor with many virtues, pushing the limits of discovery.

Maybe, then, although the ACRU report "The Truth about Jim Crow," "The Origins of Gun Culture," and the Iroquois influence theory debates

---

[49] David Waldstreicher to Andrew M. Schocket, "Re: Re: If You're Really Looking for More Punishment ...," personal communication, October 5, 2020.

[50] Legal scholar James Lindgren credited layperson Clayton Cramer as the original article's "most thorough and persistent critic"; Lindgren, "Fall from Grace," 2199.

[51] Joseph Locke and Ben Wright, eds., *The American Yawp: A Massively Collaborative Open U.S. History Textbook*, vol. 1 (Stanford: Stanford University Press, 2019).

have proven little, examining them can prompt historians to ponder ways to better our practices, or at least to consider their efficacy. We could heed the advice of Kathryn Schulz, who argues that the investigation of our mistakes can be among our most fruitful endeavors.[52] I usually tell my students not to end a paragraph, much less an entire piece, with a quotation. We should not cede our last word to someone else, thereby intellectually subcontracting our conclusions. But given the spirit of this volume—that we should not be so certain in our own convictions—and the organizational auspices under which this volume is published, here I close with words from a report about the apparent hoax of mesmerism, written by a distinguished commission at the behest of Louis XVI, headed by none other than APS co-founder Benjamin Franklin. To wit, "Perhaps the history of the errors of mankind, all things considered, is more valuable and interesting than that of their discoveries."[53]

---

[52] Kathryn Schulz, *Being Wrong: Adventures in the Margin of Error* (New York: Ecco, 2010).

[53] Benjamin Franklin, *Report of Dr. Benjamin Franklin, and Other Commissioners, Charged by the King of France, with the Examination of Animal Magnetism, as Now Practised at Paris* (London: J. Johnson, 1785), 18.

Chapter 4

Novel Democracy: Readers, Evidence, and the Commonplace Book of Elizabeth Phillips Payson, 1806–25

Gordon Fraser

Is the well-documented crisis of democracy in the United States and elsewhere partly a crisis of novel reading?[1] Some scholars have suggested as much. Sustained, attentive reading provides "a democratic foundation for critical, inferential reasoning. ... This is the basis of a collective conscience," writes Maryanne Wolf in *Reader Come Home*, her warning about the intellectual, political, and moral hazards of distracted, digital reading.[2] Philosopher Martha Nussbaum, moreover, has identified the novel in particular as the literary genre that enables the nuanced development of a democratic conscience. She writes: "Responsible lucidity can be wrested from ... darkness only by painful, vigilant effort, the intense scrutiny of particulars."[3] Nussbaum has suggested that novels uniquely enable readers to develop this "[r]esponsible lucidity" for two reasons. First, novels stage for readers a commitment "to the ethical significance of uncontrolled events, to the epistemological value of emotion, [and] to the variety and non-commensurability of important things." Second, novels demand "a deep and sympathetic investigation of" ethics, and the compari-

---

[1] See Steven Levitsky and Daniel Ziblatt, *How Democracies Die* (New York: Crown, 2018).

[2] Maryanne Wolf, *Reader, Come Home: The Reading Brain in a Digital World* (New York: Harper, 2018), 200–201.

[3] Martha Nussbaum, *Love's Knowledge: Essays on Philosophy and Literature* (New York: Oxford University Press, 1990), 148.

son of ethical positions to lived experience.[4] In short, novels enable their readers to take a nuanced approach to evidence, inviting them to consider how unpredictable events shape individual lives as they are actually lived and to weigh incommensurate values—important preconditions for self-governance.

Typically, evidence is treated as the near-exclusive domain of science and law. As Sheila Jasanoff observes, "science claims a monopoly on revealing truths" drawn from evidence, while "the law can claim a parallel monopoly on defining the nature of evidence" as a means of approximating the truth.[5] Moreover, in the anglophone world, the domains of science and law developed in tandem in the seventeenth and eighteenth centuries, as Steven Shapin observes.[6] Yet novelistic storytelling provides a very different means of assessing evidence because it presumes that evidence itself will be insufficient. Novels—and works that take similar narrative form, such as biographies—speculate about the motivations of people and the causes of events based on a few starting assumptions or known facts. In the late eighteenth and early nineteenth centuries, some believed that readers trained in such speculation would develop the habits of mind necessary for self-governance. Indeed, the anglophone novel and novel-reading habits grew up alongside American democratic institutions.[7]

But any case indicating that novels are necessary for self-governance has significant hurdles to clear. The first and most obvious is that people who suggest that novels are necessary for *anything* tend to be proven wrong, as book historian Leah Price has demonstrated. Across their history, novels have been blamed for enabling vice, eliminating vice, weakening concentration, strengthening concentration, and causing blindness.[8] Moreover, as Simon During has observed, the relationship between novel reading and democracy has been paradoxical. On the one hand, democracy elevates individual experience over more traditional ways of understanding social relations, such as "learning, hierarchies, and morality." The primacy of individual experience in the fictional secular prose narrative means that the novel is an ideal genre for a post-Enlightenment democracy. If novels

---

[4] Nussbaum, *Love's Knowledge*, 26–27.

[5] Sheila Jasanoff, *Science and Public Reason* (London: Routledge, 2012), 15.

[6] Steven Shapin, *A Social History of Truth: Civility and Science in Seventeenth-Century England* (Chicago: Chicago University Press, 1994), 122.

[7] Only twenty-two domestic novel imprints appeared in the United States in the 1780s. In the next decade, that number grew almost ten-fold, to 197 imprints. See Robert A. Gross and Mary Kelley, eds., *A History of the Book in America, Vol. 2* (Chapel Hill: University of North Carolina Press, 2010), 442. My calculations are based on the North American Imprints Program.

[8] Leah Price, *What We Talk about When We Talk about Books* Kindle Edition (New York: Basic, 2019), Introduction.

hadn't existed, democrats might just have invented them. On the other hand, all printed literature in the late eighteenth century tended to be written and read by relatively well-educated people.[9] This was certainly true in the United States, where educated, White New Englanders read far more avidly than Southerners—White, Black, or Indigenous.[10] In this sense, the novel was hardly a democratic, leveling genre. Ian Watt made this observation in his classic study, noting that novels in the late eighteenth century were "not, strictly speaking, a popular literary form." The costs of recreational reading were simply too high for widespread popularity until well into the nineteenth century.[11] And, even today, when the material costs of sustained reading are relatively low, novel reading remains a niche activity.[12]

In the pages to follow, then, I will return to the scene of reading in the first few decades of the United States, focusing on how reading secular prose narratives about the lives of individuals—novels and biographies, primarily—enabled readers to assess evidence. I am concerned with whether readers in the Early Republic really did, in practice, approach the world with a more "[r]esponsible lucidity" based upon the "intense scrutiny" of often fictional particulars. I will suggest that, despite all of the hand-wringing by Early Republican elites about the fraudulence of narratives, novels and biographies were valuable because they enabled readers to solve an otherwise unsolvable evidentiary problem. Readers learned to fill in the blanks about human intention by scrutinizing human

[9] Simon During, *Against Democracy: Literary Experience in the Era of Emancipations* (New York: Fordham University Press, 2012), 6.

[10] In the generation before the Revolution, the literacy gap between White New Englanders and White Southerners was not as great as has often been imagined. According to one study, 79 percent of the White men of Perquimas County, North Carolina, could sign their names, in comparison to 85 percent of White men in some regions of New England. By 1840, White literacy in North Carolina stood at 72 percent, whereas White literacy in New England was nearly universal. See Robert A. Gross, "Reading for an Extensive Republic," in *A History of the Book in America, Vol. 2*, eds. Robert A. Gross and Mary Kelley (Chapel Hill: University of North Carolina Press, 2010), 516–44, especially 526. Widespread literacy would not reach the native southeast until the 1820s. In the eastern Cherokee Nation by 1835, one out of every two households contained at least one person able to read the written Cherokee language, and one out of every six contained at least one person able to read written English. Barry O'Connell, "Literacy and Colonization: The Case of the Cherokees," *A History of the Book in America, Vol., 2*, eds. Robert A. Gross and Mary Kelley (Chapel Hill: University of North Carolina Press, 2010), 495–515, especially 513.

[11] Ian Watt, *The Rise of the Novel: Studies in Defoe, Richardson, and Fielding* [1957] (London: Bodley Head, 2015), 42.

[12] Only about 73 percent of people in the United States have read a book of any kind in the past year, according to a Pew study. See "Non-Book Readers," Pew, 2019, accessed August 20, 2020, https://www.pewresearch.org/fact-tank/2019/09/26/who-doesnt-read-books-in-america/. In 2012, fewer than half of the people in the United States had read a book-length work of fiction in the past year. This group was disproportionately composed of university-educated White women. See "A Decade of Arts Engagement," National Endowment for the Arts: NEA Research Report #58 (Washington: NEA, 2015), 71, accessed August 25, 2020, https://www.arts.gov/sites/default/files/2012-sppa-jan2015-rev.pdf.

action. Such books enabled readers to think more clearly about politics in the broadest sense—to assess the motivations and emotional lives of others and to weigh the relative values of noncommensurate goods.

Because this chapter is necessarily brief, I examine the story of a single reader in relation to the larger reading landscape of the Early Republic. I take up the case of Elizabeth Phillips Payson (1762–1829), who kept a detailed record of her reading habits between 1806 and 1825 in a commonplace book now held at the Schlesinger Library of Harvard University.[13] In examining her notes, I compare her reading habits to those of others in her time. Because my findings extrapolate from a single instance, however, they will be no more than suggestive. And yet I think that Payson's reading habits reveal the possibilities for novel reading in a nascent democracy because she was an extraordinarily sophisticated reader. She was initially generous in her assessment of each author or work but would turn scrupulously critical before completing most commonplace entries. She read widely and in multiple languages. She questioned her own assumptions and investigated the claims of books, including novels, by turning to living people who might be able to confirm or contradict the claims she found on the published page. Payson was as close to an ideal reader, I think, as any real reader could be.

And as an ideal-real reader, Payson demonstrates the limits of a lucid, responsible reading practice. She made errors of fact, for instance. More important, the political culture of the early United States placed significant limits on the ability of women to participate in self-governance regardless of the sophistication with which they could take the measure of the political world. Novels might be important to a democracy, but the United States had not yet become a democracy in the modern sense. Citizenship was a speculative social practice rather than a clear legal one, and even most acknowledged citizens could not vote or hold office.[14] Even if the reading practices honed by novels and biographies are ideal for democratic citizens, in short, these books nonetheless cannot materialize political power for their readers.

---

[13] Commonplace Book of Elizabeth Phillips Payson, Arthur and Elizabeth Schlesinger Library on the History of Women in America, Radcliffe College, Cambridge, MA, accessed April 25, 2020, https://curiosity.lib.harvard.edu/reading/catalog/42-990014562750203941_RADSCHL:4118841. Although Payson has been discussed by numerous scholars, her life has not been widely investigated. I believe her to be the Charlestown, Massachusetts, daughter of Rev. Phillips Payson and Elizabeth Payson. See "Elizabeth Payson, 10 September 1829," Ancestry.com, Massachusetts, Wills and Probate Records, 1635–1991 (Provo, UT, 2015). This Elizabeth Payson's grave can be found in the Rumney Marsh Burial Ground in Revere, Massachusetts.

[14] Carrie Hyde, *Civic Longing: The Speculative Origins of US Citizenship* (Cambridge, MA: Harvard University Press, 2018), 3–17.

Yet I suggest that although the link between novel reading and democracy was not a realized ideal from the past, it is nonetheless a recoverable hope from that past. In other words, those who advocated the reading of secular prose narratives about the messy, complicated lives of individuals recognized the limits of such a practice but advocated it anyway. Recognizing this hope from the past is important today because we are in the midst of a crisis of fact and fraudulence. Conspiracy theories spread through subcultures and mutate, and these fraudulent stories provide cover for political actors who seek near-term electoral, economic, or geopolitical advantage.[15] Meanwhile, and of equal concern to me in this essay, many of the defenders of the democratic order have become scrupulous factualists, insisting that "facts matter."[16] In essence, factualism has been arrayed against metastasizing fraudulence. The problem, of course, is that a narrow, pedantic factualism is not a particularly good means of arriving at an approximation of the truth. Evidence is often only partial. Experts can be wrong. And most political questions are not matters of fact or expertise but of values and interests.[17] Novels—and the novelistic approaches to storytelling found in biographies—provide a means of extrapolating from known facts or probable circumstances. They fill in the evidentiary blanks about matters of human intention. Narratives, Early Republican theorists believed and I agree, are an important means of training oneself to read one's fellow human beings in the absence of a full evidentiary picture of their motivations, desires, and aims.

THE INNER LIFE OF A TYRANT

Overheated criticisms of fiction in particular abounded at the close of the eighteenth century.[18] Yet among some political theorists and authors, there

---

[15] Gordon Fraser, "Conspiracy, Pornography, Democracy: The Recurrent Aesthetics of the American Illuminati," *Journal of American Studies* 54, no. 2 (2020): 273–94.

[16] Ronald Bailey, "Facts Matter After All," *Reason*, January 3, 2018, accessed April 15, 2020, https://reason.com/2018/01/03/facts-matter-after-all-hooray/. See also the "Fact Checker," *Washington Post* last updated January 20, 2021. https://www.washingtonpost.com/graphics/politics/trump-claims-database/?utm_term=.27babcd5e58c&itid=lk_inline_manual_2&itid=lk_inline_manual_2.

[17] Sam Fallon, "The Rise of the Pedantic Professor: When Academic Self-Regard Becomes an Intellectual Style," *Chronicle of Higher Education*, March 1, 2019, accessed April 15, 2020, https://www.chronicle.com/article/The-Rise-of-the-Pedantic/245808.

[18] English theologian Vicesimus Knox (1752–1821) believed that novels shortened attention spans and made their readers dupes: "The graces of the chaste matron Truth, are suffered to pass unobserved, amidst the gaudy and painted decorations of meretricious fiction." Vicesimus Knox, "No. XIV. On Novel Reading," in *Essays, Moral and Literary*(London: Charles Dilly, 1795), 68–72, quotation on 71. Edmund Burke (1729–1797) warned of a revolutionary French legislature writing "fiction" into law: "We have never dreamt that parliaments had any right ... to force a currency of their own fiction in the place of that which is real." Edmund Burke, *Reflections on the Revolution in France*, ed. L. G. Mitchell (Oxford: Oxford World's Classics, 1993), 153.

was also a surprising support for fiction as necessary to a self-governing people. Writing in the voice of a fictional woman defending the writing of fiction, and cribbing John Locke (1632–1704) in the process, the novelist Charles Brockden Brown (1771–1810) explained that "human nature" is more influenced "by example than by precept," and so novels were a powerful means of understanding individual behavior in practice.[19] John Adams (1735–1826), moreover, regarded fiction reading as one means of training oneself for governance. As historians Nancy Isenberg and Andrew Burstein explain, Adams modeled much of his diary writing on the prose of novelists, and he encouraged novel reading by his oldest son, John Quincy Adams (1767–1848).[20] And Susanna Rowson (1762–1824), herself a popular novelist, defended the practice of writing novels by suggesting that the "slight veil of fiction" enables one to tell stories that preserve "happiness," prevent "errors," and exert an "influence on mankind in general."[21] The advocates of fiction reading believed that it offered numerous benefits to a self-governing people.

These theorists observed a rise in the popularity of novels and biographies in their own era. In the first decades after the American Revolution, the United *States* of America had many more readers of secular literature than its predecessor colonies, and novel and biography reading grew in particular. This readership varied by region, race, gender, and level of education, but the explosion of recreational reading has nonetheless been correlated by numerous scholars with the emergence of republican institutions.[22] In *The Algerine Captive* (1797), the author and jurist Royall Tyler (1757–1826) described an American returning to the United States after seven years as a prisoner in North Africa. "One of the first observations [he] … made, upon his return to his native country," Tyler began, "was the extreme avidity, with which books of mere amusement were purchased

---

[19] A. [Charles Brockden Brown], "A Student's Diary… No. VI. Novel Reading," *The Literary Magazine and American Register* (March 1804): 403–08, quotation on 405. For Brown's borrowing from Locke, see Thomas Koenigs, "'Whatever May Be the Merit of My Book as a Fiction': *Wieland*'s Instructional Fictionality, *ELH* 79, no. 3 (2012): 717, 741n9. See also Thomas Koenigs, *Founded in Fiction: The Uses of Fiction in the Early United States* (Princeton, NJ: Princeton University Press, 2021); and Gillian Brown, *The Consent of the Governed: The Lockean Legacy in Early American Culture* (Cambridge, MA: Harvard University Press, 2001).

[20] Nancy Isenberg and Andrew Burstein, *The Problem of Democracy: The Presidents Adams Confront the Cult of Personality* (New York: Penguin, 2020), 40. See also "From Thomas Jefferson to Robert Skipwith, with a List of Books for a Private Library, 3 August 1771," *Founders Online*, National Archives, https://founders.archives.gov/documents/Jefferson/01-01-02-0056.

[21] Susanna Rowson, "Charlotte Temple, A Tale of Truth," in *Charlotte Temple and Lucy Temple*, ed. Ann Douglas (New York: Penguin, 1991), xlix–l.

[22] The classic study of this phenomenon remains Cathy N. Davidson, *Revolution and the Word: The Rise of the Novel in America* (Oxford: Oxford University Press, 2004).

and perused by all ranks of his countrymen." Tyler continued: "When he left New England, books of Biography, Travels, Novels, and modern Romances, were confined to our sea ports. ... On his return from captivity, he found ... country booksellers, fostering the new born taste of the people, had filled the whole land with modern Travels and Novels."[23] Tyler's protagonist was fictional, but the transformation he described was real. Indeed, Tyler had been part of it. *The Algerine Captive* was published in New Hampshire by a printing house that had been in operation for only four years.[24] The rise of the novel coincided with the rise of a novel form of government.

But advocates of novels recognized in these texts more than mere popularity. The virtue of reading secular narratives about the lives of individuals was that it enabled the reader to manage an evidentiary problem that plagues democratic societies. Novels trained people to "read" the inner lives and intentions of others. In a hierarchical society, the inner lives of others matter less than their stated aims and relative power. But in a democracy, a society in which relative equals argue and collaborate, reading others is a necessity.[25] But the inner lives of others are inscrutable. People hint at these inner lives through discussion, action, and occasional outbursts of unintended speech. These evidentiary fragments do not provide an observer with a complete picture. Enter fiction. By piecing together the complete story of an individual's inner life, novels arm their readers with a system for filling in the evidentiary gaps they encounter when they observe only the external behaviors of other people.

In fact, this faith in the power of fictionality to answer otherwise unanswerable questions was made most visible by fiction's literary alternatives, the authors of which claimed to salvage the power of fictionality to answer evidentiary questions while discarding fiction's chief flaw—its fraudulence. In the early American republic, this attempt to discard fiction itself but to salvage its ability to fill in evidentiary gaps manifested in the biography and the *chronique scandaleuse*, the story of a scandal. In his

---

[23] Royall Tyler, *The Algerine Captive; or, The Life and Adventures of Doctor Updike Underhill: Six Years a Prisoner among the Algerines* (Walpole, NH: David Carlisle, Jun., 1797): v–vii.

[24] Gross and Kelley, eds., *A History of the Book in America, Vol. 2*, 442. Newspaper publication was growing as well. By 1775, there were roughly thirty-seven newspapers in business in the thirteen British colonies that would become the United States.

[25] Alexis de Tocqueville writes, "The language, dress, and daily activities of men in democracies are refractory to the idealizing imagination. Such things are not poetic in themselves, and even if they were, they would cease to be so because they are too well known to anyone to whom the poet might speak about them. Thus the poet is forced constantly to delve beneath the surface revealed by the senses to catch a glimpse of the soul itself." In other words, artists in a democracy cease to valorize princes and instead examine the inner lives of individuals. Alexis de Tocqueville, *Democracy in America*, ed. Oliver Zunz, trans. Arthur Goldhammer (New York: Library of America, 2004), 559.

Autobiography (1791), Benjamin Franklin promises that his life narrative will bring readers into contact with "the nearest thing to having experience of one's own," precisely the value he ascribes elsewhere to novels such as *Pamela* (1740) and *Moll Flanders* (1721).[26] At the same time, popular novels, such as *The Power of Sympathy* (1789), *Charlotte Temple* (1791/1794), and *The Coquette* (1797), promised to be more than novels. They were based on true stories, or "founded in fact," and thus were fictionalized chronicles of scandals that had appeared in newspapers or private letters.[27]

But autobiographies and scandalous chronicles were nonetheless essentially novelistic. They filled in evidentiary gaps—from missing facts to faulty memories—with supposition and invention. Indeed, much popular narrative writing was novelistic in this way, ascribing intentions to historical actors when intention could not possibly be known based on the available evidence. And this writing was, indeed, popular. Consider, as a case in point, the extant records of the Brentwood Social Library, a private circulating library in New Hampshire incorporated in 1802. The eight most popular titles in the library's collection accounted for 44 percent of the total checkouts. Half of these titles were either a novel or a biography. Seven of the eight could be described as a novel, a biography, or a work of history.[28] In other words, readers sought out accounts that filled in evidentiary gaps to create plausible stories about the lives and motivations of other people.

The narratives that appeared in novels and biographies provided what Benjamin Rush (1746–1813) called "the perception of things as they appear to the divine mind," or a God's-eye-view of human behavior.[29] Rush was a vehement opponent of novel reading, but he was concerned with the novel's fraudulence rather than with its narrative mode. He recommended, as an alternative, "history, biography, and travels," which could be narratively similar in their God's-eye-view of human behavior but deployed suppositions only as a means of filling in evidentiary gaps between factual certainties. Rush's concern was that entirely fraudulent stories—such as novels—produced an "abortive sympathy" in their readers. Novel readers

---

[26] For a discussion, see Koenigs, "'Whatever May Be the Merit of My Book as a Fiction,'" 720.

[27] [Hannah Webster Foster], *The Coquette; or, The History of Eliza Wharton; A Novel; Founded in Fact* (Boston: E. Larkin, 1797). Koenigs, "'Whatever May Be the Merit of My Book as a Fiction,'" 719.

[28] Papers of the Brentwood, N.H., Social Library: Records [manuscript], 1809–1850, American Antiquarian Society, Worcester, MA. There were 325 total library withdrawals reported during this period. The eight most popular titles, in order, were: Oliver Goldsmith's *Animated Nature* (1774), Charles Rollin's *Ancient History* (1730), Johann Lorenz von Mosheim's *Ecclesiastical History* (English, 1765), August von Kotzebue's *The Constant Lover; or, William and Jeanette* (American edition, 1799), "*Life of Washington*," Henry Hunter's *Sacred Biography* (American edition, 1794), Benjamin Franklin's *Autobiography* (1793), and John Lendrum's *History of the American Revolution* (1795).

[29] Benjamin Rush, *Thoughts upon Female Education* (Philadelphia: Prichard and Hall, 1787), 15.

were likely to spend their sympathetic energies on fictional characters rather than on their fellow human beings.[30]

In essence, then, the enemies of novels and their boosters saw in fictionality the same fundamental virtue—it provided a complete, God's-eye-view of human intention that no other mode of accumulating and arranging evidence could provide. The readers of these sorts of narratives, whether novels or biographies, could understand the inner lives of their fellow human beings, albeit provisionally and speculatively. This understanding mattered to people in a society deeply concerned about the development of common, democratic practices and fearful about backsliding into tyranny. Such worries were common. In Brentwood, New Hampshire, where members of the local circulating library would busily read biographies and novels, a minister warned in 1801 that it was not clear whether members of the community would "be so happy as to retain our civil liberty, and free elective government, administered with economy; and not experience oppression."[31] Only time, he suggested, could tell whether the United States would backslide into despotism.

And novelistic writing and reading practices—if not novels themselves—were regarded by many as a key bulwark against that despotism. One could never understand the inner life of a future Napoleon based on fact alone. Biographers and novelists will fill in the blanks based on plausible suppositions, and readers will learn to "read" the behaviors of future demagogues and tyrants by reading stories about them. Both biographers and novelists were careful to note their scrupulous verisimilitude in making these suppositions. Much depended on their ability to educate readers in the reading of others. Willem Lodewyk Van-Ess, who completed a biography of Napoleon Bonaparte (1769–1821) while the French emperor was still blasting his way across Europe, made clear that understanding the character of his subject required a scrupulous extrapolation from known facts. "To render any character instructive, it must be impartially given," Van-Ess explained. Because understanding the French emperor was a matter of life and death, his biographer must join neither the "the flatterers or the enemies of Buonaparté."[32]

The novelist Richard Cumberland (1732–1811) took much the same position, explaining that he could "force beings into nature, that no well-bred reader ever met with." But, he continued, this would be a mistake.

---

[30] Rush, *Thoughts upon Female Education*, 9, 12.

[31] Solomon Aiken, "Sermon, Preached at the Ordination of ... Ebenezer Flint, A.B." (Exeter, NH: Henry Ranlet, 1801), 17.

[32] Willem Lodewyk Van-Ess, *The Life of Napoleon Buonaparté, Vol. I* (London: W. Day, 1808), advertisement.

"I have lived long enough," he writes, "to see wonderful revolutions effected by an intemperate abuse of power, and shall be cautious how I risk privileges so precious upon experiments so trivial." For Cumberland, the novelist must be *more* scrupulous in attending to likelihoods than even the historian or biographer. Cumberland explained that a biography of Alexander the Great (356–323 BCE) could end with the man dying in a drunken stupor, as many in the eighteenth century believed he had in fact died. But since most despots and warlords do not die in this way, a novelist would be advised to end the life of a despotic character more plausibly.[33]

Novelistic writing—the God's-eye-view of human behavior provided to varying degrees by novelists and biographers—ostensibly educated people for self-governance. Such writing made readers scrupulous observers of human behavior and reasoners about human motivation. This was, at least, the theory. But what did such reading look like in practice?

READING WITH ELIZABETH PHILLIPS PAYSON

Consider a commonplace book kept between 1806 and 1825 by a Massachusetts woman named Elizabeth Phillips Payson (1762–1829).[34] Payson's commonplace contained a detailed record of her reading, as well as written reflections on it. Some books she read and reflected on alone. Others, she reflected on in conversation with the "Female Reading Society" of Charlestown, Massachusetts, a group of about fifteen women who gathered regularly between November 1812 and September 1817 to discuss books such as the German epic poem *Oberon* (1780) and a two volume *History of Rome* (1769).[35] Payson's commonplace is an extraordinary record of early nineteenth-century reading, and numerous scholars have relied on it in their research.[36] I am interested in Payson here because her scrupulous reading and note-taking practices (her notes on the history of Rome run to twenty densely written pages) provide a real-life manifestation of idealized theories of reading. In other words, if reading stories about individuals

---

[33] Richard Cumberland, *Henry* [1795], in *The Novels of Swift, Bage, and Cumberland* (London: Hurst, Robinson, and Co., 1824), 514.

[34] Commonplace Book of Elizabeth Phillips Payson. I will cite according to Payson's original numbering scheme, but include the digitized PDF page numbers in [brackets].

[35] These books were Christoph Martin Wieland, *Oberon* (Weimar: Hoffman, 1780) and Oliver Goldsmith, *The Roman History, from the Foundation of the City of Rome, to the Destruction of the Western Empire* (London: Baker, Leigh, Davies, and Davies, 1769), although it is unclear which editions the Society worked from. See Commonplace Book of Elizabeth Phillips Payson, 102 [32], 107 [36], 142 [71].

[36] See, for instance, Mary Kelley, *Learning to Stand and Speak: Women, Education, and Public Life in America's Republic* (Chapel Hill: University of North Carolina Press, 2006), 138, 163–64.

really did train readers to be carefully democratic observers of human behavior, Payson's example would almost certainly demonstrate this training. And Payson read precisely those genres most believed to teach readers to read their fellow human beings: scandalous chronicles, novels, and biographies. I'll begin with scandal.

In 1813, Payson read Hannah Foster's (1759–1840) *The Coquette* (1797), a fictionalized account of Elizabeth Whitman (1752–1788), the daughter of a Connecticut clergyman who died in childbirth after checking into a Massachusetts inn under an assumed name. Various rumors swirled around Whitman. In one account, she had married in secret but died before her husband could reach the inn. In another account, she had been seduced and abandoned by a rake. But Foster's novel of a decade later fictionalized Whitman's story even as it promised to explain it.[37] *The Coquette* was, ostensibly, "founded in fact," and yet it was a fiction. Indeed, it is a key example of the novel-as-scandalous chronicle that proved popular in the late eighteenth and early nineteenth centuries.

In her two-page, hand-written reflection on the novel, Payson worked from memory as she often did. (Her quotations are frequently mistaken by a word or two, indicating that she tended to write down evocative phrases after setting the relevant book aside.) Payson regards *The Coquette* as a roman à clef—a novel with a key. She explains that it is, "A novel founded literally of facts as several of the characters are well known by any persons at the time." Payson apparently believed that Foster had changed the names of the scandal's participants but reported its factual elements without embellishment. As Bryan Waterman has observed, this was not actually the case. Foster's novel diverges considerably from the actual Whitman story.[38] But Payson makes a curious decision when she tries to decode the novel, a decision she does not make elsewhere in her commonplace. She leaves blank spaces. "The heroine whose name was [blank] I was very intimate with a dissipated fellow at the time," Payson reflects. She adds: "Not long after having been seduced by [blank] she left her father's house and came to Danvers." Payson only correlates one character with a real-life person. She writes: "The principle male character [illeg.] known by the name of Boyer, is known to be the Rev.d. Dr. Buckminster of Portsmouth." Payson's identification repeats local lore. Joseph Buckminster (1751–1812) would remain associated with the scandal, although decisive evidence of

---

[37] As late as the 1870s, some readers continued to regard Foster's novel as essentially factual. See Bryan Waterman, "Elizabeth Whitman's Disappearance and her 'Disappointment,'" *William & Mary Quarterly* 66, no. 2 (2009): 325–64, especially 325.

[38] Waterman, "Elizabeth Whitman's Disappearance," 331.

his involvement has not been discovered.[39] Yet Payson's blank spaces seem designed to be filled in later. Aside from a single instance, she does not use the common practice of drawing a line to indicate a censored name. Instead, she leaves considerable room—often continuing to write on the next line—as if she intended to fill in the full name of each participant when she ultimately discovered it. In essence, her commonplace reflection reveals a reader who expects that a "novel founded literally of facts" can be decoded, and she leaves the space to decode it.

Payson was a sophisticated and skeptical reader, and I don't think that her acceptance of Foster's novel as factual reveals a naïve credulity. Instead, Payson in her writing accepts what at the time would have seemed incontestable. Elizabeth Whitman had been a real person, and the people of Danvers really had "erected a monument to her memory," as Payson notes in her commonplace. At the same time, Payson's inclusion of blank spaces marks her unanswered questions. She provides herself, quite literally, with the space to fill in the blanks left by this story of a seduced New England woman. Who was her seducer? Who were the other participants in the scandal? Payson's reading of *The Coquette* is scrupulously provisional. Readers, such as Payson, may have imperfectly distinguished between fiction and fact, and yet they did not wholly surrender their investigative impulses. They could withhold judgment—sometimes indefinitely.

But what of avowed fictions? Payson could be a scathing critic. When she read *Waverley* (1814), by Sir Walter Scott (1771–1832), she began as she typically did with a generous reading. She copied out those passages she found particularly evocative or valuable. In a few cases, these were truisms about moral action: "If the path of gratitude & honour were always smooth & easy there would be little merit in following it." In other cases, the truisms applied to social convention: "We are ever connect uniformity of dress with the military character." But Payson's commonplacing only lasts for half a page. Then, she gives her first assessment: "The above are extracts from W. which are not however suitable criterions by which to judge the work; for where is that field or forest however wild that does not produce something to charm the eye, the ear, or the taste[?]"[40] Payson

---

[39] It is possible Payson heard this claim rather than read it. Waterman found the earliest printed reference to Buckminster to have appeared in 1823, a decade after Payson wrote her reflection on the novel. Of course, an earlier printed reference to Buckminster may have been lost. In addition, it is possible that she is confusing the suspected Joseph Buckminster with his son, Dr. Joseph Stevens Buckminster (1784–1812), who died the same year. The elder Buckminster had not received a doctorate of divinity, but the younger Buckminster would have been four years old when Whitman died in childbirth. See Waterman, "Elizabeth Whitman's Disappearance," 332; and Commonplace Book of Elizabeth Phillips Payson, 73 [144].

[40] Commonplace Book of Elizabeth Phillips Payson, 45 [107].

found *Waverley* to be a weedy, boring mess of a novel. She concluded that Scott's decision to publish anonymously this book—his first novel—was probably for the best.

Payson's ultimate assessment of *Waverley* appears in the final paragraph of her reflection. She writes:

> This book was generally speaking very dry & uninteresting. The Author seems to be very deficient in decorations for his productions, but in the advertisements it is said "supposed to have been written by W. Scott whose name alone is sufficient to induce many to peruse works otherwise inspired, so much do we natural[ly] expect from those who have formerly pleased["]; but the idea is certainly incorrect ^{tho} ~~for~~ the same piece of land will produce weeds as well as the nicest fruit. However, it is but justice to Scott to say that to those who have read his works no ^{farther} [than his poetry], contradiction of the report is unnecessary—[41]

In other words, those who have not read beyond Scott's poetry never need learn that his novel is without significant merit. Scott here is the field, as able to produce fruit as to produce dry, boring weeds. And *Waverley* is a weed. Yet although Payson's critique of the novel is essentially a matter of preference—she read the novel to be entertained, but she was bored—her complaints and her commonplacing practices reveal what virtues she found in novels as a genre.

Liberated from the requirement of strict factualism, novels could nonetheless in theory provide "something to charm the eye, the ear, or the taste." Moreover, charming writing was to Payson not merely decorative, although it was that, as well. Consider those passages Payson *does* find charming: "If the path of gratitude & honour were always smooth & easy there would be little merit in following it," or "We ~~are~~ ever connect uniformity of dress with the military character."[42] In essence, Payson is seeking in novels the sort of insights she might find in narratives founded in fact or in biographies. She is seeking the sort of insights about living that Benjamin Franklin promised readers in his own autobiography: that his life narrative will bring readers into contact with "the nearest thing to having experience of one's own."[43] Payson was following the conventional practices of eighteenth-century commonplacing by recording expressions

---

[41] Commonplace Book of Elizabeth Phillips Payson, 46 [108].

[42] Commonplace Book of Elizabeth Phillips Payson, 45 [107].

[43] Benjamin Franklin, *Autobiography and Other Writings*, ed. Ormond Seavey (New York: Oxford University Press, 1993), 75. For a discussion, see Koenigs, "'Whatever May Be the Merit of My Book as a Fiction,'" 720.

that seemed particularly true and apt, but she was locating these apt truths in an avowedly fictional work—albeit a boring one.[44]

Across both of these novels—*Waverley* and *The Coquette*—Payson reads with what Nussbaum might call "responsible lucidity."[45] She aims to wrest from these works of fiction deeper truths about the lives of New Englanders such as herself, about social conventions more broadly, and about right action in the face of moral difficulty. She also aims to observe distinctions between those fictions that extrapolate from known facts (as she believes she finds in *The Coquette*) and those fictions that invent facts to theorize about moral and social questions (such as *Waverley*). But, in both cases, Payson regards the act of reading prose narratives about the lives of individuals as a worthwhile endeavor, even when such narratives are poorly written or essentially fraudulent. As she explains: "where is that field or forest however wild that does not produce something to charm the eye, the ear, or the taste[?]"[46] Reading narratives brought Payson into contact with uncontrolled events and non-commensurate values, asking her to make judgments about them.[47] By adopting a God's-eye view of human affairs through her reading, even a factually inaccurate or deeply boring God's-eye view, Payson was able to consistently and repeatedly take the measure of these affairs.

And this persistent effort applied to biography, as well. Sometime after 1812, she read a biography of Catherine the Great (1729–796).[48] Payson's analysis of Catherine's character is nuanced and skeptical, although in some ways less skeptical than that of the biographer whose work she read. That biographer clearly lingered on Catherine's murderous scheming and rumored sexual license, as many did following the death of the Russian ruler. (Catherine II, later Catherine the Great, took power in a July 1762 coup d'état against the rule of her husband, Peter III.)[49] Payson

---

[44] For a discussion of topoi, or places in the mind, recorded in eighteenth-century commonplace books, see David Allan, *Commonplace Books and Reading in Georgian England* (Cambridge, UK: Cambridge University Press, 2010), 37.

[45] Martha Nussbaum, *Love's Knowledge*, 148.

[46] Commonplace Book of Elizabeth Phillips Payson, 45 [107].

[47] Martha Nussbaum, *Love's Knowledge*, 26–27.

[48] Commonplace Book of Elizabeth Phillips Payson, 138–41 [67–70] and unnumbered page [30]. Because Payson did not quote directly from the text, I have not been able to determine with certainty which biography she read. That said, Payson identifies this two-volume biography as the eighth book read by the Female Reading Society, which likely places her reading in the summer of 1813. It is possible that they read the *Authentic Memoirs of the Life and Reign of Catherine II* (London: Crosby, 1797), but I have only found that book in one volume. Although Payson could read French and set on a course of improving her French in 1819, I am not sure whether other Society members could. The widely available two-volume biography by François Buisson, *Vie de Catherine II, Impératrice de Russie* (Paris: Buisson, 1797), is a possible selection. Payson's decision to leave out any direct quotation from the biography could theoretically be explained by a language barrier.

[49] Robert E. Jones, *Emancipation of the Russian Nobility, 1762–1785* (Princeton, NJ: Princeton University Press, 2015), 99–100.

writes that Catherine "admitted all to her company at all times & in all situations both before & after [her husband's] death for whom she had any partiality. This was I think her greatest I had almost said only failing (excepting the great crime for which we can never forgive her murder)." Payson condemns Catherine for failing to fulfill her duties as a wife— duties that surely included sexual fidelity and refraining from the murder of her husband.[50]

But Catherine had a great many virtues, as well, and Payson spends a long time lingering on these virtues in her analysis of the late Russian leader. Catherine was a patron of the arts, paying "great attention to every species of literature supported several schools out of her private purse & gave great encouragement to the arts & science." Payson continued by observing that Catherine was a savvy, cunning, and effective ruler, if a despotic one:

> Catherine carried the nation through every difficulty & so great was her perspicasity [sic] that she seemed to have as it were a foreknowledge of most of the important events that happened, though there were many attempts made to form a conspiracy it could not be effected for it seemed as if she was in every part of this vast empire at the same time, where she discovered anything of the kind, instead of punishing the guilty as they deserved she would place them in some more elevated situation, pay them very liberally for any services they might render her & thus gain them over to her cause.[51]

In short, Payson regarded Catherine as a savvy ruler, one who maintained her rule by winning adversaries to her side when necessary. Cunning, pragmatic, observant, and careful, Catherine had all the qualities that allow a political leader to survive in a ruthless political world. "Her character in general," Payson concluded, "confirms me in a long entertain[ed] opinion that female judgement, [prowess?], foresight, knowledge &c. &c. is not to be surpassed by the other sex where their privileges are equal; their endowments by nature I believe to be the same, & the fashion of the day & custom only makes the difference."[52] Payson, who had read histories of Greece and Rome, as well as numerous biographies of emperors, kings, and generals, had a working knowledge of eighteenth- and nineteenth-century ideas about what made an effective political or military leader. And she had concluded that these virtues were as accessible to women as to men. Now, in a biography of Catherine the Great, Payson found proof

---

[50] Commonplace Book of Elizabeth Phillips Payson, 138 [67].
[51] Commonplace Book of Elizabeth Phillips Payson, 139 [68].
[52] Commonplace Book of Elizabeth Phillips Payson, 141 [70].

of her long-held suspicion that women were just as capable of wielding power.

But these observations do not constitute the totality of Payson's writing on the subject of the Russian ruler. Only a few pages earlier, in her observations on Oliver Goldsmith's history of ancient Greece, Payson paraphrased Goldsmith quoting the Athenian statesman Solon (c. 630–560 BCE) on the subject of tyranny: "A tyranny I said resembled a fair garden it is a beautiful spot while we are in it but wants a way to get out."[53] Tyrants are charismatic and appealing for many reasons, particularly for their ability to impose order on a seemingly wild and disordered world. They can turn a wilderness into a garden. But this is the problem with tyrants, as well. Upon entering the fair garden of a dictator, one finds the exits blocked. Payson agreed, and she kept this in view as she considered the legacy of Catherine the Great—a woman who proved that women could be tyrants but did not prove that tyrants could be just.

Indeed, after concluding that Catherine's example demonstrates the capacity of women for autocratic rule, Payson clarifies her view. "C_ was not by no means perfect in her domestic character she was supposed to be at the head of the conspiracy against her husband & that she was very capricious must be acknowledged in all who read her history for it was very evident from the frequency with which she changed her favorites with whom she would be at one time indecorously intimate but change in a moment to any more fascinating or that was a greater admirer of her charms."[54] Catherine's fickleness here was not just a failure of personal morality, although Payson as the New England daughter of a Congregationalist minister was certainly concerned with that. Inconstancy, as she observed elsewhere in her commonplace, was a particular failing of autocrats, as was susceptibility to flattery.[55] Catherine brought courtiers into her orbit and expelled them on a whim. She spent lavishly on frivolities even while her soldiers fought battles in far-off places and epidemic disease killed thousands of ordinary people.[56] In other words, she was a Caesar. Catherine's greatness, such as it was, flowed from her capacity for violence and survival, and from her indifference to suffering.

---

[53] Commonplace Book of Elizabeth Phillips Payson, 136 [65]. Originally, Goldsmith wrote: "*A tyranny*, he would say, *resembles a fair garden; it is a beautiful spot while we are within: but it wants a way to get out at.*" The quotation ostensibly comes from Solon (c. 630–c. 560 BCE). See Oliver Goldsmith, *History of Greece, Vol. I, Eleventh Edition* (London: Rivington, 1812), 27.

[54] Commonplace Book of Elizabeth Phillips Payson, 70 [141].

[55] See, for instance, her discussion of Caligula (12–41 CE). Commonplace Book of Elizabeth Phillips Payson, 110 [39].

[56] "There was at one time so great pestilence that 8,000 persons died in one day," Payson observed. Commonplace Book of Elizabeth Phillips Payson, 69 [140].

Payson's (and Solon's) metaphor of the garden, then, is useful. Freedom is an overgrown mess, producing weeds alongside good fruit. Reading widely and freely, Payson was variously entertained, bored, informed, and misled. *Waverley* failed to entertain, although it offered a few useful observations on character and social convention. *The Coquette* appeared to be factual, but Payson never did decode the novel's references to real people because those references were fraudulent. And Catherine the Great momentarily ensorcelled Payson, although the latter woman reminded herself of the fickle dangerousness of Caesars before even concluding her commonplace entry. Yet in reading widely, weighing evidence, and considering character in light of readerly experience, Payson demonstrated the "responsible lucidity" of the readers of narratives.[57] Payson's experience was enlarged by reading narratives about the experiences of others. In short, Payson came as close to embodying the ideal reader as theorists of reading— whether proponents of the novel, such as Charles Brockden Brown, or proponents of biography, such as Benjamin Rush—could ever hope to find in the real world.

THE LIMITS OF READING FOR DEMOCRACY

But Payson's scrupulous reading habits demonstrate the limits on a democracy of readers. First, she was a rarity. Most commonplace books from the period reveal readers with a far more limited range of interests.[58] And although Americans in the late eighteenth and early nineteenth centuries read more than people elsewhere, reading in the United States nonetheless remained a niche activity.[59] Second, Payson was a woman. Early American republicanism was fraternal, and it excluded highly educated women more consistently even than the patriarchal system of the Colonial era.[60] Legal exclusions, moreover, were not the only means by which women were kept from the arena of study, debate, and governance. Payson's reading group, the "Female Reading Society" of Charlestown, Massachusetts, ultimately disbanded. Payson explained: "In Sept[r] [1817] Sickness & death having visited many families rendering it thereby impracticable for many of the ladies to attend it was agreed to suspend the meeting for the present."[61]

---

[57] Nussbaum, *Love's Knowledge*, 26–27.

[58] For an example of a more narrowly focused commonplace book, see Jane Bemis commonplace book, 1821, Mss octavo volumes B, American Antiquarian Society, Worcester, MA.

[59] Gross, "Reading for an Extensive Republic," 516–44.

[60] Rosemarie Zagarri, *Revolutionary Backlash: Women and Politics in the Early American Republic* (Philadelphia: University of Pennsylvania Press, 2007), 1–11, 155–57.

[61] Commonplace Book of Elizabeth Phillips Payson, unnumbered page [31].

In other words, the women in the reading society had significant caring responsibilities, which effectively excluded them even from debate and discussion within their single-gender group. Such reading and discussion depend upon a degree of autonomy that is not consistently available to most people, particularly people whose lives are restricted by law or custom.

But eighteenth- and early nineteenth-century theorists of reading did not imagine that it made societies perfect. They imagined that reading narratives could make self-governing societies better. Benjamin Rush believed that reading biographies and histories would dispel the "weak and ignorant" character that made people unable to govern themselves. A thriving republic, he believed, depended upon individuals who understood one another and freely agreed to live lives of mutual responsibility. Charles Brockden Brown's taste in reading was more eclectic, and he regarded novels as important to the development of individuals in a free society. He explains: "[A] just and powerful picture of human life in which the connection between vice and misery, and between felicity and virtue is vividly pourtrayed, is the most solid and useful reading that a moral and social being ... can read."[62] In other words, people in a free society should read stories about people. They should, like Payson, weigh up the consequences of human action and the motivations of individuals caught in conflict with one another. Critics, such as Rush and Brown, differed on whether individuals should read novels, but they agreed that individuals should read texts that were essentially novelistic.

A novelistic relation to evidence could never prove a case in a courtroom or establish for scientists a natural law. There is simply too much speculation and too little fact in a novelistic story for it to be dispositive. And yet stories about people nonetheless enable readers to speculate responsibly about human motivation, about incommensurate values, and about relationships between individuals. A reader can, like Payson, draw provisional conclusions about the inner life of a tyrant or about the motivations that shape a public scandal. A republic of novel readers is one in which people hold views not merely on matters of policy but on the relations between individuals. Granted, a republic of novel readers hardly constitutes a realized social reality from the past that can be studied and recovered. Instead, it was a dream. And it was a dream that, I think, deserves to be maintained—particularly now.

Among the many crises that plague American democracy today, one of the most significant is the metastasizing spread of fraudulent stories

---

[62] A. [Brown], "A Student's Diary [No. VI]," 405.

about sinister conspiracies. Many believe these stories. Many others cynically spread these stories for electoral or geopolitical advantage. In academic and journalistic circles, one response has been relentless fact-checking.[63] Yet although scrupulous fact-checking might be a necessary response to the spread of fraudulent conspiracy theories, it is not a sufficient response. Evidence is often only partial, demanding that individuals speculate about the relations between known facts. And the experts who are frequently called upon to speculate responsibly often turn out to be wrong despite their best efforts.[64] Even more important, most political questions are not matters of fact or expertise at all. They are matters of values and interests.[65] Novels—and novelistic approaches to storytelling—provide a means of extrapolating from known facts or probable circumstances. They fill in the evidentiary blanks about matters of human intention, training readers to provisionally theorize about the motivations of their fellow human beings.

In essence, such stories are honestly political. The scrupulous factualist attempts to educate political adversaries, to explain why one view is wrong and another is right. And yet, as Hannah Arendt has observed, such education "can play no part in politics," a field in which we must contend with equals. She continues: "[T]he word 'education' has an evil sound in politics; there is a pretense of education, when the real purpose is coercion without the use of force."[66] In short, the factualist aims to explain why the fraudulent conspiracist is wrong. But the conspiracist doesn't necessarily want to be right. The conspiracist has endorsed a story that fulfills various needs—the need for security, virtue, or power, for instance. Scrupulously collected evidence can sometimes reveal to an observer the correct answer to a question of fact. But it cannot resolve a question of politics, which requires an understanding of human intention and the negotiation with, or struggle against, an equal. Understanding our human equals—from Napoleon Bonaparte to Catherine the Great to Elizabeth Whitman—demands storytelling, speculation, and responsible lucidity.

Granted, the problem with a novelistic prescription for an illness of democracy is that novels are weak medicine. Most people do not read

---

[63] See also the "Fact Checker," *Washington Post*, last updated January 20, 2021, https://www.washington-post.com/graphics/politics/trump-claims-database/?utm_term=.27babcd5e58c&itid=lk_inline_manual_2&itid=lk_inline_manual_2.

[64] To take a recent example, we might consider how missteps at the US Centers for Disease Control and Prevention compounded failures by elected officials. See Caroline Chen et al., "Key Missteps at the CDC," *ProPublica*, February 28, 2020, accessed July 20, 2020, https://www.propublica.org/article/cdc-coronavirus-covid-19-test.

[65] Fallon, "The Rise of the Pedantic Professor."

[66] Hannah Arendt, *Between Past and Future*, ed. Jerome Kohn (New York: Penguin, 2006), 173–74.

novels.[67] And because novels are written by people who do not themselves
have any special insight into the motivations and intentions of others,
the God's-eye-view of human affairs adopted by the novelist is always
speculative. And yet I suggest that speculating about the intentions of others,
continually reassessing one's readings of those intentions, and sometimes
withholding judgment is the only path to sustainable self-governance. Stories about other people remain, I suggest, the only means of contending with
the complex problem of other people. Attempts to reduce the complexity
of individuals to their psychology, their economic conditions, their voting
habits, their Google searches, or their level of education will consistently fail
because people are, quite simply, complicated. Their motivations remain
opaque, often even to themselves. In contending with our equals, we must
aim to understand them as equals. I do not fully know myself, nor do I
know you. And it is only by speculating responsibly, and extrapolating
from the paltry evidence available, that I can come close to an approximation
of our aims, desires, and intentions.

---

[67] "A Decade of Arts Engagement," 71.

Chapter 5

Archival Profusion, Archival Silence, and Analytic Invention: Antebellum Charleston's African American Debaters

Angela G. Ray

In the scholarly field of rhetoric and argumentation, frequently config-
ured in the United States as a subset of the discipline of communication,
the concept of evidence is malleable.[1] Rhetoricians are wary, for instance, of paeans to "evidence-based decision-making" if those using that
term presume that evidence can directly determine decisions. Instead,
evidence is the basis of argument, rhetorical scholars assert, and argument
is an interactive, culturally specific process of critical engagement that
requires judgment in order to generate decisions in conditions of uncertainty
and variability.[2] For evidence to function persuasively, people to whom it
is presented must accept it as valid support for the claim it grounds; such
acceptance relies on the often-unstated values, beliefs, and assumptions
of people involved in an exchange and on the sociocultural milieu in which
the evidence is mooted.[3] As a result, in analyzing argument—formal and

---

[1] See, e.g., Colleen Derkatch, *Bounding Biomedicine: Evidence and Rhetoric in the New Science of Alternative Medicine* (Chicago: University of Chicago Press, 2016), 12.

[2] David Zarefsky, *Rhetorical Perspectives on Argumentation* (Cham, Switzerland: Springer Nature, 2014); David Zarefsky, "What Does an Argument Culture Look Like?" *Informal Logic* 29, no. 3 (2009): 296–308; Wayne A. Baughman, David W. Dorsey, and David Zarefsky, "Putting Evidence in Its Place: A Means Not an End," *Industrial and Organizational Psychology* 4 (2011): 62–64. See also Chaïm Perelman and Lucie Olbrechts-Tyteca, *The New Rhetoric: A Treatise on Argumentation*, trans. John Wilkinson and Purcell Weaver (Notre Dame, IN: University of Notre Dame Press, 1969).

[3] See Stephen Toulmin, *The Uses of Argument*, updated edition (Cambridge, UK: Cambridge University Press, 2003), 89–100.

informal, as well as verbal, visual, and performative—rhetoricians critically identify as evidence all types of phenomena that arguers offer to support claims. Important pedagogical texts in the field, which must codify volumi-nous scholarship to make it functionally useful, illustrate this tendency clearly; for example, Karlyn Kohrs Campbell and her colleagues identify five common forms of evidence—statistics, narratives, analogies, visual images, and expert testimony—and then explore the logical and affective power of each in specific situations for particular audiences. Advising nascent producers and analysts alike, they note the argumentative strengths in blending forms, such as complementing the statistical emphasis on scope, extent, and frequency with the imaginative power of crystallizing narratives.[4]

The tendency of scholars of rhetoric and argumentation to foreground the utility of evidence within temporally and culturally specific contexts— and thus to define anything as evidence that might be presented as such— emphasizes the persuasive potential of evidence rather than its intrinsic value. Thus, rhetoricians typically highlight the selection of evidence appro-priate for audiences and situations instead of proffering normative stan-dards; indeed, they argue that standards are always determined within contexts. As David Zarefsky puts it, "in an argument culture, practice begins in awareness of the specific circumstances of the case and of the constraints and opportunities it presents."[5] This type of disciplinary train-ing, foregrounding cultural variability, does not rest on the notion that all evidence is of equal quality or validity. On the contrary, if the usefulness of evidence is always determined in situ, then no evidence is presumptively sound or unsound and must always be evaluated. Weighing the merits of evidence is a fundamental critical skill: It entails analyzing its provenance, the methods of its generation, and its correspondence to the beliefs of people involved in a situation in which influence is possible.

This quizzical approach to evidence can assist arguers in all walks of life, but it is the recognizable basis for scholarly inquiry, humanistic and scientific alike. Whereas rhetorical scholars analyze the evidence and arguments of others with a healthy skepticism, the approach also grounds our own inquiry. This chapter is concerned primarily with what Richard Shiffrin, Stephen M. Stigler, and Kathleen Hall Jamieson describe as expert judgment: conventionalized, field-specific assessments of evidence.[6] How

---

[4] Karlyn Kohrs Campbell, Susan Schultz Huxman, and Thomas R. Burkholder, *The Rhetorical Act: Thinking, Speaking, and Writing Critically*, 5th ed. (Stamford, CT: Cengage Learning, 2015), chapter 4; see also Edward Schiappa and John P. Nordin, *Argumentation: Keeping Faith with Reason* (Boston: Pearson, 2014), chapters 3–4. An emphasis on practical pedagogy is a long-standing trait of rhetoric and argumentation.

[5] Zarefsky, "What Does an Argument Culture Look Like?" 299.

[6] See Richard Shiffrin, Stephen M. Stigler, and Kathleen Hall Jamieson, "Evaluating Evidence Requires Expert Judgment," in this volume.

can trained scholars make good judgments about the quality and validity of evidence? Specifically, the chapter is about the challenges to historians of rhetorical practice in amassing, assessing, and representing evidence within the technical arena of historical investigation and publication. Writing of historical research more broadly, Marjatta Rahikainen and Susanna Fellman note that history is distinguished by "the challenges of evidence and the problems, both concrete and conceptual, with deciphering and interpreting remnants of the past." Historians know well that "sources are more or less fragmentary, defective, faulty, imperfect and insufficient." At the same time, they long to know what happened in the past, and although the past, as Carolyn Steedman puts it, "cannot be retrieved," it "may be represented." Representing the past carries a profound ethical responsibility, to present-day readers and to lives lived before us.[7] Even as we recognize the limitations of sources—whether voluble or reticent—we seek to make plausible claims of fact. Such claims are arguable to be sure but also, we hope, accurate to the highest standards of evidence-gathering and history-making at the time of their utterance.

This chapter is thus in part a meditation on the theme of evidence and its utility in grounding factual claims about the past, and it also proffers an argument for scholars to consider all evidence as a protean rhetorical form and all use of evidence as a rhetorical process. It thus develops from the presumption that abstract questions are productively explored within specific contexts, and it tracks the challenges of moving from evidence to claim within an ongoing research project, a historical study of a debating society that was organized and run by young, free men of color in Charleston, South Carolina, not long before the Civil War. The information that can be amassed about this group through physical and digital archives is paradoxically plentiful yet truncated, bold yet taciturn. After describing the project and its evidentiary archive, I identify three key attributes of the evidence and investigate the production of analytic claims grounded upon it: how a scholar might adduce meaning from silence, respond to or resist an impulse to narration, and construct questions from contradiction.

ARCHIVAL INVENTION

Studies of nineteenth-century popular education are burgeoning, as scholars across the humanities seek to understand how people of the past created

---

[7] Marjatta Rahikainen and Susanna Fellman, "Introduction," in *Historical Knowledge: In Quest of Theory, Method and Evidence,* eds. Susanna Fellman and Marjatta Rahikainen (Newcastle upon Tyne: Cambridge Scholars, 2012), 1; Rahikainen and Fellman, "On Historical Writing and Evidence," in *Historical Knowledge,* eds. Fellman and Rahikainen, 20; Carolyn Steedman, *Dust: The Archive and Cultural History* (New Brunswick, NJ: Rutgers University Press, 2002), 69.

learning opportunities for themselves and their communities. For example, *Thinking Together: Lecturing, Learning, and Difference in the Long Nineteenth Century*, a 2018 volume I edited with Paul Stob, brings together scholars and scholarship from four disciplines and investigates topics as varied as women's public performance of dramatic reading and the covert learning of soldiers in Civil War prisons.[8] Interests in such subjects are often motivated by questions about learning among populations underrepresented in traditional educational venues, and studies are made more feasible and more nuanced by the increasing availability of digital resources such as searchable facsimiles of nineteenth-century newspapers or personal papers and online finding aids from archival repositories. Sources of evidence to support these investigations are characterized by variety in every attribute: genre, form, style, length, and purposes of producers. Sources are print, scribal, and material, and they include newspaper advertisements and reports; ephemera such as posters, circulars, and tickets; letters, diaries, and organizational records; handwritten performance texts; photographs and engravings; and even rare objects like magic lantern slides. For some topics a scholar can find a surfeit of evidentiary sources, but for others, archives are reserved or silent; the content and availability of sources—both physical and electronic—are never neutral, resulting from decisions made across time about comparative value; the political and financial goals of governments, universities, or corporations; and mundane features of search engines that highlight some histories and obscure others.[9] Using what is available and accessible—depending on factors such as language, copyright laws, or institutional economic privilege—scholars build their own project-specific collections drawing on an array of resources. This process is less about discovering what is there—although unearthing is part of it—than about constellating, recombining, and juxtaposing sources, providing an example of what Debra Hawhee, in describing rhetorical invention, has called "a discursive-material-bodily-temporal encounter,"

---

[8] Angela G. Ray and Paul Stob, eds., *Thinking Together: Lecturing, Learning, and Difference in the Long Nineteenth Century* (University Park: Pennsylvania State University Press, 2018); see Sara E. Lampert, "The 'Perfect Delight' of Dramatic Reading: Gertrude Kellogg and the Post–Civil War Lyceum," in *Thinking Together*, eds. Ray and Stob, 130–49; and Ronald J. Zboray and Mary Saracino Zboray, "The Portable Lyceum in the Civil War," in *Thinking Together*, eds. Ray and Stob, 23–40.

[9] See, e.g., Arlette Farge, *The Allure of the Archives*, trans. Thomas Scott-Railton (New Haven, CT: Yale University Press, 2013); Elizabeth Yale, "The History of Archives: The State of the Discipline," *Book History* 18 (2015): 332–59; Jim Casey, "Parsing the Special Characters of African American Print Culture: Mary Ann Shadd and the Limits of Search," in *Against a Sharp White Background: Infrastructures of African American Print*, eds. Brigitte Fielder and Jonathan Senchyne (Madison: University of Wisconsin Press, 2019), 109–27; Tessa Hauswedell, Julianne Nyhan, M. H. Beals, Melissa Terras, and Emily Bell, "Of Global Reach Yet of Situated Contexts: An Examination of the Implicit and Explicit Selection Criteria That Shape Digital Archives of Historical Newspapers," *Archival Science* 20 (2020): 139–65.

an "interruptive and connective hooking-in to circulating discourses."[10] Thus the inventional process is a crafting of claims that speak from the scholar's own experience and speak through and to the conceptual–theoretical questions of one's own time.

As a participant in interdisciplinary inquiry into nineteenth-century US popular learning, I have studied the development of networks for public lecturing in the Northeast and Midwest, emphasizing the interplay of social reform and commercial lecturing of the immediate post-Civil War period.[11] Recently I have turned my attention to the antebellum debating society, a cultural form that in some locations impelled the lecture circuit. In such societies, antebellum Americans, usually but not exclusively young, White, male, Protestant, and with professional aspirations, gathered together—both within and outside of formal educational institutions—to debate political, historical, or academic questions that were broadly common across the country, from "Ought Texas to be admitted into the Union?" to "Was Brutus justifiable in the part he took in the assassination of Caesar?"[12] Participants learned skills useful for professional advancement and public participation, and they took pleasure in homosocial camaraderie and the give-and-take of the verbal contest. Although the connections between training in debate and public participation for young White men have long been known, twenty-first-century scholarship, notably literary scholar Elizabeth McHenry's *Forgotten Readers*, historian Mary Kelley's *Learning to Stand and Speak*, and rhetorician Carly Woods's *Debating Women*, has complicated long-standing assumptions about race and gender in nineteenth-century debate.[13]

With experience in researching antebellum men's debating societies from small-town Massachusetts to frontier Illinois, and hence with an understanding of common debating questions and society organization, I sought to apprehend popular debating practice and its functions more

---

[10] Debra Hawhee, "Kairotic Encounters," in *Perspectives on Rhetorical Invention*, eds. Janet M. Atwill and Janice M. Lauer (Knoxville: University of Tennessee Press, 2002), 24.

[11] Angela G. Ray, *The Lyceum and Public Culture in the Nineteenth-Century United States* (East Lansing: Michigan State University Press, 2005).

[12] Angela G. Ray, "How Cosmopolitan Was the Lyceum, Anyway?" in *The Cosmopolitan Lyceum: Lecture Culture and the Globe in Nineteenth-Century America*, ed. Tom F. Wright (Amherst: University of Massachusetts Press, 2013), 26–27, 30–32.

[13] Elizabeth McHenry, *Forgotten Readers: Recovering the Lost History of African American Literary Societies* (Durham, NC: Duke University Press, 2002); Mary Kelley, *Learning to Stand and Speak: Women, Education, and Public Life in America's Republic* (Chapel Hill: University of North Carolina Press, 2006); Carly S. Woods, *Debating Women: Gender, Education, and Spaces for Argument, 1835–1945* (East Lansing: Michigan State University Press, 2018).

broadly, initially by expanding the geographic scope of my inquiry.[14] Using research funds from my employer, I traveled to North Carolina, where I spent time in the David M. Rubenstein Rare Book and Manuscript Library at Duke University and the Southern Historical Collection at the University of North Carolina at Chapel Hill. There I viewed several manuscript minute books, personal letters, and other documents outlining debating activities of young White men in the South, similar in form and content to materials I had seen elsewhere. Acting on two intriguing sentences in Michael O'Brien's *Conjectures of Order*, a two-volume study of antebellum Southern intellectual life, at Duke I requested a handwritten, bound volume of proceedings of the Clionian Debating Society from Charleston, South Carolina, dated 1851–58. O'Brien identifies the Society members as free Black men.[15] Although he emphasizes the consistency of the organization's debating topics with other groups of its time, I was captivated by the specifics of the comparatively detailed minutes, which describe the selection of debating questions, decisions on debates, regular speeches, officer elections, discussions of governance, and purchases or donations of books and pamphlets for a Society library. The handwriting of the Society secretaries was welcoming in its extraordinary legibility, signaling a high level of care and personal effort in representing the competence of the scribe and in crafting accessible prose. Viewing the variable line weight of the ink on the original page—a trace of the long-ago gesture of writing—enhanced readability and fostered an imaginative connection.[16] I also recognized the rarity of a surviving minute book produced by free Black men at the hearth of secession as civil war loomed.

The volume begins with a suggestive phrase at the top of the first page: "Continuing Proceedings of the Clionian Debating Society" (Figure 5.1).[17] Using the guest Wi-Fi available in the Rubenstein Library, I launched a quick search for this document's predecessor. Knowing that most extant records of nineteenth-century debating societies are incomplete, I typed "Clionian Debating Society" into WorldCat as an act of due diligence but without much hope. To my surprise, I found an entry for the proceedings

---

[14] Angela G. Ray, "The Permeable Public: Rituals of Citizenship in Antebellum Men's Debating Clubs," *Argumentation and Advocacy* 41, no. 1 (2004): 1–16; Angela G. Ray, "Learning Leadership: Lincoln at the Lyceum, 1838," *Rhetoric and Public Affairs* 13, no. 3 (2010): 349–87; Ray, "How Cosmopolitan," 30–32.

[15] Michael O'Brien, *Conjectures of Order: Intellectual Life and the American South, 1810–1860*, vol. 1 (Chapel Hill: University of North Carolina Press, 2004), 424.

[16] See Tamara Plakins Thornton, *Handwriting in America: A Cultural History* (New Haven, CT: Yale University Press, 1996), 3–41.

[17] Clionian Debating Society (Charleston, SC), Proceedings, 1851–1858, David M. Rubenstein Rare Book and Manuscript Library, Duke University, Durham, NC (hereafter CDS-Duke).

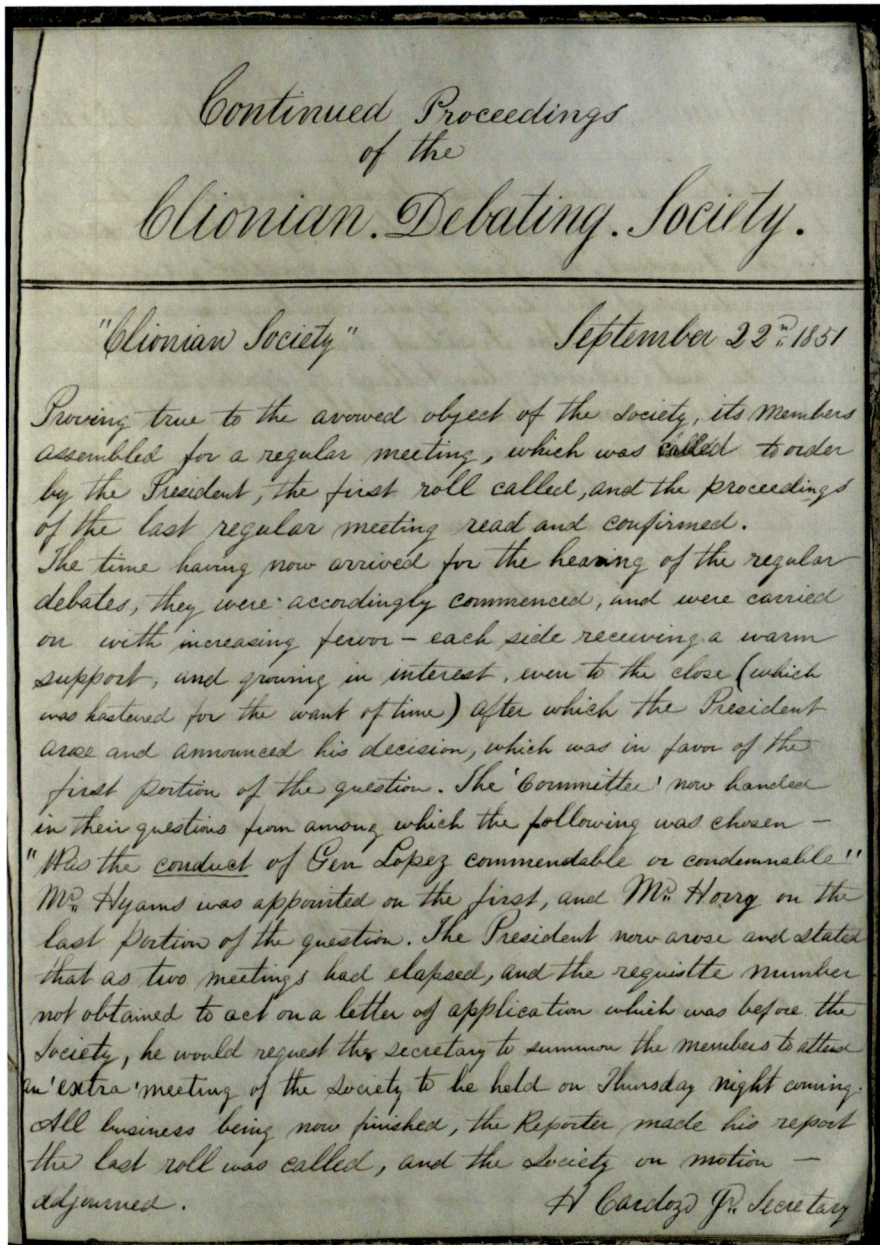

Figure 5.1. Entry for September 22, 1851, in Clionian Debating Society (Charleston, SC), Proceedings, 1851–1858.

of a group with the same name, held at the Charleston Library Society, for the dates 1847–51; conveniently, this volume was reproduced on microfiche in 1981, and the reproduction can be borrowed through interlibrary loan.[18] I was intrigued but cautious. The microfiche was at my university library by the time I returned from North Carolina, and I promptly ascertained that the two minute books were produced by the same people and that together they covered the Society's entire history, from inception through dissolution. A visit to the original of the first volume, located in Charleston, followed shortly.

MEANING FROM SILENCE

Historical studies of the free Black community in Charleston and in South Carolina by scholars, such as Marina Wikramanayake, Michael P. Johnson and James L. Roark, Edmund L. Drago, Bernard E. Powers Jr., Amrita Chakrabarti Myers, and John Garrison Marks, offer a fine-grained depiction of the environment in which the Clionian Debating Society was created and operated—the varied origins of members of the community, their precarious sociopolitical situation, their religious commitments, their economic travails and successes, their benevolence and self-help societies, their color consciousness, and their intricate relationships with the slaveocracy, including, in some cases, the ownership of human chattel.[19] The South Carolina legislature had required legislative action for manumissions since 1820, and ownership of others by the free Black community in Charleston—especially among the generation preceding the debaters—ranged from compassionate care for family and friends to the exploitation of bonded labor.[20]

---

[18] Clionian Debating Society (Charleston, SC), Proceedings, 1847–1851, Charleston Library Society, Charleston, SC (hereafter CDS-CLS).

[19] Marina Wikramanayake, *A World in Shadow: The Free Black in Antebellum South Carolina* (Columbia: University of South Carolina Press, 1973); Michael P. Johnson and James L. Roark, *Black Masters: A Free Family of Color in the Old South* (New York: W. W. Norton, 1984); Michael P. Johnson and James L. Roark, eds., *No Chariot Let Down: Charleston's Free People of Color on the Eve of the Civil War* (New York: W. W. Norton, 1984); Edmund L. Drago, *Charleston's Avery Center: From Education and Civil Rights to Preserving the African American Experience*, rev. ed. W. Marvin Dulaney (Charleston, SC: History Press, 2006); Bernard E. Powers Jr., *Black Charlestonians: A Social History, 1822–1885* (Fayetteville: University of Arkansas Press, 1994); Amrita Chakrabarti Myers, *Forging Freedom: Black Women and the Pursuit of Liberty in Antebellum Charleston* (Chapel Hill: University of North Carolina Press, 2011); John Garrison Marks, *Black Freedom in the Age of Slavery: Race, Status, and Identity in the Urban Americas* (Columbia: University of South Carolina Press, 2020).

[20] Larry Koger, *Black Slaveowners: Free Black Slave Masters in South Carolina, 1790–1860* (Jefferson, NC: McFarland and Co., 1985), 143, 148–49, 226; Loren Schweninger, *Black Property Owners in the South, 1790–1915* (Urbana: University of Illinois Press, 1990), 104–08; Larry Koger, "Black Masters: The Misunderstood Slaveowners," *Southern Quarterly* 43, no. 2 (Winter 2006): 52–73; Powers, *Black Charlestonians*, 39; Myers, *Forging Freedom*, 122–28. For the Act of 1820, see David J. McCord, ed., *The Statutes at Large of South Carolina*, vol. 7 (Columbia, SC: A. S. Johnson, 1840), 459–60.

Learning within Charleston's free Black community had profound and multifaceted power for group survival and personal autonomy, what Myers aptly names the "freedom experience."[21] Thus a study of the Clionian Debating Society is highly localized and yet has national and global implications. Analysis of an exemplary organization can crystallize educational, social, economic, and political dynamics of a tumultuous time. The Society is exemplary in two senses: it is simultaneously an example of an ordinary social form and a distinctive organization. The remarkable minute books are dramatic and newsworthy. Living in a state and a political climate in which the legislature, in 1834, had outlawed teaching any enslaved person to read or write, outlawed school keeping by any Black person, free or enslaved, and severely constrained the learning of any free person of color, these young men, who attended clandestine schools, were sprinkling their carefully crafted English prose with Latin phrases, debating the ongoing Crimean War in Europe, and praising their members for delivering speeches envisioning the evangelization of Africa.[22] They elected new officers three times per year, creating scope for members' involvement; they developed a small library for their own use; and they communicated with local patrons and with supporters at a distance, such as Charleston native Daniel Alexander Payne, then in Baltimore, who was soon to become the sixth bishop of the African Methodist Episcopal Church.[23]

The detailed minutes are also careful. Their reticence about sectional politics invites a scholar to adduce meaning from absence and to speculate comparatively and analogically, relying on knowledge of other debating societies of the time and of the precarious circumstances faced by this group.[24] The minutes eschew racial descriptors, and terms like *slavery*, *emancipation*, and even *the South* never appear. When in April 1850 the minutes report the Society's intention to purchase "Five political speeches recently delivered in the Senate," they do not pinpoint the state or national legislature and do not reveal the topics; the speeches may have been delivered as part of the turbulent debates in the US Congress on the Compromise of 1850.[25] Yet in 1848 the group had debated the justifiability of the Mexican–American War—surely a topic difficult to extricate from

[21] Myers, *Forging Freedom*, 110; see also 3, 8, 12–13, 69, 84, 127, 174.
[22] CDS-CLS, Nov. 9, 1847; CDS-Duke, Mar. 14, 1854, Jan. 1, 1855. See the Act of 1834 in McCord, *Statutes at Large of South Carolina* 7: 468–69.
[23] CDS-CLS, May 21, 1849, May 29, 1850.
[24] Angela G. Ray, "Warriors and Statesmen: Debate Education among Free African American Men in Antebellum Charleston," in *Speech and Debate as Civic Education*, eds. J. Michael Hogan, Jessica A. Kurr, Michael J. Bergmaier, and Jeremy D. Johnson (University Park: Pennsylvania State University Press, 2017), 32–33.
[25] CDS-CLS, April 10, 1850. Recent speeches by US senators like John C. Calhoun, Lewis Cass, Henry Clay, Stephen A. Douglas, William H. Seward, and Daniel Webster were available as pamphlets.

the question of slavery—and in 1854 a member donated a book by a College of Charleston professor that intervened in disputes about whether human beings derived from a single origin or multiple origins, a controversy fundamental to pro- and antislavery disputes.[26] These moments are unusual; the minutes more often identify questions debated, the names of debaters, the verdicts rendered, and the procedures for Society governance, and they reiterate time and again the significance of learning. For example, in 1851 the minutes recorded a member's speech that asserted "the importance of Learning in preparing Man to act his part in the great drama of life."[27] Such statements prompt questions that take the inquiry outside the confines of the Society minutes and even beyond the context of the members' dangerous situation in antebellum Charleston. What were the great dramas of their lives?

IMPULSE TO NARRATION

The two minute books name fifty-four people (fifty-two men and two women) connected with the debating society, as members, honorary members, or supporters. In an effort to understand the trajectory of their lives in relation to learning, I sought evidence in sources outside the minute books: not only secondary literature about the place and time but also the extant proceedings of other educational and benevolent societies operated by the free Black community in Charleston, court records, and government records from federal censuses to applications for military pensions.[28] The body of evidentiary materials thus amassed is voluminous but indiscriminate: the details of the lives of those connected to the Society must largely be intuited from general information about the local community and from haphazard snippets of often contradictory information. The most common delineation emerges from moments when the individuals interacted with institutional power in the person of census takers or military or court officials, illustrating the aptness of Elizabeth Yale's observation that "archives are where individual lives intersect with the apparatus of the state."[29] Despite the irregular appearance of the debaters and their benefactors in extant public records, community and genealogical sources provide persuasive evidence that the

---

[26] CDS-CLS, June 7, 1848; CDS-Duke, Dec. 6, 1854. See Ray, *Lyceum and Public Culture*, 123–28, 317nn3–4, 318n11.

[27] CDS-CLS, April 14, 1851. Stephen J. Maxwell was the speaker.

[28] The investigative process is outlined in Angela G. Ray, "Rhetoric and the Archive," *Review of Communication* 16 (2016): 50–56.

[29] Yale, "History of Archives," 333; Steedman, *Dust*, 68; Rahikainen and Fellman, "On Historical Writing and Evidence," 24.

Society comprised young men, most in their teens and twenties. In time, a few of these men would serve in the Union Army; others would be elected as representatives in Reconstruction-era state legislatures; and many would become ministers, schoolteachers, skilled artisans such as tailors and barbers, and supporters of schools for Black Southerners.

For example, Simeon W. Beaird, the debating society's first president, ran a covert school for Black youth in antebellum Charleston, and during and after the war he lived for a time in Augusta, Georgia, where he taught Black schoolchildren, preached as a Methodist minister, and, as a Republican political leader, was elected to Georgia's state constitutional convention in 1867 (Figure 5.2). In 1870 he led a delegation to the White House to explain the dire situation of African Americans in Georgia.[30] Although Beaird's major governmental, ministerial, and educational positions and actions are possible to trace, other features of his life, such as when and why he moved to Augusta, thus far defy narration.

On the other hand, wartime activity is especially clear for Society member Conrad D. Ludeke. In June 1860 he told Charleston friends of his intention to leave South Carolina, and in April 1861, only eight days after the war began, he enlisted in the Union Army in New York City, interpreted by the enlisting officer as a White man with a dark complexion (Figure 5.3). Ludeke mustered out in 1866 in New Orleans at the rank of captain. Whereas many stories of Ludeke's life are accessible to study— including friends' reminiscences of his childhood, reports of his health and his two marriages, and even his wife Julia's description of the last day of his life—these emerge primarily from his voluminous military pension file at the National Archives, a source constructed with a range of persuasive purposes by Ludeke, his survivors, and federal government investigators and their deponents.[31] Awareness of the context of production is essential in the assessment of these sources' evidentiary power and their utility in reconstructing an impression of Ludeke's life, ambitions, and experiences.

Other Society members with fewer connections to governmental institutions are more difficult to track. Simeon's brother Enoch G. Beaird, for example, inherited a "white quilt with fringe" from his mother, Rachel

---

[30] See Ray, "Warriors and Statesmen," 25–35; and J. T. Trowbridge, *The South: A Tour of Its Battle-fields and Ruined Cities* (Hartford, CT: L. Stebbins, 1866), 490–91.

[31] Ray, "Rhetoric and the Archive," 50–52; entry for June 19, 1860, Friendly Association (Charleston, SC) Records, 1853–1869, South Carolina Historical Society (SCHS), Charleston, SC; Conrad D. Ludeke, Compiled Military Service Records (Co. B, 82nd New York Infantry, Co. C, 90th New York Infantry, and Co. C, 1st New Orleans Infantry), Records of the Adjutant General's Office, 1780s–1917, Record Group 94, National Archives and Records Administration, Washington, DC (NARA); Conrad D. Ludeke, Military Pension Application File, Records of the Department of Veterans Affairs, 1773–1985, Record Group 15, NARA.

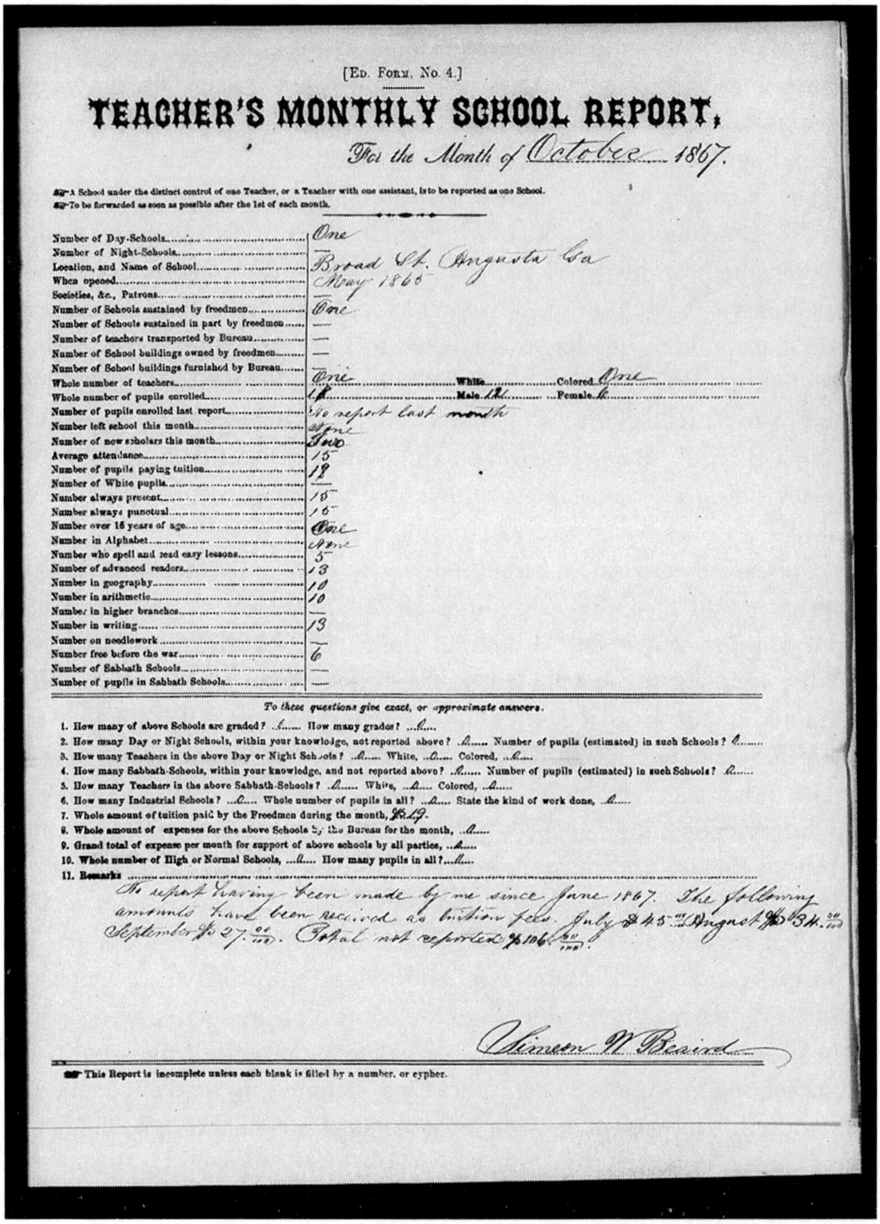

[Ed. Form, No. 4.]

TEACHER'S MONTHLY SCHOOL REPORT,

For the Month of October 1867.

A School under the distinct control of one Teacher, or a Teacher with one assistant, is to be reported as one School.
To be forwarded as soon as possible after the 1st of each month.

Number of Day-Schools	One
Number of Night-Schools	—
Location, and Name of School	Broad St. Augusta Ga
When opened	May 1865
Societies, &c., Patrons	—
Number of Schools sustained by freedmen	One
Number of Schools sustained in part by freedmen	—
Number of teachers transported by Bureau	—
Number of School buildings owned by freedmen	—
Number of School buildings furnished by Bureau	—
Whole number of teachers	One White Colored One
Whole number of pupils enrolled	18 Male 12 Female 6
Number of pupils enrolled last report	No report last month
Number left school this month	None
Number of new scholars this month	Two
Average attendance	15
Number of pupils paying tuition	18
Number of White pupils	—
Number always present	15
Number always punctual	15
Number over 16 years of age	One
Number in Alphabet	None
Number who spell and read easy lessons	5
Number of advanced readers	13
Number in geography	10
Number in arithmetic	10
Number in higher branches	—
Number in writing	13
Number on needlework	—
Number free before the war	6
Number of Sabbath Schools	—
Number of pupils in Sabbath Schools	—

To these questions give exact, or approximate answers.

1. How many of above Schools are graded? 0 How many grades? 0
2. How many Day or Night Schools, within your knowledge, not reported above? 0 Number of pupils (estimated) in such Schools? 0
3. How many Teachers in the above Day or Night Schools? 0 White, 0 Colored, 0
4. How many Sabbath-Schools, within your knowledge, and not reported above? 0 Number of pupils (estimated) in such Schools? 0
5. How many Teachers in the above Sabbath-Schools? 0 White, 0 Colored, 0
6. How many Industrial Schools? 0 Whole number of pupils in all? 0 State the kind of work done, 0
7. Whole amount of tuition paid by the Freedmen during the month, $19.
8. Whole amount of expenses for the above Schools by the Bureau for the month, 0
9. Grand total of expense per month for support of above schools by all parties, 0
10. Whole number of High or Normal Schools, 0 How many pupils in all? 0
11. Remarks No report having been made by me since June 1867. The following amounts have been received as tuition fees. July $45.00/100 August $34.00/100 September $27.00/100. Total not reported $106.00/100.

Simeon W. Beaird

This Report is incomplete unless each blank is filled by a number, or cypher.

Figure 5.2. Simeon W. Beaird, Teacher's Monthly School Report, October 1867. At this time eighteen pupils—twelve boys and six girls—were enrolled in Beaird's private day school for Black children on Broad Street in Augusta, Georgia. Six had been free before the war. Beaird reported thirteen as "advanced readers."

Records of the Superintendent of Education for the State of Georgia, Bureau of Refugees, Freedmen, and Abandoned Lands, 1865–1870, M799, reel 21, Record Group 105, National Archives and Records Administration, Washington, DC.

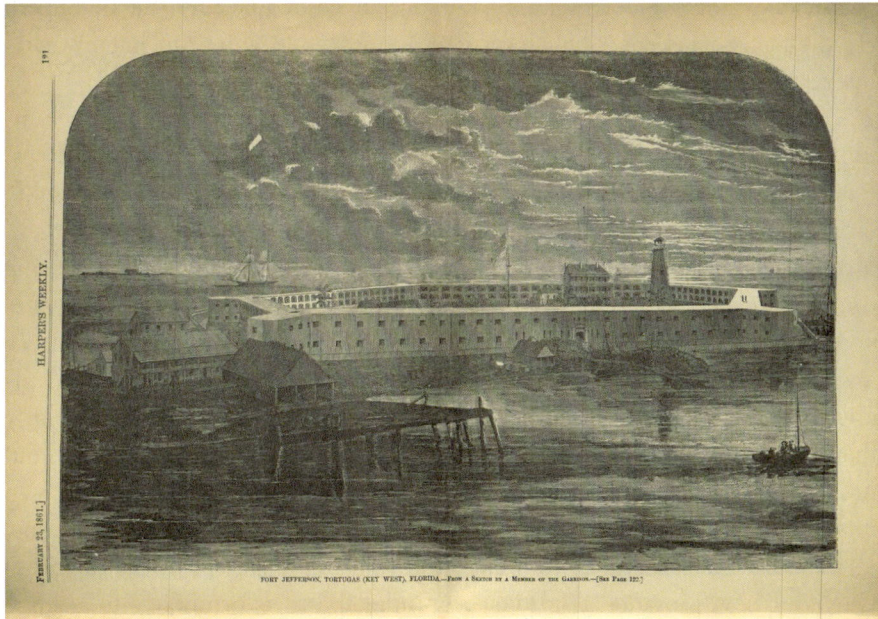

Figure 5.3. "Fort Jefferson, Tortugas (Key West), Florida," *Harper's Weekly*, February 23, 1861, p. 121. As an officer in the Ninetieth New York Infantry, Conrad D. Ludeke served on garrison duty at Fort Jefferson in 1862. Many soldiers fell victim to typhoid fever here, including Ludeke's friend William R. Hill. In May 1863, shortly before the regiment participated in the Union siege of Port Hudson, Louisiana, Ludeke wrote to Hill's widow and sent her a lock of Hill's hair.

Reprinted courtesy of Northwestern University Library, Evanston, Illinois.

Beaird, at her death in 1867; he is listed as a tailor in the city directories of Washington, DC, from the 1860s until his death in 1903. He, too, executed a will, bequeathing all of his bank deposits and other belongings to his landlady of thirty years, Sarah E. Washington, who, he wrote, "has never failed to give me wise counsel and substantial aid in my struggles and undertakings through life."[32] Other debaters had shorter lives: Robert L. Deas, an active Society member who donated several pamphlets of educational and religious speeches, died in Charleston in April 1865, a fact recorded respectfully in the records of the Friendly Association, a

---

[32] Rachel Beaird, last will and testament, in *Georgia, Wills and Probate Records, 1742–1992*, database online (Provo, UT: Ancestry.com, 2015); Enoch G. Beaird, last will and testament, in *Washington, D.C., Wills and Probate Records, 1737–1952*, database online (Provo, UT: Ancestry.com, 2015); Rachel Beaird died in Augusta in early 1867; Enoch Beaird died in Washington on June 21, 1903. A representative city directory listing Enoch Beaird is William H. Boyd, comp., *Boyd's Directory of Washington and Georgetown … 1867* (Washington, DC: Wm. H. Boyd, 1867), 663.

local benevolent society for free persons of color to which he belonged. He died possessed of a house on Charlotte Street, which he left in a life interest to his mother.[33]

Although the evidence of these men's lives is sparse by some reckonings, it is comparatively ample considering their era and circumstances. Further, the ready availability of searchable databases that can quickly produce facsimiles of newspaper articles, or census records, or records of births, marriages, and deaths, or entries in city directories has made locating traces of people like Enoch Beaird far easier than it was only a few years ago. Although scholars rightly interrogate the limitations of digital archives and searchable databases, as well as the correlation between digital availability and corporate financing, certain kinds of information—especially that of interest to genealogists—has made some stories more feasible and provided hints of others that remain untold.[34] It would be a mistake to imagine that these materials supply more than glimpses of lived experience, and usually glimpses of factors most relevant to the state, but the historian Giovanni Levi provides a salutary reminder that it is erroneous to assume that "if we don't know everything, all things of the Other, we know nothing." Instead, he says, "We know *something*. This is our work."[35] Recognizing that comprehensive knowledge is not a viable goal and hence that any narration must emphasize gaps, we can responsibly record what we do know and why and how we know it. In my project, extant evidentiary material can ground a persuasive case for the significance of a rhetorical education—in speaking, writing, reading, debating—in helping to produce the South's postwar Black male leadership. The self-assertion of the minute books, in their propositional content as well as in the sheer fact of their creation, supports a claim that these young men were performing freedom for themselves and their community despite external circumstances.

QUESTIONS FROM CONTRADICTION

Yet the Society members were not alone in this practice of education and uplift, and tracing other connections leads to evidentiary complexities that

---

[33] The memorial page reads: "In Memory / Of / Robert. Lyles. Deas. / Who departed this life / on the 27th of April 1865"; Friendly Association Records, SCHS. See also Robert L. Deas, will, transcribed in *Wills of Charleston County, South Carolina*, vol. 50 (1862–68), 334, South Carolina Department of Archives and History, Columbia (SCDAH), available in *South Carolina, Wills and Probate Records, 1670–1980*, database online (Provo, UT: Ancestry.com, 2015).

[34] See, e.g., Casey, "Parsing the Special Characters of African American Print Culture," 109–27; Hauswedell et al., "Of Global Reach," 139–65.

[35] Levi quoted in Rahikainen and Fellman, "On Historical Writing and Evidence," 35.

generate new questions. Although the Society was supported by honorary members—primarily older, local free men of color who were leaders in religion and trade—it also benefited from the generosity of others in the community. Two women, Frances Pinckney Bonneau and Emma Farbeaux, are named in the minutes as donors of books and money. Bonneau, the daughter of a respected community leader and teacher and then a teacher herself, gave the Society a book of Irish poetry. She would later marry one of the group's members, Richard S. Holloway.[36] Using a financial gift from Farbeaux, the Society purchased two volumes of French historian Charles Rollin's *Ancient History*, and she later donated "three very valuable books written by distinguished Authoresses."[37] Farbeaux's influence on the young men's reading can be adduced by a temporal juxtaposition: Shortly after her donation of the works of unnamed women writers, the Society purchased Elizabeth Starling's *Noble Deeds of Woman* for its library, which otherwise focused on the lives and works of men like Benjamin Franklin.[38] The Clionians thrice appointed committees to write letters of thanks to Farbeaux, and on one occasion she facilitated the group's communication with Daniel Payne.[39] The Clionian minutes thus represent Farbeaux as a revered bene-factor, well connected and eminently worthy of the young men's deference and esteem.

Searching for records of Farbeaux's life produces evidence of other stories, not only nuggets of information that provide glimpses across time but also ambiguities and overt contradictions that crystallize the complexities of the status of free people of color in the late antebellum period. Because she testified in a US circuit court case in Philadelphia in 1856—bearing witness in the hall of the American Philosophical Society, then being rented by the court—the lineaments of her midcentury life are accessible in public records (Figure 5.4).[40] Her legal status in the antebellum era—as domestic servant or enslaved laborer—is ambiguous. In the court case, which landed at the US Supreme Court in 1858 as *Pennsylvania v. Ravenel*, the property and regular movements of a wealthy White woman, Eliza Neufville Kohne, were characterized in detail, since the dispute concerned whether Kohne, a native of Charleston, had been domiciled in Pennsylvania and hence

---

[36] CDS-CLS, Mar. 10, 1851. See Myers, *Forging Freedom*, 101–02; and Thomas S. Bonneau, will, transcribed in *Wills of Charleston County, South Carolina*, vol. 39 (1826–34), 905–07.
[37] CDS-CLS, Jan. 7, Aug. 14, 1850.
[38] CDS-CLS, Dec. 2, 1850. The Society purchased Franklin's *Life* at the same time.
[39] CDS-CLS, Sept. 13, 27, 1849, Jan. 7, May 29, Aug. 14, 1850.
[40] Harvey Bartle III, *Mortals with Tremendous Responsibilities: A History of the United States District Court for the Eastern District of Pennsylvania* (Philadelphia: St. Joseph's University Press, 2011), 59, 87–97; the court rented the APS hall from 1854 to 1863.

Figure 5.4. Theodore Poleni, *Independence Hall, Philadelphia, 1876*, lithograph (Philadelphia: Thomas Hunter, 1875). The building at the far left is the American Philosophical Society's Philosophical Hall, which the US District Court for the Eastern District of Pennsylvania rented from 1854 to 1863. In October 1856 Emma and Jacob Farbeaux testified here in the case *Pennsylvania v. Ravenel*.

Print Collection, American Philosophical Society, Philadelphia; reprinted by courtesy.

whether her estate owed Pennsylvania taxes. An aged widow, she had resided seasonally in Charleston and Philadelphia and had owned property in both places. Farbeaux's testimony that Kohne regarded Charleston as her home proved critical to the disposition of the case; at the same time, the testimony of Farbeaux and other witnesses reveals that she—and her mother and grandmother before her—had been enslaved in Kohne's natal family. Although in 1849 Farbeaux paid South Carolina capitation tax as a free person of color, her formal legal condition at midcentury remains uncertain. Farbeaux's responsibilities in the elderly Kohne's household included reading to her and working as her amanuensis, writing Kohne's letters "for 5 or 7 years before her death" in 1852.[41] At the time Farbeaux

---

[41] US Supreme Court, *The Commonwealth of Pennsylvania, Plaintiff in Error, vs. William Ravenel, Executor of Eliza Kohne, Deceased*, Transcript of Record, no. 114, filed Feb. 25, 1857, 11; State Free Negro Capitation Tax Books, ca. 1811–1860, SCDAH.

was writing to the Clionian debaters and supporting them through donations, her daily labor also involved the writing and reading common to secretarial aid.

Yet this was not Emma Farbeaux's only appearance in court records. In 1842 she had been arrested in Charleston owing to a report by a local White man, James Simons, who said that she, an enslaved person, had been taken north of the Potomac and then returned to South Carolina and thus was liable to seizure and sale in accordance with an 1835 state statute. In a case in which she was described as Kohne's "female slave called Emma," Charleston attorney James Petigru successfully argued that Kohne's right to property, that is, property in Emma, rendered the statute contrary to the state constitution. Long before the 1844 resolution of the case, however, Petrigru assisted Kohne in quietly manumitting her coach-man Jacob Farbeaux in Baltimore, under Maryland's more flexible manumission laws, as Kohne was traveling northward toward Philadelphia. Records from the late 1840s list Emma's surname as Farbeaux, and she and Jacob would be married until his death in 1874.[42] How had his manumission affected Emma?

Petrigru, deposed in the Pennsylvania case in 1856, noted that legal restrictions "in latter times ... in So. Ca. ... against the migration of colored people" caused a change in the Kohne household's annual journeys, with "servants" from Charleston accompanying Kohne to Baltimore, where they were met by servants from Philadelphia. Kohne, noted Petigru, "summoned her servants in Charleston to her" in Philadelphia in 1850 to care for her in her illness, knowing full well that "if she recovered her health she would find difficulty in taking them back to Charleston." Jacob and Emma Farbeaux, whom even the US Supreme Court labeled, uncertainly, as "servants or slaves," would have known of that difficulty, too.[43] Jacob testified that he had left Charleston on June 10; Emma reported traveling

---

[42] R. H. Speers, *Cases at Law, Argued and Determined in the Court of Appeals of South Carolina*, vol. 2, *From November, 1843, to May, 1844, Both Inclusive* (Columbia, SC: A. S. Johnston, 1844), 762; Jane H. Pease and William H. Pease, "Law, Slavery, and Petigru: A Study in Paradox," in *The Moment of Decision: Biographical Essays on American Character and Regional Identity*, eds. Randall M. Miller and John R. McKivigan (Westport, CT: Greenwood Press, 1994), 39, 45–46; James Louis Petigru to Howard and Read, April 5, 1842, and James Louis Petigru to "My dear Legare" (Hugh Swinton Legaré), April 5, 1842, both in James Louis Petigru Papers, 1822–1948, South Caroliniana Library, University of South Carolina, Columbia; James Louis Petigru to William George Read, April 27, 1842, in Pettigrew Family Papers (1816–1842), David M. Rubenstein Rare Book and Manuscript Library, Duke University; Jacob Fabbor [sic], certificate of freedom, May 30, 1842, on p. 21 of Baltimore County Court, Certificates of Freedom, 1841–1848, MdHR 40131-5, C290-5, Maryland State Archives, accessible at http://guide.msa.maryland.gov/pages/item.aspx?ID=C290-5, image 20. For the Act of 1835, see McCord, *Statutes at Large of South Carolina* 7: 470–74.

[43] *Pennsylvania v. Ravenel*, 62 U.S. 106.

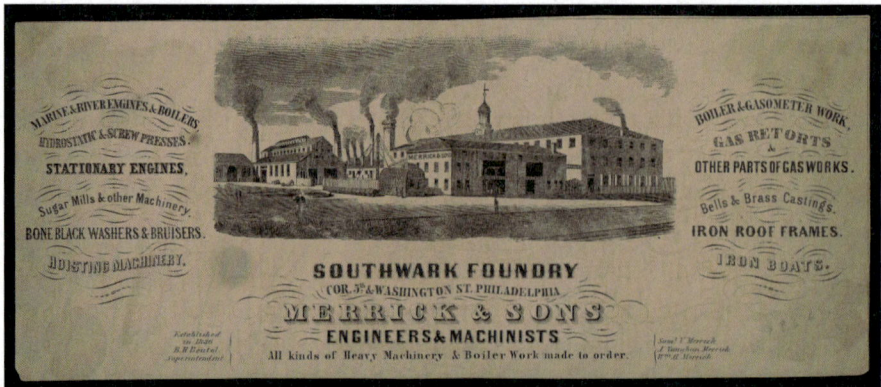

Figure 5.5. *Southwark Foundry, cor. 5th & Washington St., Philadelphia*, c. 1856, wood engraving with letterpress. Jacob Farbeaux worked as a messenger for Merrick and Sons, and he was among those injured in a calamitous boiler explosion at the foundry in April 1864.

LC-DIG-pga-13635, Prints and Photographs Division, Library of Congress, Washington, DC.

to Philadelphia in September. Emma Farbeaux's last gifts to the Clionian Debating Society, the three books by "distinguished Authoresses," were minuted in August. Was she deaccessioning books before moving? How had the books come into her possession? Did she anticipate that she would not return south again?

After Kohne's death Jacob and Emma Farbeaux made a home for themselves in Philadelphia's free Black community—a community, although regularly threatened, that harbored vibrant societies for learning and sociability as well as political action. The Farbeauxes lived on Locust Street, and Jacob became a barber, an occupation long controlled by Black men in the city. He would later become a messenger for the iron founders Merrick and Sons (Figure 5.5) and an elder in the First African Presbyterian Church, then located on the east side of Seventh Street south of Shippen. The Farbeauxes maintained their connection with Daniel Payne, and in 1858 Charlotte Forten would record in her diary that, while visiting the Farbeaux home, "Mrs. F.[arbeaux] read to me the interesting account of the A.[nti] S.[lavery] Meetings."[44] Emma Farbeaux's skills in reading aloud

---

[44] Brenda Stevenson, ed., *The Journals of Charlotte Forten Grimké* (New York: Oxford University Press, 1988), 310. Jacob Farbeaux was listed in city directories from the 1850s until his death in 1874. See, e.g., *McElroy's Philadelphia Directory, for 1855* (Philadelphia: Edward C. and John Biddle, 1855), 164; *McElroy's Philadelphia City Directory for 1865* (Philadelphia: A. McElroy, 1865), 222; Isaac Costa, comp., *Gopsill's Philadelphia City Directory for 1873* (Philadelphia: James Gopsill, 1873), 480. On Jacob Farbeaux's participation in the First African Presbyterian Church on Seventh Street, see "Things about Philadelphia," *[Philadelphia] Christian Recorder*, Oct. 18, 1862, p. 166; and entries for Jan. 27, Feb. 3, March 22, April 21–22, May 19, 1863, April 7–8, May 31, 1864, Jan. 8, 15, 17, April 30, and Aug. 9, 1865, in Emilie Davis Diaries, 1863–1865, Collection 3030, Historical Society of Pennsylvania, Philadelphia. See also Julie Winch, introduction to *The Elite of Our People: Joseph Willson's Sketches of Black Upper-Class Life in Antebellum Philadelphia*, ed. Julie Winch (University Park: Penn State University Press, 2000), 20, 32–33; and Erica Armstrong Dunbar, *A Fragile Freedom: African American Women and Emancipation in the Antebellum City* (New Haven, CT: Yale University Press, 2008).

thus made the leap to a resistant politics. The family also persisted in educational ambitions: whereas Jacob himself could "read and write a little," his daughter Martha Farbeaux, born in South Carolina, would be among the first graduates of the Institute for Colored Youth, the first high school for Black students in the city, and she would become a teacher there.[45]

Evidence of Emma Farbeaux's midcentury life indicates her support for learning and her own productive literacy. Yet her presence in court records signals the precarity of her legal status—as servant or slave—and highlights the uncertainties of Black freedom in relation to marriage, domestic service, and interstate mobility. This evidence grounds claims of ambiguity, even as that ambiguity throws into even higher relief the rhetorical power of the debating society's minute books to support an interpretation of the Society's varied activities as an insistent assertion of liberty.

CLANDESTINE MEMORY

Extant sources provide an evidentiary basis to claim that the Clionian Debating Society was an organization of the type that communication scholar Catherine R. Squires has named an *enclave*, a form of minoritarian public that can produce "ideologies of self-determination" and offer "a source of history, pride, or community connections" even within "conditions of intense oppression."[46] This enclave may have been psychologically protective, but it was not intellectually insular. Skills that members practiced in comparative safety can be found enacted elsewhere for community leadership or against external threats. Yet the significance of the Society for its members and friends, at the time and subsequently, must be adduced through a process of selection and interpretation of available evidence, and by recurrence to basic analytic questions: What are the characteristics of the authorial persona represented in this source? To whom was this addressed, and for what purposes? In whose interests was this document

---

[45] On Jacob Farbeaux's literacy, see *Pennsylvania v. Ravenel*, Transcript of Record, 12. On Martha Farbeaux, see *Objects of the Institute for Colored Youth, with a List of the Officers and Students, and the Annual Report of the Board of Managers, for the Year 1866* (Philadelphia: Ringwalt and Brown, 1866), 19; Fanny Jackson Coppin, *Reminiscences of School Life, and Hints on Teaching*, Introduction by Shelley P. Haley (New York: G. K. Hall and Co., 1995), 149, 155; and Benjamin C. Bacon, *Statistics of the Colored People of Philadelphia* (Philadelphia: T. Ellwood Chapman, 1856), 5–6. The 1921 death certificate of Martha Farbeaux Minton, with information provided by her daughter Mary, identifies Martha's father as Jacob Farbeaux and her mother as Catharine Perot; *Pennsylvania, Death Certificates, 1906–1963*, database online (Provo, UT: Ancestry.com, 2014).

[46] Catherine R. Squires, "Rethinking the Black Public Sphere: An Alternative Vocabulary for Multiple Public Spheres," *Communication Theory* 12 (2002): 459, 460.

created, saved, and made accessible? Sources with tangential links to the debating society require a similar process of assessment even as they generate new questions. In recognizing that the creation, preservation, and circulation of sources that we denominate as evidence are all rhetorical acts, we also find that the same is true of scholarship.

As a rhetorical performance, scholarship is consequential in ways not always easy to anticipate. If history writing is understood not as antithetical to memory practice but as a form of it—albeit a specialized form with its own communal expectations for methods, evidence, claims, and arguments—then generating histories of minoritarian communities of the past has the potential to alter public memories and public attitudes about the past and the present alike.[47] Rhetorical choices of evidence made by scholars—even, or perhaps especially, when the evidence grounds apparently straightforward claims of fact—can create impressions that, as Carole Blair and Neil Michel note, can "seep into public discourse" as presumptively "correct" readings of the past.[48] Thus the responsibility is significant. And so, we turn our analytic questions upon ourselves: If even the identification of a source as a resource for evidence represents a rhetorical choice, how are we selecting our evidence? How and for what purposes is a source deemed credible? When should we attempt to fill the silences, and when should the silences speak their own truths? How do we responsibly tell stories with scattered information while resisting an impulse to narrate unsubstantiated connections? When do we present our major claim in the form of questions? In short, how do we, how can we, how should we represent the past for our present?

---

[47] On history as memory, see Kirt H. Wilson, "Debating the Great Emancipator: Abraham Lincoln and Our Public Memory," *Rhetoric and Public Affairs* 13, no. 3 (2010): 459–60.

[48] Carole Blair and Neil Michel, "Reproducing Civil Rights Tactics: The Rhetorical Performances of the Civil Rights Memorial," *Rhetoric Society Quarterly* 30, no. 2 (2000): 32; see also Ronald H. Carpenter, *History as Rhetoric: Style, Narrative, and Persuasion* (Columbia: University of South Carolina Press, 1995), 1.

Chapter 6

Isaac Ray and the Case: Narrative, Data, and Early Psychiatric Method

Lindsey Grubbs

In an 1847 article for the *American Journal of Insanity*, Isaac Ray noted a "curious fact": "metaphysicians whose special province it is to observe and analyze the mental phenomena, have shown much less knowledge of mind as affected by disease, than writers of poetry and romance whose ideas are supposed to be the offspring of imagination, rather than a sober observation of facts."[1] Ray, author of the influential *Treatise on the Medical Jurisprudence of Insanity* (1838) and, in 1844, founding member of the Association of Medical Superintendents of American Institutions for the Insane, was a central figure in the professionalization of American psychiatry.[2] As Ray's article seems to acknowledge, literary material played a significant role in the development of the field.

The influence of literary thought on the development of American psychiatry was clear from its earliest days. In 1786, physician Benjamin Rush addressed the American Philosophical Society to advocate for the expansion of medicine's jurisdiction into matters of morality. Likening himself to a Greek hero penetrating the underworld, he proposed two new diagnoses: *micronomia*, "the partial or weakened action of the moral

---

[1] Isaac Ray, "Shakespeare's Delineations of Insanity," *American Journal of Insanity* 3, no. 3 (April 1847): 289.

[2] For a biography, see John Starrett Hughes, *In The Law's Darkness: Isaac Ray and the Medical Jurisprudence of Insanity in Nineteenth-Century America* (New York: Oceana Publications, 1986); for a more recent evaluation, see Courtney E. Thompson, *An Organ of Murder: Crime, Violence, and Phrenology in Nineteenth-Century America* (New Brunswick, NJ: Rutgers University Press, 2021).

faculty," and *anomia*, its complete absence.[3] Rush supported this theory primarily through anecdote, narrating, for instance, the case of a woman who lost the capacity to tell the truth when ill but was restored to verity by a cold snap—evidence of the physical nature of moral capacity—but also citing multiple Shakespearean plays. Over twenty years later, well established as a physician for the insane, Rush still relied on literary evidence alongside his own cases. Arguing that reason can return to the mad, he wrote, "Such cases must be common in all countries; or Cervantes, who copied all his characters from nature, would not have restored Don Quixote to the use of his reason in the close of his life of folly and madness."[4] Like Ray, he took for granted that at least some literary artists observe and report human nature with such specificity and accuracy that their characters could stand in as medical evidence.

Although Rush's "anomia" was not widely adopted, this early example introduces two key concepts that would prove essential to the rise of the medicine of the mind: the expansion of diagnostic jurisdiction, and the narrative basis of that expansion. Across the nineteenth century, alienists (the professionals who would one day be called *psychiatrists*) and asylum superintendents gained professional legitimacy in part by arguing that madness encompassed more than total alienation from reason, and thus only specialists could draw the lines between states like simulated insanity, hidden insanity, partial insanity, or moral insanity. Phillippe Pinel developed *manie sans délire* at the turn of the century to denote madness without delusion. This concept was tweaked and imported into English as "moral insanity" in 1835 by the British ethnologist James Cowles Prichard, who defined *moral insanity* as "madness consisting in a morbid perversion of the natural feelings, affections, inclinations, temper, habits, moral dispositions, and natural impulses, without any remarkable disorder or defect of the intellect or knowing and reasoning faculties."[5] As this description makes

[3] Benjamin Rush, *An Inquiry into the Influence of Physical Causes upon the Moral Faculty: Delivered before the American Philosophical Society, Held in Philadelphia on the Twenty-Seventh of February, 1786* (Philadelphia: Haswell, Barrington, and Haswell, 1839), 10.

[4] Benjamin Rush, "Lecture XVI. On the Study of Medical Jurisprudence. Delivered November 5th, 1810," in *Sixteen Introductory Lectures, to Courses of Lectures upon the Institutes and Practice of Medicine* (Philadelphia: Bradford and Innskeep, 1811), 374.

[5] James Cowles Prichard, *A Treatise on Insanity and Other Disorders Affecting the Mind* (Philadelphia: Haswell, Barrington, and Haswell, 1837), 16. It is important to note that *moral* had several definitions at the time, and here, did not signify that the madness regarded morality but instead specified "emotional" as opposed to intellectual disorder. Rush's anomia names one facet of the later, broader moral insanity, but, significantly, also forecasts the turn away from intellectual insanity. For more on moral insanity see Cristina Hanganu-Bresch and Carol Berkenkotter, *Diagnosing Madness: The Discursive Construction of the Psychiatric Patient, 1850–1920* (Columbia: University of South Carolina Press, 2019); Jodie Boyer, "Religion, 'Moral Insanity,' and Psychology in Nineteenth-Century America," *Religion and American Culture: A Journal of Interpretation* 24, no. 1 (2014): 70–99; Susanna L. Blumenthal, *Law and the Modern Mind: Consciousness and Responsibility in American Legal Culture* (Cambridge, MA: Harvard University Press, 2016).

clear, behavioral rather than physical evidence is required to diagnose moral insanity. Thus, the evidence that mental scientists used to support these more subtle diagnoses was necessarily narrative.

In the United States, Ray was the primary booster of the doctrine of moral insanity.[6] Ray was a lifelong advocate for the diagnosis, which he understood to have implications for criminal and civil law: a controversial position that was the subject of professional and public battles over the jurisdiction of medicine and the boundaries of human agency and pathology throughout his long career. He believed that the backward-looking and precedent-respecting legal system was incompatible with new, forward-looking discoveries in medicine—specifically, the doctrine of moral insanity.[7] Ray's *Treatise* was influential both in the United States and Great Britain, going through five editions between 1838 and 1871, and he became a popular expert witness as he argued for a move beyond the dualism of the "wild beast" test, under which a ruling of insanity only prevented legal guilt when the defendant was totally alienated from reason. At the time of its initial publication, his *Treatise* was the most comprehensive work in English at the intersection of psychiatry and law, and it was used widely, including being quoted at length in the successful defense of Daniel M'Naghten for the assassination of the Prime Minister's secretary.[8] (The public outcry over this decision led to the "M'Naghten rule" in Britain, which made it more difficult to find defendants insane.) Unlike earlier physicians called to court to make statements about injury and death, Ray and his colleagues claimed jurisdiction over moral responsibility. Including vast swaths of behavior in his professional remit and advocating for the inclusion of this expertise into law, he was a key figure in the professionalization of psychiatry in America.

To support this effort, Ray emphasized the modernity of his approach. He graduated from the Medical School of Maine at Bowdoin in 1827 at the age of twenty. Strongly influenced by the Paris school's clinical approach and phrenological materialism, he held mechanistic views of mental disorder that linked behavior indisputably to anatomic pathology. Ray believed all disease was evidence of structural change and advocated for increased autopsy.[9] Against the systematizing and theoretical positions of earlier

[6] Susanna L. Blumenthal, "The Mind of a Moral Agent: Scottish Common Sense and the Problem of Responsibility in Nineteenth-Century American Law," *Law and History Review* 26, no. 1 (2008): 132.

[7] Hughes, *In The Law's Darkness*, viii.

[8] For a classic account of the insanity defense in the United States, see Daniel Robinson, *Wild Beasts and Idle Humors* (Cambridge, MA: Harvard University Press, 1996); on Ray's influence on the legal system, see Hughes, *In The Law's Darkness*, 58; Karen Haltunnen, *Murder Most Foul: The Killer and the American Gothic Imagination* (Cambridge, MA: Harvard University Press, 1998), 217.

[9] Hughes, *In The Law's Darkness*, 7–10.

physicians (including Rush), he claimed a Baconian approach in which theory must grow out of observation rather than shaping it.[10] By relating cases that could demonstrate the lines between true and false illness, determine when a sane person feigned madness, and when a mad person passed as sane, Ray worked to a solve a tangle of medical, legal, and social problems that required a conception of madness more fine-grained than total alienation from reason. According to Ray, because the mad were isolated in asylums, not even general medical practitioners, let alone agents of the law, had enough experience with the insane to have accurate judgment. Believing the legal application of psychiatry to be lagging far behind clinical understanding, he articulates the diagnostic crux of the problem. He writes, "The only difficulty, or diversity of opinion, consists in determining who are really insane, in the meaning of the law."[11] Seizing authority over this diagnostic question, Ray denigrated speculation, offering observation as a counterweight to imagination. Notably, when establishing the legitimacy of this observational method, Ray claimed a lineage not from the European philosophers often associated with the prehistory of psychiatry, but from Shakespeare and Walter Scott.[12] These literary figures provided the model of the kind of narrative evidence needed to accurately capture human character.

Through readings of Ray's work, this chapter examines the role of narrative as data in early American psychiatry, asking how "subjective" stories were transformed into "objective" fact, and how this transformation enabled the growth of the field. In support of broadening categories of mental disorder, alienists relied on a methodology that is apparent in Rush's early text and the cornerstone of Ray's: telling, sharing, and sorting narrative material in support of new theories. Facing patients without clear biological markers of disease, then, physicians relied on narratives of behavior to systematize the medicine of the mind, and drew on familiar characters, like Hamlet or King Lear, and genres, like the Gothic, as they composed the case studies that shaped the boundaries of pathological and moral mental function, defining diagnostic boundaries imbued with moral import. All the while, Ray and his peers relied on the rhetoric of organic disorder and objectivity, obscuring the subjective in these accounts. In what follows, I first examine the multiple forms of narrative data that Ray uses to support

---

[10] Blumenthal, *Law and the Modern Mind*, 34; Sarah Blackwood, *The Portrait's Subject: Inventing Inner Life in the Nineteenth-Century United States* (Chapel Hill: The University of North Carolina Press, 2019), 22–23.

[11] Isaac Ray, *A Treatise on the Medical Jurisprudence of Insanity*, 3rd ed. (Boston: Little, Brown, and Co., 1853), 3.

[12] Ray, "Shakespeare's Delineations of Insanity," 289.

his physiologic theories in the *Treatise*. Then, I turn to his discussion of explicitly fictional medical case material, clarifying the appeal of creative work for the psychiatric diagnostician. Ultimately, I demonstrate how the porosity between medical and literary cases incorporated creative, Gothic, and even sensational tales into the new science as objective fact rather than subjective story.

NARRATIVE DATA

The asylum was a major source of data in the nineteenth-century human sciences. Asylum records took the multiple, messy narratives of patient admissions—physician assessment, personal testimony, family complaint, and legal proceedings—and compressed them into forms and tables meant to keep track of patient intake and release.[13] From these institutional genres emerged what Theodore Porter calls psychiatry's turn to a "numerical method" and "statistical hope" around 1820, as superintendents began to circulate their findings in tabular form in annual reports that they shared with the public and among one another. As they spoke with patients and families at intake, Porter writes, "The alienists labored to create, from scenes they never witnessed, data that could be lifted from all context and combined with results from other institutions."[14] This essay stresses, though, the extent to which the narratives themselves were seen as decontextualizable information that could be shared and aggregated as data.

It was this narrative, not numerical, data that formed the basis of Ray's *Treatise*. Ray's insistence on the centrality of scientific observation and personal experience to medical knowledge leads us to a central irony of Ray's career: He wrote his influential work without much experience treating the mad. After working in general private practice for over ten years, it was Ray's *theoretical* interest in the science of the mind that led him to compose the *Treatise*. Acknowledging that he makes controversial claims, he assures readers they are based on "well-observed, well-authenticated facts."[15] But Ray did not take on his position as superintendent of the Maine Insane Hospital until 1841, three years after he published his text.[16] This earlier book includes observations not Ray's own. He translated European physicians, phrenologists, and philosophers like Pinel, Étienne-

---

[13] Theodore Porter, *Genetics in the Madhouse: The Unknown History of Human Heredity* (Princeton, NJ: Princeton University Press, 2018).

[14] Porter, *Genetics in the Madhouse*, 20, 57.

[15] Ray, *A Treatise on the Medical Jurisprudence of Insanity*, xi.

[16] Hughes, *In The Law's Darkness*, 56.

Jean Georget, Franz Joseph Gall, and Johann Hoffbauer and included cases by English writers like Prichard and John Haslam. He writes that illustrative cases "are well worth the consideration of every honest and unprejudiced inquirer, for he will find in them a kind of information which he can obtain from no other quarter" and allow the reader to "see for himself" (100–01), gaining first-hand sensory experience second-hand—or even third- or fourth-hand, as the cases Ray pulls from others texts were often themselves borrowed. Although physicians' observations of their patients are included, so, too, are references to news stories, biographies, and other popular literature. According to the *Treatise*, then, practical experience could be gained not only through patient care but also through reading—and reading all kinds of texts. This method was not unique to Ray, as cases often moved through multiple texts, and may have been multiply translated: for example, Ray translates a French text by Gall in which Gall has translated a German news story (203). These authors relied on the style of thinking that John Forrester has called "reasoning in cases," which, like Kuhn's "exemplar," "shows the way in which shared examples are what ground the productive collective labour of a scientific community."[17] Through scientific journals, published texts, popular newspapers and magazines, and personal correspondence, case studies circulated between physicians and continents as data points that could be aggregated and entered into works of classification by experts.[18]

The term *data* entered English in the seventeenth century and was capacious enough to span genres. At the beginning of the eighteenth century the term was mostly used in mathematics and theology to designate those things that were mutually agreed upon and beyond argument, but by the end of the century it had been adopted in a variety of fields and included evidence gathered through experimentation and other knowledge-building practices.[19] Ray uses *data* several times in the *Treatise*. Its first appearance poses "data" against "facts": uneducated juries are not capable of making decisions based on competing expert testimony about madness because diagnosis is not "purely a matter of facts" but "on the contrary, it is a matter of inference to be drawn from certain data" and thus is a "professional question of a most delicate nature."[20] Although "facts" are portrayed as

---

[17] John Forrester, "If p, Then What? Thinking in Cases," *History of the Human Sciences* 9, no. 3 (August 1, 1996): 6.

[18] Carol Berkenkotter, *Patient Tales: Case Histories and the Uses of Narrative in Psychiatry* (Columbia: University of South Carolina Press, 2008), 23.

[19] Daniel Rosenberg, "Data Before the Fact," in *"Raw Data" Is an Oxymoron*, ed. Lisa Gitelman (Cambridge, MA: MIT Press, 2013), 33.

[20] Ray, *A Treatise on the Medical Jurisprudence of Insanity*, 56–57.

self-explanatory and comprehensible to a jury, professionals are required to process "data" into information that can be put to use by lay people. *Data* also appears twice to describe *imbecility*, in which there is a problem with "the power of the mind to examine the data presented to it by the senses and therefrom to deduce correct judgments" (79). Finally, it appears in a chapter on the "Duration and Curability of Madness," in which Esquirol calculates probability of cure from "data" gathered from hospitals (310). But this data could be explicitly narrative, as, after relating several case studies of cure, Ray concludes, "The above facts and considerations will furnish the data, on which the physician is to form an opinion relative to the duration and curability of any given case of insanity" (314). Ray thus thinks of data as many early nineteenth-century (and twenty-first century) writers did: as the raw, immutable information that meant little on its own but could be computed, reasoned, or deduced into knowledge. In his rendering, the "facts" of case studies are information that, when aggregated, becomes the data upon which psychiatrists can craft medical theory with concrete applications. As Daniel Rosenberg writes, "Facts are ontological, evidence is epistemological, data is rhetorical."[21] Data is the premise for argumentation—data points are not up for debate, they are for debating *with*. Ray sees his case studies, then, not as subjective accounts but as objective data points upon which the work of reason can be done in support of his larger argument for the existence of a psychiatric specialty and its expansion into the judicial realm.

The medical case has a long history as a knowledge-building genre. When Rush trained in Scotland during the eighteenth century, medical schools required students to learn clinical genres as they copied patient case reports and their professors' lectures.[22] Medical journals like *Medical Observations and Inquiries* circulated in Edinburgh in the latter half of the eighteenth century, aiming to "revive the Hippocratic method of composing various narratives of particular cases, in which the nature of the disease, the manner of treating it, and the consequences are to be specified."[23] Sharing information from singular cases in a standard format, the case attempted to chip away at medical mysteries, and the rise of new kinds of medical publications allowed for these cases to be widely shared, forming a repository of clinical experience. The historian Gianna Pomata finds the earliest precedents of the medical case in the Hippocratic *Epidemics*, in

---

[21] Rosenberg, "Data Before the Fact," 18.

[22] On the role of the case study genre in the Scottish Enlightenment, see Carol Berkenkotter, *Patient Tales: Case Histories and the Uses of Narrative in Psychiatry* (Columbia: University of South Carolina Press, 2008), chapter 1.

[23] Quoted in Berkenkotter, *Patient Tales*, 23.

which several authors described patient consultations. These texts, she suggests, have a "self-conscious cognitive purpose," indicating future directions for study and attempting to build a series of cases that could help develop medical rules.[24] For Pomata, this knowledge-building genre dissipated with the rise of Galenic medicine, as Galen's theory-driven practice used cases not to build knowledge, but as anecdotal illustrations proving his overarching system of medicine. This was the transition that Ray claimed to reverse, as he rejected theory-guided for observational methods. Despite Ray's theoretical reorientation toward empiricism, however, he drew on established narrative forms.

Ray's chapter on moral mania, which is at the core of his project in the *Treatise*, was particularly reliant on narrative structure. Ray notes that the diagnosis of moral mania must be longitudinal, fusing clinical observation with patient history. Any attempt to give a clear definition of this form of madness would fail, he suggests, because that definition would include much of mankind, and so a patient cannot be compared to a "fancied standard of mental soundness" but instead "his natural character should be diligently investigated" (143). In place of definitions, Ray calls for investigations drawing on family, friends, or community members, each of whom makes claims about the previous character of the patient. It is "not the abstract act or feeling which constitutes *a symptom; it is the departure from the natural and healthy character, temper and habits, that gives it this meaning*" (145, emphasis in original). A symptom, then, only becomes a symptom when plotted.

To Ray, these stories of personality change stood in for the autopsies he prized so highly, proving the organic nature of insanity: they are "symptoms of a deviation from the normal condition—of pathological changes in the action of the cerebral organism" (39). Ray believed proper jurisprudence required that insanity be viewed as brain disease. But while some of the insane were found to have lesions upon autopsy, many did not. Ray writes, though, that it would be "absurd" to think that the lack of lesions meant

---

[24] Gianna Pomata, "The Medical Case Narrative: Distant Reading of an Epistemic Genre," *Literature and Medicine* 32, no. 1 (2014): 8–9, http://muse.jhu.edu/article/548071. See also J. Andrew Mendelsohn, "Empiricism in the Library: Medicine's Case Histories," in *Science in the Archives: Pasts, Presents, Futures*, ed. Lorraine Daston (Chicago: University of Chicago Press, 2017), 85–109. The term *case* is not monolithic and means different things to different scholars. Pomata, for example, speaks of "case records" as practice-based, close-to-the ground observational commentary and opposes it to the use of medical stories as "examples and anecdotes," which are used in support of a larger theoretical point and are not "cases" (11). In this chapter, I use *case* capaciously to designate clinical stories or stories believed to have clinical significance. I include both "case records" written by physicians as part of their practice, as well as paradigmatic case studies, intended to give a salient example. Indeed, it is this range of contexts that make the case such a fascinating genre, particularly as individual physicians' case narratives enter print circulation and are drawn upon as paradigmatic case studies that their fellow physicians put to use.

that the disorder had been "spiritual" rather than "physical" (138). At-tempting to prove physiological disorder without anatomical evidence, Ray instead relied on narratives of behavior.[25] Because we know that derange-ment of the brain creates an abnormal mind, he argues, we can claim the reverse: the "effect indicates the existence of the cause" (135). Speaking of the uncontrollable desire to steal, for example, he writes that it is hard to prove that this is a disorder of the brain, but the "presumptive evidence" is strong. This evidence falls in five categories, each supported by case history. For example, that a strange shape of the head is "often observed" is evidenced by Gall and Spurzheim's case of a "rickety" boy who steals; that maniacs often steal is attested by cases from Gall and Prichard; and that the desire is occasionally brought on by a head wound, is proven in a case by Acrel of a man who begins to steal after trepanation (188–89). Similarly, after providing a series of cases of erotic mania, he writes "many more cases like these might be quoted, but the above are sufficient to illustrate a truth as generally recognized as any other in pathology, and to convince the most skeptical mind, that if insanity—or, in more explicit terms, if morbid action in the brain inducing a deprivation of moral liberty—ever exists, it does in what is called erotic mania" (195).

Ray learned this anatomo-narrative method from the phrenological science to which he subscribed, particularly in his early career. In 1835 he wrote that he hoped to cast the "light of phrenology into the dark passages of our Criminal Law."[26] Phrenology was still a respectable science when Ray encountered it, as men of science like Gall and Spurzheim imagined a science that could link behavioral patterns to anatomical evi-dence.[27] But for all its anatomical rhetoric, phrenology was a narrative science. If a person's skull had an unusual protuberance, the only way to draw a connection to a particular personality trait was through stories of that person's life and behavior. The rhetoric of quantification and clinical evidence was lain over the storytelling science, which distanced itself from the kind of subjectivity that the reliance on narrative implied. The narratives that undergirded phrenology were drawn not only from personal experience but from literary and popular genres, whose tropes were imported into the science and afforded the cover of objectivity.

Although phrenology became an object of ridicule across the 1830s, and Ray began to publicly distance himself from it, his career-long faith

---

[25] On the use of literature in investigating physiology as opposed to anatomy, see Sari Altschuler, *The Medical Imagination: Literature and Health in the Early United States* (Philadelphia: University of Pennsylvania Press, 2018), 11.

[26] Quoted in Hughes, *In The Law's Darkness*, xiii.

[27] Hughes, *In The Law's Darkness*, 18; Thompson, *An Organ of Murder*.

that pathological behavior illuminated anatomical defects remained. Ray
did not find the absence of evidence of nervous pathology upon autopsy
disqualifying: Nervous disorder is physiological, requiring the animation
of human action. Thus, analyses of the mind in action—of human behavior—are the most appropriate method for clinical assessment. While Ray
biographer Hughes argues that he had "completely sublimated" phrenology
by the time he published his *Treatise* in 1838, Ray's intro has what Hughes
calls a "bittersweet yet veiled eulogy" for phrenology, "The only metaphysical system of modern times which professes to be founded on the observation
of nature and which really does explain the phenomena of insanity with a
clearness and verisimilitude that strongly corroborate its proofs."[28] Phrenology still seems very much alive, however, in the *Treatise,* which contains
many cases from phrenologists, including Gall, Spurzheim, and Combe.
Moreover, he retained his faith in the method: narratives of behavior were
the way to access the workings of mental physiology.

Examining the narrative voice of Ray's accounts of relatively well-
established and comparatively uncontroversial categories, like "idiocy"
or "imbecility," demonstrates a diagnostic ideal: a depersonalized case
composite that can capture a "kind." These chapters in Ray's text are
largely devoid of actual cases. At times, patients disappear altogether, as
Ray writes of idiocy in generalities: "In idiocy the features are irregular";
"The senses are very imperfect at best"; and "Idiocy's wretched subjects
seldom live beyond their twenty-fifth year" (73, 75). In these formulations,
the facial features, the senses, and idiocy itself take grammatical precedence
over the human subject. Elsewhere, he compresses entire "classes" of
patients into fictional composites to describe a type. Describing febrile
delirium, for example, he writes,

> The patient lies on his back, his eyes, if open, presenting a dull and
> listless look, and is almost certainly talking to himself in a low, muttering
> tone. Regardless of persons or things around him, and scarcely capable
> of recognising them when aroused by his attendants, his mind retires
> within itself to dwell upon the scenes and events of the past which pass
> before it in a wild and disorderly array, while the tongue feebly records
> the varying impressions, in the form of disjoined, incoherent discourse,
> or of senseless rhapsody. (299)

Attributing specific details and accounts of interior mental life to a person
who does not exist, Ray outlines a pathological category by creating an
exemplary fictional character. Fictional characters have an obvious appeal

[28] Quoted in Hughes, *In The Law's Darkness*, 32.

for a diagnostic project. As literary scholar Catherine Gallagher writes, "Characters' peculiar affective force ... is generated by the mutual implication of their unreal knowability and their apparent depth, the link between their real nonexistence and the reader's experience of them as deeply and impossibly familiar. ... We seem to encounter something with the layers of a person but without the usual epistemological constraints on our knowledge."[29] This is most true, she notes, of third-person omniscient narrators—the point of view taken by many psychiatric cases. Allowing writers to imagine away the "usual epistemological constraints" on knowledge of the other, fictional psychiatric cases offers a window to the interior.

Ray attempts the same kind of universalizing narrative early in his discussion of "moral mania," but in the face of skepticism and controversy, must support the generic type with a profusion of data points, allowing the case *series* to stand in place of a clear case *description*. Whereas his chapter on "Idiocy" spans only five pages and "Dementia" ten, Ray takes sixty-seven pages to sketch out the nascent, controversial "moral mania." Much of this space is taken up with cases as, through sheer volume, he works to prove that the moral maniac is a kind of person who exists. To support the existence of "total" moral mania, for example, he includes seven cases that demonstrate the range of his sources and the complex traffic of medical material: one from Pinel, one that Combe took from a historical source, a case "from Metzger" but found in Hoffbauer, several cases from Prichard, and one "case" that is actually an abridgement of six chapters of Lord Dover's *Life of Frederic the Second, King of Prussia*. The rest of the chapter lays out case upon case to prove the existence of various "partial moral manias," like pathological theft, lying, eroticism, incendiarism, and the "propensity to destroy."

Ray's "propensity to destroy"—an irresistible impulse to murder—is especially densely supported with popular, rather than medical, cases. Michel Foucault discusses the power of cases to create pathological categories through the "entirely fictious entity" of "homicidal monomania," to which he attributes the "psychiatrization" of law in the nineteenth century. Homocidal monomania—Ray's "propensity to destroy"—describes a form of insanity in which the only symptom was the perpetration of a horrific, motiveless act, often the violent murder of a child, which Foucault suggests was justified through "a series of cases whose pattern was about the same" from 1800–35, which were highly publicized and cited in psychiatric

---

[29] Catherine Gallagher, "The Rise of Fictionality," in *The Novel, Volume 1: History, Geography, and Culture*, ed. Franco Moretti (Princeton, NJ: Princeton University Press, 2007), 356–57.

literature.[30] The invisible quality of this supposed disease required psychiatric expertise, and doctors were asked to become "specialists in motivation."[31] The narrative possibilities for physicians and patients alike were
shaped by newspaper circulation: among Ray's cases of the irresistible
urge to murder he cites the "celebrated" case of Henriette Cornier, who
violently killed her neighbor's child without motive or explanation. Three
of the other cases in this section refer to people who reported being
irresistibly drawn to murder after reading Cornier's case.[32] Such sensational
stories became cases as they moved from newspaper to medical treatise,
taking on a medical narrator.

In Ray's text, this narrator is a complicated one with an inconsistent
voice: Sometimes he introduces a source text and quotes it at length, other
paragraphs are fully quoted from sources named in footnotes but not in
the text, still others are abridgements or rewritings in his own language.
This muddy form suggests the extent to which medical genres were in flux
at this time. Still, certain patterns in the case genre—although not identical
across original authors—bear noting. L. S. Jacyna writes that the case
format has become so ubiquitous and naturalized that its "status as a
literary genre has been effectively suppressed."[33] Examining the genre of
the case study as developed in clinical medicine, Jacyna notes that the
narrator's identity is "deeply problematic" as the cases show a "striking
reluctance to admit the presence of the self" (39). The narrator of a case
knows things that no single person could know: "It is evidently a fictive
entity akin to the omniscient narrator of a novel; yet the enigmatic nature
of this subject is effectively obscured by a variety of conventional narrative
devices" (40). Weaving information gained from patient testimony, family
interviews, and clinical examination into one omniscient third-person narrative, "the particularity of other voices is suppressed to create the fiction
of a succession of events occurring within the ambit of a single observer"

---

[30] Michel Foucault, "About the Concept of the 'Dangerous Individual' in 19th-Century Legal Psychiatry,"
trans. Alain Baudot and Jane Couchman, *International Journal of Law and Psychiatry* 1, no. 1 (February
1978): 5–6, https://doi.org/10.1016/0160-2527(78)90020-1. Foucault suggests that the entrance of psychiatry into law was founded exclusively on dramatic cases of horrific motiveless murders, and that "Criminal
psychiatry first proclaimed itself a pathology of the monstrous" (5), and only from there did it disperse
into more minor forms of deviance and civil matters. In the American context, at least, this does not appear
to have been the full story. Many early cases were over civil matters like wills, and Ray's text speaks as
much to civil as to criminal matters (see Blumenthal, *Law and the Modern Mind*, 2, on the centrality of
civil law to early psychiatric jurisprudence). Homicidal mania for Ray is only one of many examples proving
that moral insanity exists.

[31] Foucault, "About the Concept of the 'Dangerous Individual,'" 10.

[32] Ray, *A Treatise on the Medical Jurisprudence of Insanity*, 202, 208, 210, 219.

[33] L. S. Jacyna, *Lost Words: Narratives of Language and the Brain, 1825–1926* (Princeton, NJ: Princeton
Univeristy Press, 2009), 25.

(41). In one example of such a structure, Ray offers a case by "Dr. Michu" that begins: "A country woman, twenty-four years of age, of a bilious sanguine temperament, of simple and regular habits, but reserved and sullen manners, had been ten days confined with her first child, when suddenly, having her eyes fixed upon it, she was seized with the desire of strangling it. The idea made her shudder."[34] The case blends knowledge drawn from a physician ("bilious sanguine"), from the patient ("was seized with the desire"), and potentially from her community ("regular habits" and "sullen manners") into one omniscient narrator. For Jacyna, this fictive narrator, who speaks from an impossible position of knowledge, uses story to "claim to *objectivity*" (39–40). The narrator of Ray's *Treatise*, though, often stumbles in their omniscience, bringing in the voices of other practitioners and, sometimes, patients.

When the voice of the patient does appear in Ray's text, it is typically to provide the narrator with an impossible interior knowledge they could gain in no other way. The patient's voice provides the missing evidence required to prove moral mania—namely, that the person had no motive for their behavior, and that it was done by them against their own will. The need for this testimony is part of the transition marked by Foucault, in which the nineteenth century demands not only a law and its violation for punishment, but an account of the self through "confessions, memories, intimate disclosures."[35] A case of erotic moral mania taken from Gall and translated by Ray, for example, describes a "very intelligent lady" tormented "with the most inordinate desires" (193). The pathological nature of the desires, though, requires a lack of motive and a personal distaste for the behavior that could only be proven by direct testimony from the woman herself: "'Everywhere,' she exclaimed, 'I see nothing but the most lascivious images; the demon of lust unremittedly pursues me, at the table, and even in my sleep. I am an object of disgust to myself, and feel that I can no longer escape either madness or death" (194). Presenting cases through an omniscient narrator, interjected with statements of intent that prove the medical point required, Ray and his sources craft a fiction of interior legibility from which the patient's voice cannot be fully extricated.

FICTIONAL CASES

This narrative approach to knowledge-building meant that science was open to overtly fictional material. Paradoxically, physicians' use of fictional

---

[34] Ray, *A Treatise on the Medical Jurisprudence of Insanity*, 211–12.
[35] Foucault, "About the Concept of the 'Dangerous Individual,'" 2.

material like Shakespeare may have seemed more stable than patient testimony, as fictional sources—or fictionalized, ventriloquized cases reported by other physicians—enabled the fantasy of legibility that would break down in an actual human encounter. Rush's citations of Shakespeare, for example, suggest that literature's verisimilitude allowed it to be placed alongside clinical cases. Moreover, in the transatlantic market of medical cases, internationally known exemplars like those offered by Shakespeare, Milton, and Cervantes certified alienists as culturally knowledgeable and provided a shared base of material on which medical theory could be collaboratively built by those with European training.[36] Alongside the case studies circulating between early scientists of the mind, then, were a library composed by other reliable observers of the human condition. As Daston and Park argue, in mid-eighteenth-century literature, "truth to fact" was subsumed by "verisimilitude—not truth itself, but the appearance of truth, which relied on conventions of plausibility, decorum, and seemliness."[37] This literary plausibility furnished exemplary cases for medical theory.

Writing several decades later, at a time when popular literature was more cheaply and rapidly produced, Ray's reliance on literature was more ambivalent. He writes that psychiatrists could detect simulation so effectively because simulators drew their "mad" behavior not from first-hand experience, but from literature and popular culture. These simulators tended toward "caricature" because they relied on "the representations of mania put forth in the works of novelists and poets," which are "of all their attempts to copy nature, the least like their model."[38] Presented with true madness, the lay public would be fooled: "The real disease would not present insanity enough for them."[39] Shakespeare, though, was one of the "admirable exceptions" to the failure of literary models of mania. In an 1847 article for the still young *American Journal of Insanity*, Ray further develops this claim, arguing for the accuracy of Shakespeare's representations of madness and diagnosing familiar characters.[40] Benjamin Reiss has argued that asylum superintendents, including Ray, Amariah Brigham, and A. O. Kellogg, used William Shakespeare to gain the cultural authority necessary to establish specialist knowledge of mental science. "It was William Shakespeare," Reiss writes, "more than Phillippe Pinel, Benjamin

---

[36] See Altschuler, *Medical Imagination*; Benjamin Reiss, *Theaters of Madness: Insane Asylums & Nineteenth-Century American Culture* (Chicago: University of Chicago Press, 2008).

[37] Lorraine Daston and Katharine Park, *Wonders and the Order of Nature, 1150–1750* (New York: Zone Books, 1998), 212.

[38] Ray, *A Treatise on the Medical Jurisprudence of Insanity*, 351.

[39] Ray, "Shakespeare's Delineations of Insanity," 307–8.

[40] Ray, "Shakespeare's Delineations of Insanity."

Rush, or Amariah Brigham, who did the most to justify the authority of the asylum superintendents."[41] In the twenty years beginning in 1844, the *American Journal of Insanity* published thirteen substantial articles on Shakespeare, in which psychiatrists claimed that Shakespeare's views on insanity coincided with their own in viewing insanity as a physical disease. Shakespeare held popular appeal in Jacksonian America, and, Reiss argues, his use in psychiatry served not just to establish the cultural bona fides of the members of a profession aspiring to the middle and upper classes, but also to argue that their medical views came from the same observation of the "natural" and "real life" in which Shakespeare excelled.[42]

Ray attributes a remarkable degree of realism to Shakespeare's "delineations of insanity," asserting that Shakespeare's characters are not "copies" but "real, mortal men."[43] He hypothesizes, "assuming Lear to be an historical portrait instead of a poetical creation, we should say there existed in his case a strong predisposition to insanity" (292). Reading *Lear* as a medical case, he asks who could read the play without "feeling that he has read a new chapter in the history of mental disease, of most solemn and startling import?" Lear's raving, Ray explains, can be "physiologically explained" as resulting from "cerebral excitement" (298). Relying upon the belief that behavior proves physiologic alteration, Ray turns his diagnostic eye on Shakespeare's characters, concluding that Lear is a maniac and Hamlet a monomaniac.

Diagnosing Shakespeare's characters was not mere entertainment. The skills of literary genius were the same observational skills that Ray attempted to cultivate. In his praise of Shakespeare, Ray aligns the skill of asylum physicians closely with that of literature. Shakespeare, he claims, had an uncanny ability to move from observation to inference, which Ray casts in terms of medical theory-building (in the terms of his *Treatise*, Shakespeare worked not just in facts but in data). Shakespeare "observed [the insane] as the great comparative anatomist of our age observed the remains of extinct species of animals,—from one of the smallest bones, reconstructing the whole skeleton of the creature, reinvesting it with flesh and blood, and dividing its manners and habits."[44] Establishing the value of literary thinking, he writes,

> No one would look into Locke, or Kant, or Steward, to find any light on
> the subject of insanity; but in the pages of Shakespeare and Scott, are

[41] Reiss, *Theaters of Madness*, 80.
[42] Reiss, *Theaters of Madness*, 92–93.
[43] Ray, "Shakespeare's Delineations of Insanity," 290.
[44] Ray, "Shakespeare's Delineations of Insanity," 291.

delineations of this disorder that may be ranked with the highest triumphs
of their masterly genius. The cause of this difference is obvious. The one
looks at mind in the abstract; the other, in the concrete.[45]

Thus, Ray and his peers should learn to write and to think not like moral
philosophers, but like Shakespeareans.

Luckily, Shakespeare himself furnished the training materials for
these professionals, as Ray stresses that Shakespeare does not just represent
insanity, but trains others in its detection.

> We are left in no doubt as to his views of what is and what is not genuine
> insanity; and by holding before us an elaborate picture of each, he enables
> us to compare them together, and to judge of his success for ourselves....
> Not more true to nature is the representation of Lear writhing under the
> stroke of real insanity, than is that of Edgar playing upon the popular
> curiosity with such shams and artifices as would most effectually answer
> the simulator's purpose. (304)

Turning patrons of his plays into "practised observers," Ray imagines,
Shakespeare demonstrates that overwrought emotionality is evidence of
simulation more than of true insanity—the same kind of "practical" training
he hopes to provide readers of his own *Treatise*. Despite Hamlet's claim
that he would "put an antic disposition on," he writes, "Poetically, dramatically, and pathologically true, is this exhibition of Hamlet is his interview
with Ophelia."[46] Hamlet serves as evidence that partial and moral insanity
exist—and have existed for centuries—and that medical experts capable
of managing them are required. He writes, "it is enough to state it as a
scientific fact, that Hamlet's mental condition, furnishes, in abundance,
the pathological and psychological symptoms of insanity, in wonderful
harmony and consistency" (309).

Diagnosing Shakespeare's characters and establishing their truth-to-
nature, Ray argues that the bard's texts are required reading in the American
courtroom:

> Had the great jurist, in forming his opinions on this subject meditated
> upon the pictures of Shakespeare as well as the principles of Lyttleton
> and Coke, it would have been better for his own reputation, and better—
> ah, how much better—for the cause of humanity. Would that we were
> able to say that the Courts of our own times have entirely avoided his
> error, and studied the influence of insanity upon human conduct more by

---

[45] Ray, "Shakespeare's Delineations of Insanity," 289.
[46] Ray, "Shakespeare's Delineations of Insanity," 316.

the light of Shakespeare and of nature, than of metaphysical dogmas and legal maxims. (332)

Portraying his own methods as Shakespearean and using the authority of Shakespeare to argue for his place in the court, Ray creates a literary lineage for his own medical theories. Ray offers a provocative suggestion when he closes his article on Shakespeare with a turn to the novel. "[T]he novelist," he writes, "possesses an advantage over the poet in the broader limits within which he may exercise his art, untrammelled by the restrictions imposed upon the other by severer rules of composition and the comparative brevity of his efforts" (331). In his suggestion that the looser structure of prose fiction provides new opportunities for developing a literary mental science, Ray gestures toward the developing genres of psychological fiction—and to his own case style.

Ray's narrative-diagnostic concerns are familiar to literary critics tracing the development of Gothic genres across the early nineteenth century. Early American fiction was deeply interested in questions of responsibility, as articulated by Jeannine DeLombard, who writes that "Responsibility, criminal and otherwise, was at the core of the conjoined national and individual selfhood that accompanied the novel as it arose amidst cognate print forms like popular trial reports, criminal biographies, and scaffold speeches."[47] In a society increasingly concerned about the frightening disjuncture between appearance and character, the Gothic, in particular, provided generic elements that dramatized attempts to read interior character from external signs. Karen Haltunnen cites the 1830s as an important period in the transition between religious narratives to secular, Gothic narratives of individual "moral aliens," disseminated by the profusion of literatures beyond the execution sermon.[48] In creating these narratives, psychiatric science and the development of a national American literature were linked pursuits, mutually invested in developing narrative technologies capable of capturing personality and interpreting culpability. In his reading of the monologic medical case, Jacyna writes that the intent of the narrator is clear: "it seeks to derive a moral from the story recounted that is applicable to some scientific problematic."[49] For Ray, that problematic was the existence of moral insanity and its legal

---

[47] Jeannine Marie DeLombard, *In the Shadow of the Gallows: Race, Crime, and American Civic Identity* (Philadelphia: University of Pennsylvania Press, 2012), 183. See also David Zimmerman, "Charles Brockden Brown and the Conundrum of Complicity," *American Literature* 88, no. 4 (2016): 665–93; Haltunnen, *Murder Most Foul*.

[48] Haltunnen, *Murder Most Foul*, 2.

[49] Jacyna, *Lost Words*, 40.

repercussions—a question of responsibility like that posed by American literature. Ray and his peers were, alongside sensational authors like Edgar Allan Poe, among those popularizing Gothic genres, imagining unwell minds lurking behind healthy faces, and asking readers to render judgments about individual and social complicity. In other words, although Ray's source material may have been Shakespearean, his own genre was the Gothic.

CONCLUSIONS

When comparing medical case studies with literary narratives, the first impulse may be to put them in opposition—one is reductive, the other is humanizing; one is particular, the other is universal; one is informational, the other is aesthetic. For historian Gianna Pomata, medical cases are an "epistemic genre"—which she contrasts with the "literary genre"—to refer to "specifically those kinds of texts that are linked, in the eyes of their authors, to the practice of knowledge-making (however culturally de-fined)."[50] The epistemic genre is that "specific kind of genre whose function is fundamentally cognitive, not aesthetic or expressive--that kind of genre whose primary goal is not the production of *meaning* but the production of *knowledge*" (3). In this chapter, I have examined the blurred line between literary and epistemic genres in the professionalization of psychiatry in the United States during the nineteenth century. As Ray and his colleagues built a bank of data from which they could fashion medical theory, they looked not just to the clinic but to historical biography, sensational news story, and literary texts. Regardless of their original context or purpose, accounts of human behavior that Ray read as sufficiently truthful could furnish medical evidence. Discriminating among texts, then, Ray engaged his own aesthetic sensibilities. Linking portraiture to discourses of mental science in the nineteenth century, Sarah Blackwood argues that the aesthe-tic is instrumental in producing the sense of the interior often claimed by psychological science. She cautions: "The art form is generally (and often incorrectly) considered a reflective or symptomatic genre, a form through which we see dominant cultural ideals and assumptions expressed rather than debated or produced."[51] Ray's incorporation variety of aesthetic genres demonstrates the extent to which he relied on popular and literary genres

---

[50] Pomata, "Medical Case Narrative," 2. Pomata acknowledges that the line between the two categories is often muddy, but insists on the utility of the distinction.

[51] Blackwood, *The Portrait's Subject*, 19.

as the data that he could process into fact. He thus claimed the authority to transform literary genres into epistemic ones, facilitating the importation of "meaning" into "knowledge." As literary genres infused the epistemic genre of the case, they shaped beliefs about morality and culpability through moralistic and aesthetic—as much as scientific—appeals.

Chapter 7

The Limits of Control: Anthropology, the Pascua Yaqui Tribe, and Federal Recognition in the United States[1]

Nicholas Barron

I n the context of the United States, anthropology has long been called upon to aid in the adjudication of disputes regarding the political status of Indigenous groups. In the absence of a discrete documentary record, anthropologists and their ethnographic and ethnohistorical findings serve as an alternative archive for those trying to make heads or tails of the complex mosaic that is Native history. However, this is hardly an uncomplicated endeavor. Positioned as expert witnesses, scholars are often compelled to translate their findings into the stricture of federal law. Of course, anthropologists working in an applied capacity have long recognized the difficulty of such a task. As Nancy Lurie once remarked regarding her own

[1] The impetus for this essay was born of the "Evidence: The Uses and Misuse of Data" symposium organized by Adrianna Link and Kyle Roberts of the American Philosophical Society. I am deeply indebted to Link and Roberts for allowing me to participate in this event as well as my co-panelists Alexander Campolo and Jaco de Swart for their stimulating contributions and Link for her illuminating comments. Although this essay is quite different in content compared to my conference paper, the themes and questions that permeated the symposium deeply informed the writing of this essay. Additional words of thanks are owed to Susana Sepulveda who read and provided wonderfully constructive comments on several drafts as well as David Dinwoodie whose comments on the theoretical framing and the evolving relationship of anthropology to recognition were illuminating. I must also thank the anonymous reader who pushed for a more explicit engagement with science and technology studies as well as Richard Handler who, in addition to raising critical questions on a previous draft, suggested the current title. Research for this chapter was supported by the American Philosophical Society, Andrew W. Mellon Foundation, the Center for Regional Studies at the University of New Mexico, the Robert L. Platzman Memorial Fellowship, and the Edward H. and Rosamond B. Spicer Foundation.

participation in the US Indian Claims Commission during the 1950s, "A court of law ... is not intended nor able to discern the technical merits of highly complex, academic differences of opinion."[2] Countless scholars have illustrated with great acuity the difficulty that comes with attempting to bring the intricacies and nuances of scholarly concepts and debates before courts and governmental bodies.[3] Taking inspiration from these incisive critiques as well as the theoretical insights of science and technology studies, I explore an instance in which the anthropologist/ethnohistorian is no longer the one doing the translating as it were. To be more precise, I consider a case in which the ideas of a social scientist, encased in books and articles, are taken up by others—particularly government officials—for unforeseen ends.

From the perspective of Indigenous communities, the operationalizing of extant ethnographic and ethnohistorical knowledge presents an ambiguous prospect. On the one hand, anthropological archives and expertise have been operationalized by Native actors and their non-Native interlocutors to affirm hard-won cultural identities, territories, and political statuses. On the other hand, these same sources of knowledge have been used by others to obstruct such affirmations. In many instances, opposing parties find themselves invoking and debating the meaning of the same set of historical objects (e.g., a document, map, monograph, etc.), arriving at wildly opposing interpretations.[4]

Such has been the case for the Pascua Yaqui Tribe, one of several federally recognized American Indian Tribes of the US–Mexico borderlands. Unlike many other tribes in the US, the Pascua Yaqui have not relied primarily on the courts or formal bureaucratic mechanisms of recognition (e.g., the Federal Acknowledgment Process) to establish their political

---

[2] Nancy Oestreich Lurie, "Problems, Opportunities, and Recommendations," *Ethnohistory* 2, no. 4 (1954): 359–60.

[3] James Clifford, *The Predicament of Culture: Twentieth-Century Ethnography, Literature, and Art* (Cambridge, MA: Harvard University Press, 1988); David W. Dinwoodie, "The Canadian Anthropological Transition and Land Claims," in *Histories of Anthropology Annual Volume 6*, eds. Regna Darnell and Frederic W. Gleach (Lincoln: University of Nebraska Press, 2010), 31–47; Les W. Field, "Unacknowledged Tribes, Dangerous Knowledge," *Wicazo Sa Review* 18, no. 2 (2003): 79–94; Francesca Merlan, "Anthropology and Policy-Preparedness," *The Asia Pacific Journal of Anthropology* 14, no. 4 (2013): 323–38; Elizabeth Povinelli, *The Cunning of Recognition: Indigenous Alterities and the Making of Australian Multiculturalism* (Durham, NC: Duke University Press, 2002); Arthur Ray, *Aboriginal Rights Claims and the Making and Remaking of History* (Montreal: McGill-Queen's University Press, 2016).

[4] Clifford, *The Predicament of Culture*; Field, "Unacknowledged Tribes, Dangerous Knowledge"; Ray, *Aboriginal Rights Claims and the Making and Remaking of History*; Christian W. McMillen, *Making Indian Law: The Hualapai Land Case and the Birth of Ethnohistory* (New Haven, CT: Yale University Press, 2007).

status.[5] Rather, the Pascua Yaqui have channeled their campaign for federal acknowledgment through Congress, first in the late 1970s and again in the early 1990s. In both instances, Pascua Yaqui representatives and federal officials invoked the name of Edward Spicer, a twentieth-century American anthropologist and ethnohistorian of the greater Southwest. As a scholar, Spicer devoted his career to studying Yaqui communities on both sides of the border. As an advocate, Spicer committed himself to maintaining the cultural and social distinction of the Pascua Yaqui with whom he worked from 1935 until his death in 1983.

In the campaign to secure federal recognition, Pascua Yaqui representatives and federal officials presented and interpreted the meaning of Spicer's depictions of this borderlands people. More specific, the Bureau of Indian Affairs (BIA) attempted to use Spicer's characterization of the Pascua Yaqui as "political refugees" to argue that the group's history of transnational movement disqualified them for recognition as a "historic tribe"—a politically consequential term that I expand on in the text that follows. Conversely, the Pascua Yaqui argued that the BIA's reading of Spicer was both limited and inaccurate. I am less concerned with resolving this dispute than I am with the implications of transporting Spicer's depictions of Yaqui culture and history into new arenas, especially those arenas that are particularly germane to the functioning of state and tribal relations.

By historicizing the conditions under which Spicer developed his portrayals of the Yaqui, I show how an attempt to contest essentializing depictions of Native history during the 1970s was, ironically, operationalized by the federal government in the 1990s to undermine the Pascua Yaqui Tribe's effort to exercise their rights as a sovereign people. This paradox is revealed by tracking the life history of a scholarly object of knowledge from the corridors of the academy to the chambers of Congress, from one realm of the shared terrain of science and politics to another. Such an approach does not mean the abandonment of event-based analyses,

---

[5] Historically, Yaqui peoples have referred to themselves as *Yoeme* among themselves. In the presence of *Yoris* (White people), the term *Yaqui* is most commonly used, see Edward H. Spicer, *People of Pascua*, eds. Kathleen M. Sands and Rosamond B. Spicer (Tucson: University of Arizona Press, 1988), 99. The origin of the term is unclear. According to Andrés Pérez de Ribas, in 1645, Jesuits encountered a group of Indians who said, "Don't you see we are *hiaqui*, 'the ones who make sounds'?," quote in David Delgado Shorter, *We Will Dance Our Truth: Yaqui History in Yoeme Performances* (Lincoln: University of Nebraska Press, 2009), 7. Because this essay explores intercultural engagements, I follow the recent historical literature and retain the use of the term *Yaqui*, Brenden W. Rensink, *Native but Foreign: Indigenous Immigrants and Refugees in the North American Borderlands* (College Station: Texas A&M University Press, 2018); Jeffrey M. Schulze, *Are We Not Foreigners Here?: Indigenous Nationalism in the US–Mexico Borderlands* (Chapel Hill: University of North Carolina Press, 2018).

nor does it mean the erasure of the scholar as a historical figure. Rather, it means a humble recognition of the limits of control that scholars have over their ideas as they take material form and are mobilized within the power-laden fields of sociopolitical life.

A SHARED TERRAIN

This study contributes to enduring themes in science and technology studies, namely, the interrelations of scientific knowledge and sociopolitical life. In their influential book, *Leviathan and the Air Pump*, historians Steven Shapin and Simon Schaffer describe the history of science and the history of politics as operating on a shared "terrain." Within this metaphorical "terrain," Shapin and Schaffer propose three ways in which science and politics interrelate:

> First, scientific practitioners have created, selected, and maintained a polity within which they operate and make their intellectual product; second, the intellectual product made within that polity has become an element in political activity in that state; third, there is a conditional relationship between the nature of the polity occupied by scientific intellectuals and the nature of the wider polity.[6]

Shapin and Schaffer's metaphor of a shared terrain and their associated postulates have been given empirical texture in the works of scholars who examine how the social sciences (e.g., cartography, psychology, and statistics) have shaped the modern managerial state.[7]

US anthropology, I would argue, offers a circumscribed case of the interdigitation of science and politics in the manner described by Shapin and Schaffer. One can see this, for example, in the simultaneous rise of the so-called American school of anthropology and the codification of race as a legal category in the wake of the Civil War. During this period, the writings of anthropologists, such as Josiah Nott, Louis Agassiz, and Daniel Brinton, bore a striking resemblance to the White supremacist political interests of the postbellum period that underwrote racialized court rulings

---

[6] Steven Shapin and Simon Schaffer, *Leviathan and the Air-Pump: Hobbes, Boyle, and the Experimental Life* (Princeton, NJ: Princeton University Press, 2011), 332.

[7] Geoffrey C. Bowker and Susan Leigh Star, *Sorting Things Out: Classification and Its Consequences* (Cambridge, MA: MIT Press, 1999); Michel Foucault, *The Birth of the Clinic* (London: Routledge, 2003 [1963]). Ian Hacking, *The Taming of Chance* (Cambridge: Cambridge University Press, 1990); Theodore M. Porter, *Trust in Numbers: The Pursuit of Objectivity in Science and Public Life* (Princeton, NJ: Princeton University Press, 1995); James C. Scott, *Seeing Like a State: How Certain Schemes to Improve the Human Condition Have Failed* (New Haven, CT: Yale University Press, 1998).

such as *Plessy v. Ferguson* (1896) and the passage of immigration quotas.[8] However, in many instances, the relationship between anthropology and governance has been more than mere temporal overlap and resemblance. Thinking in terms of Shapin and Schaffer's second postulate, anthropological knowledge has been a concrete element in the political activity of the state. On a somewhat positive note, Lee Baker shows how Franz Boas's critique of the biological foundation of the race concept, constructed in direct opposition to the writings of Brinton and others, informed the arguments of National Association for the Advancement of Colored People (NAACP) lawyers as they pursued racial equality in the courts during the 1950s.[9] Unfortunately, the historical record is replete with less uplifting accounts of how the products of anthropological inquiry have been put to work. Past manifestations of the US empire at home and abroad reveal a pattern in which anthropological concepts, data, and methods have lent themselves to the waging of war and the management of subject populations.[10] A more specific strain in this history can be found in the relationship among anthropology, ethnohistory, and federal–Indian relations, where the writings and expert witness testimonies of scholars have informed legal disputes[11] and shaped the formation of policies and governmental offices.[12] Although previous case studies have largely focused on the role of anthropologists as expert witnesses and state functionaries, I will consider a case in which the products of scientific research are enrolled in Indigenous–

---

[8] Lee D. Baker, *From Savage to Negro: Anthropology and the Construction of the Race, 1896–1954* (Berkeley: University of California Press, 1998), 14–25; George W. Stocking, *Race, Culture, and Evolution: Essays in the History of Anthropology* (New York: Free Press, 1968), 49–68.

[9] Baker, *From Savage to Negro*, 150–57.

[10] David H. Price, *Anthropological Intelligence: The Deployment and Neglect of American Anthropology in the Second World War* (Durham, NC: Duke University Press, 2008); David H. Price, *Cold War Anthropology: The CIA, the Pentagon, and the Growth of Dual Use Anthropology* (Durham, NC: Duke University Press, 2016); Karin Alejandra Rosemblatt and Leandro Daniel Benmergui, "Japanese-American Confinement and Scientific Democracy: Colonialism, Social Engineering, and Government Administration," *Journal of the History of the Behavioral Sciences* 54, no. 2 (2018): 117–39; Orin Starn, "Engineering Interment: Anthropologists and the War Relocation Authority," *American Ethnologist* 13, no. 4 (1986): 700–20.

[11] Joanne Barker, *Native Acts: Law, Recognition, and Cultural Authenticity* (Durham, NC: Duke University Press, 2011); Jack Campisi, *The Mashpee Indians: Tribe on Trial* (Syracuse, NY: Syracuse University Press, 1991); James Clifford, *The Predicament of Culture: Twentieth-Century Ethnography, Literature, and Art* (Cambridge, MA: Harvard University Press, 1988); Arthur Ray, "Kroeber and the California Claims: Historical Particularism and Cultural Ecology in Court," in *Central Sites, Peripheral Visions: Cultural and Institutional Crossings in the History of Anthropology*, ed. Richard Handler (Madison: University of Wisconsin Press, 2006), 248–74.

[12] Elizabeth Guerrier, "Applying Anthropology in the Interest of the State: John Collier, the Indian Office, and the Bureau of Sociological Research," *Histories of Anthropology Annual* 3 (2007): 199–221; Curtis M. Hinsley, *Savages and Scientists: The Smithsonian Institution and the Development of American Anthropology, 1846–1910* (Washington, DC: Smithsonian Institution Press, 1981); Alice Beck Kehoe, *A Passion for the True and Just: Felix and Lucy Kramer Cohen and the Indian New Deal* (Tucson: University of Arizona Press, 2014).

state disputes by other social actors in other times and other places. As I will show, Edward Spicer was long gone when his intellectual debris (i.e., a journal article) was mobilized by the BIA. Informed by Shapin and Schaffer's notions of a shared terrain, this chapter considers the process by which Spicer's "Highlights of Yaqui History" was transported into a new niche in the historical ecology of the social sciences and federal Indian policies in the United States.

STUDYING AND RECOGNIZING THE PASCUA YAQUI

Although Spicer's work is at the center of this analysis, one cannot understand Spicer or his inscriptions apart from the history of the Pascua Yaqui Tribe. The present-day tribe is largely composed of the descendants of individuals who migrated to the United States from Sonora, Mexico, in the late nineteenth and early twentieth centuries. The full weight of this transnational history often escapes the popular imagination. Ariel Zatarain Tumbaga observes that "in Mexico, Yaquis are mostly depicted in two ways: as dancers and as warriors."[13] The same can be said of the United States and the state of Arizona. Neither depiction is without empirical grounding. The dancer image, for instance, stems from elaborate religious ceremonies, which combine aspects of pre-Colonial cosmologies and selectively incorporated elements of Catholicism brought to the Yaqui by way of Jesuit missionaries during the seventeenth century.[14] The warrior image is reflective of the centuries-long struggle of the Yaqui to negotiate the terms of Spanish and Mexican military domination.[15] Although these negotiations were by no means limited to armed resistance,[16] the figures of Yaqui resistance fighters, such as Juan Banderas and Jose Maria Leyva Cajeme, carry great symbolic weight.

However, the dancer and warrior tropes obfuscate the lived experiences of individuals and families who moved through economic networks that stretched from Arizona to California. Significant numbers came to settle in southern Arizona in and around the developing city of Tucson

---

[13] Ariel Zatarain Tumbaga, *Yaqui Indigeneity: Epistemology, Diaspora, and the Construction of Yoeme Identity* (Tucson: University of Arizona Press, 2018), 15.

[14] Larry Evers and Felipe S. Molina, *Yaqui Deer Songs, Maso Bwikam: A Native American Poetry* (Tucson: University of Arizona Press, 1980); Shorter, *We Will Dance Our Truth*.

[15] Evelyn Hu-DeHart, *Yaqui Resistance and Survival: The Struggle for Land and Autonomy, 1821–1910* (Madison: University of Wisconsin Press, 1984).

[16] Raphael Brewster Folsom, *The Yaquis and the Empire: Violence, Spanish Imperial Power, and Native Resilience in Colonial Mexico* (New Haven, CT: Yale University Press, 2014).

during the early twentieth century. In time, many aggregated into several urban villages, one of the most prominent of which became known as Pascua Village. Lacking any form of federal recognition or support as an Indigenous community, the Yaqui of Pascua managed to cultivate a niche for themselves within Tucson's budding cultural tourism industry.[17] They carefully reconstituted their traditional Lent and Easter ceremonies, syncretic forms of Indigenous Catholicism, as captivating public performances for visitors of the Southwest in search of an exotic and romantic "other." The name Pascua (Spanish for *Easter*) was bestowed by a supportive Anglo-American lawyer and chairman of the Chamber of Commerce who shrewdly recognized the touristic potential of the Yaqui ceremonies. As these annual events served as a boon to the regional economy, the Yaquis of Pascua lived humble lives, relying primarily on local philanthropy and seasonal agricultural labor.

Although the complete account of Pascua Village is beyond the scope of this piece, even a cursory overview of the community's history suggests that residents continuously crafted new ways to reposition themselves in relation to the local political establishment. Though they remained a largely impoverished people living on the economic margins, the Yaqui of Pascua were never isolated from the world around them. If anything, their ability to persist as a distinct community was the result of their efforts to forge and maintain relationship with non-Yaquis. This included Kirk Moore, President of the Chamber of Commerce and local attorney; Isabella Greenway, the state's congressional representative; the Marshall Foundation, a local philanthropic group; and Thamar Richey, an influential schoolteacher in Tucson.[18] The most enduring and consequential of these relationships involved local anthropologists associated with the University of Arizona such as Edward Spicer.

While his name may not carry the same historiographic weight of American anthropological scions like Ruth Benedict, Margaret Mead, Edward Sapir, and their progenitor Franz Boas, Edward Spicer casts a large

---

[17] See Spicer, *People of Pascua* for a succinct account of Pascua Village history. A slew of other sources address aspects of this history: Christina Leza, *Divided Peoples: Policy, Activism, and Indigenous Identities on the US–Mexico Border* (Tucson: University of Arizona Press, 2019); Eric V. Meeks, *Border Citizens: The Making of Indians, Mexicans, and Anglos in Arizona* (Austin: University of Texas Press, 2007); Mark Edwin Miller, *Forgotten Tribes: Unrecognized Indians and the Federal Acknowledgment Process* (Lincoln: University of Nebraska Press, 2004); Brenden W. Rensink, *Native but Foreign: Indigenous Immigrants and Refugees in the North American Borderlands* (College Station: Texas A&M University Press, 2018); Jeffrey Schulze, *Are We Not Foreigners Here?*

[18] Nicholas Barron, "Applying Anthropology, Assembling Indigenous Community: Anthropology and the Pascua Yaqui Indian Tribe in Southern Arizona" (PhD diss., University of New Mexico, 2019); George Pierre Castile, "Yaquis, Edward H. Spicer, and Federal Indian Policy: From Immigrants to Native Americans," *Journal of the Southwest* 44 (2002): 383–435; Miller, *Forgotten Tribes*; Meeks, *Border Citizens*.

shadow in the world of Southwest anthropology and ethnohistory.[19] His magisterial tome *Cycles of Conquest*, remains indispensable for those seeking to understand Indigenous responses to Spanish, Mexican, and Anglo-American colonization of the region.[20] Spicer's entry into this field of study began in 1935 with his graduate research, an ethnographic account of Pascua Village. Though it would be difficult to reduce any individual living in an interconnected world of ideas to a single mode of thought, one can say with relative accuracy that Spicer's approach to the Yaqui developed within the paradigm of acculturation studies.

Anthropological interest in the study of acculturation developed in a post-World War I (WWI) milieu. This period was charged by the mounting influences of both racism and nativism, two impulses that were by no means new to the United States. In addition to numerous other indicators of rising racist tensions, the 1920s saw the popular resurgence of the Klu Klux Klan, immortalized in their 30,000-member march on Washington, DC, in 1925.[21] Alongside the intensifying conflict of the color line, immigration became a worrying preoccupation of the federal government. The passage of the Johnson–Reed Immigration Act of 1924 imposed more stringent immigration quotas on Europe, which favored the flow of "white," northern and western Europeans. In the same year, the federal government established the border patrol as part of the Land Appropriation Act, making the movement of bodies along the imaginary line between the United States and Mexico a point of consternation.[22] As Franklin Delano Roosevelt's New Deal policy went into effect, a notable shift in federal Indian policy also unfolded. What had once been a relationship predicated on overt assimilation now took the form of pluralistic recognition and indirect rule.[23] This is not to say that pre-1930s United States–Indian relations were exclusively assimilatory. As the imperial pendulum swung back and forth

---

[19] See, for example, Lois W. Banner, *Intertwined Lives: Margaret Mead, Ruth Benedict, and Their Circle* (New York: Knopf, 2003); Regna Darnell, *Edward Sapir: Linguist, Anthropologist, Humanist* (Berkeley: University of California Press, 1990); Regna Darnell et al., eds., *Franz Boas as Public Intellectual: Theory, Ethnography, Activism* (Lincoln: University of Nebraska Press, 2015).

[20] Edward H. Spicer, *Cycles of Conquest: The Impact of Spain, Mexico, and the United States on the Indians of the Southwest, 1533–1960* (Tucson: University of Arizona Press, 1962).

[21] William E. Leuchtenburg, *The Perils of Prosperity 1914–32* (Chicago: University of Chicago Press, 1958), 205–11; Stanley Coben, "Ordinary White Protestants: The KKK of the 1920s," *Journal of Social History* 28, no. 1 (1994): 155–65.

[22] Mae M. Ngai, *Impossible Subjects: Illegal Aliens and the Making of Modern America* (Princeton, NJ: Princeton University Press, 2005).

[23] Akim D. Reinhardt, "A Crude Replacement: The Indian New Deal, Indirect Colonialism, and Pine Ridge Reservation," *Journal of Colonialism and Colonial History* 6, no. 1 (2005); Graham Taylor, *The New Deal and American Indian Tribalism: The Administration of the Indian Reorganization Act, 1934–45* (Lincoln: University of Nebraska Press, 1980).

between integration and differentiation, Indigenous sovereignty experienced moments of partial recognition prior to the Indian New Deal.[24] Of course, indirect rule could still entail the reproduction of metropolitan authority over Indigenous communities often behind a veil of "self-determination" and cultural "preservation."[25] Despite the relatively positive nature of the shift in federal–Indian relations, all of these developments signaled an accelerating obsession with the management of racial and cultural difference in post-WWI, American, political discourse.

Amid these developments, American anthropology began exploring issues of cultural contact and change. This marked a visible departure from the discipline's early twentieth-century preoccupation with the reconstruction of pre-Colonial lifeways.[26] Steadily, these novel and politically salient interests were grouped under the broad heading of "acculturation." In 1935, the Social Science Research Council (SSRC) commissioned several leading anthropologists to trace the parameters of this new field of inquiry. In their seminal memorandum, participants Robert Redfield, Melville Herskovits, and Ralph Linton proffered what would become the leading definition of this emergent topic: "Acculturation comprehends those phenomena which result when groups of individuals having different cultures come into continuous first-hand contact, with subsequent changes in the original cultural patterns of either or both groups."[27] With this definition, the memorandum worked to guide the anthropological study of culture in a new direction.

Previous traditions, such as the culture-area approach of Alfred Kroeber, were not prepared to account for the complexities of change among Indigenous peoples due in part to a lack of conversancy in historical analysis and attention to colonial processes.[28] To be sure, the discipline was not universally or categorically uninterested in diachronic trans-

---

[24] Gary Clayton Anderson, *Ethnic Cleansing and the Indian: The Crime That Should Haunt America* (Norman: University of Oklahoma Press, 2014).

[25] Thomas Biolsi, "'Indian Self-Government' as a Technique of Domination," *American Indian Quarterly* 15, no. 1 (1991): 23–28; Michael Herbert Fisher, *Indirect Rule in India: Residents and the Residency System, 1764–1858* (Delhi: Oxford University Press, 1991); John Iliffe, *A Modern History of Tanganyika* (Cambridge, UK: Cambridge University Press, 1979).

[26] Jacob W. Gruber, "Ethnographic Salvage and the Shaping of Anthropology," *American Anthropologist* 72, no. 6 (1970): 1289–99; Kent G. Lightfoot, *Indians, Missionaries and Merchants: The Legacy of Colonial Encounters on the California Frontiers* (Berkeley: University of California Press, 2005).

[27] Robert Redfield, Ralph Linton, and Melville J. Herskovits, "Memorandum for the Study of Acculturation," *American Anthropologist* 38 (1936): 149.

[28] See, for example, Thomas Buckley, "'The Little History of Pitiful Events': The Epistemological and Moral Contexts of Kroeber's California Ethnology," in *Volksgeistas Method and Ethic: Essays on Boasian Ethnography and the German Anthropological Tradition*, ed. George Stocking (Madison: University of Wisconsin Press, 1996), 273.

formations.[29] However, this has not prevented some from suggesting that American anthropology's inattention to the mutable nature of social life presumed the inevitable and total absorption of Indigenous communities within the "modern" world, even if individual scholars opposed assimilation on political grounds.[30] In contrast to this supposed disciplinary orthodoxy, Redfield and company specified that assimilation was but one potential facet of acculturation. According to these scholars, the results of such a process eventuate in a variety of outcomes more effectively grouped under three distinct categories: acceptance (most reminiscent of popular notions of assimilation), adaptation ("where both original and foreign traits are combined so as to produce a smoothly functioning cultural whole") and reaction (in which "contra-acculturative movements arise" due to "oppression, or because of the unforeseen results of the acceptance of foreign traits").[31] With this outline of the field of possible trajectories, the SSRC memorandum laid the foundation for the next several decades of acculturation inquiry. Although Redfield, Herskovits, and Linton would lead this charge, they would not be the only contributors.[32]

Spicer, a student of Redfield, came of age as an anthropologist amid the rise of acculturation studies. Unsurprising, his career-long historical and analytical exploration of the Yaqui Indians fit within the general definition of acculturation as laid out by his mentor. Captivated by the community's ability to maintain a sense of ethnic distinction in the face of urban assimilation, Spicer would position the Pascua Yaqui as his primary case study for the next four decades as he examined issues of acculturation in the greater Southwest.[33]

From 1936 to 1937, Edward, alongside his collaborator and wife, Rosamond, conducted fieldwork in Pascua Village. The two would return in 1939 with the support of a grant from the SSRC to continue their

[29] See, for example, Franz Boas, "The Methods of Ethnology," *American Anthropologist* 22, no. 4 (1920): 315–21; Alex Golub, "The Methods of Ethnology: SMOPS 9," *Savage Minds* blog entry, January 21, 2014, https://savageminds.org/2014/01/21/the-methods-of-ethnology-smops-9/; Herbert S. Lewis, "The Misrepresentation of Anthropology and Its Consequences," *American Anthropologist* 100, no. 3 (1998): 724.
[30] Margaret Bruchac goes so far as to claim that "early anthropologists…depicted virtually all Native peoples of North America as inherently naïve, uneducated, primitive, and helpless to resist the inevitable fading away of traditions and assimilation into mainstream (white) society." Margaret Bruchac, *Savage Kin: Indigenous Informants and American Anthropologists* (Tucson: University of Arizona Press, 2018), 178.
[31] Redfield, Linton, and Herskovits, "Memorandum for the Study of Acculturation," 149–52.
[32] Robert Redfield, *The Primitive World and Transformations* (Ithaca, NY: Cornell University Press, 1953); Melville J. Herskovits, *Acculturation: The Study of Culture Contact* (New York: J. J. Augustin, 1938); Ralph Linton, *Acculturation in Seven American Indian Tribes* (New York: D. Appleton-Century Company, 1940).
[33] See, for example, Edward H. Spicer, *Pascua, a Yaqui Village in Arizona* (Chicago: University of Chicago Press, 1940); Edward H. Spicer, ed., *Perspectives in American Indian Culture Change* (Chicago: University of Chicago Press, 1961); Spicer, *Cycles of Conquest*.

explorations. A Guggenheim Fellowship would enable the Spicers to conduct fieldwork with Yaquis of Potam, Sonora, in 1941 and 1942. Though this would mark the end of Spicer's formal and sustained ethnography with Yaqui communities on both sides of the border, he would continue to draw on this research and the case of the Yaqui until his death in 1983. In addition, the couple made periodic return trips to Potam in 1947, 1970, and 1979, and Pascua was never more than a mere ten miles down the road from the Spicers' home in Tucson.[34]

But the Yaqui were never merely an intellectual concern for Spicer. A proponent of the practical application of anthropological knowledge and methods to address real-world problems, Spicer labored for decades alongside others to devise new ways for the Yaqui to maintain some semblance of cultural distinction and self-determination in and around Tucson.[35] These efforts came to include lobbying the US government to purchase federal trust land on the outskirts of the city specifically for the Yaqui and securing funds from the Office of Economic Opportunity (OEO) to build homes on this newly secured plot of land, which would function as an unofficial reservation. Both efforts held great promise. However, by the end of the 1960s, OEO funding dried up and the Pascua Yaqui found themselves split between a poverty-ridden urban center and a half-built, limping reservation-like community.

With few options available, the Pascua Yaqui made a bold move. Leveraging the support of local politicians and lawyers, they decided to pursue federal recognition. If successful, they would be able to access the resources of the BIA. However, federal recognition of the Pascua Yaqui as an "American Indian Tribe" presented many challenges that made for a complicated pursuit.

In the case of the United States, federally recognized "Indian tribes" are imagined to be discrete, bounded entities capable of "[reflecting] their cultural consistency 'from historical times to the present.'"[36] Those communities that are able to conform to this conception are able to access the limited resources the federal government reserves for officially acknowledged tribes such as Indian Health Services and the ability to mount land

---

[34] Kathleen Sands and Rosamond Spicer, "Preface," in *People of Pascua*, eds. Kathleen Sands and Rosamond Spicer (Tucson: University of Arizona, 1988), xlv.

[35] Thomas R. McGuire, "The Advent of Sociocultural and Applied Anthropology at Arizona: A Brief Genealogy," *Arizona Anthropologist* 25 (2015): 52–69; Edward H. Spicer, ed., *Human Problems in Technological Change: A Casebook* (New York: Russell Sage Foundation, 1974); Edward H. Spicer, "Beyond Analysis and Explanation: Notes on the Life and Times of the Society for Applied Anthropology," *Human Organization* 35, no. 4 (1976): 335–43.

[36] Barker, *Native Acts*, 37; George Pierre Castile, *Taking Charge: Native American Self-Determination and Federal Indian Policy, 1975–1993* (Tucson: University of Arizona Press, 2006); Miller, *Forgotten Tribes*.

claims with the support of federal law. In this sense, "Indian tribe" is not
a mere category, it is a political ontology with material consequences for
those who do and do not fall within it. Unfortunately, it is relatively easy
for Indigenous communities to find themselves outside of the parameters
of a recognizable tribe.

Multilingualism, shifting political alliances, trade networks, and situa-
tionally dynamic cultural practices—hallmarks of the pre-Columbian Indigenous experience—are often obscured in this line of thinking as hybridity
and discontinuity are subsumed within a story of neat cultural–political
persistence and primordialism. Thus, the commonsense understanding of
the Indian tribe is incongruent with the history of the Pascua Yaqui, who
were relatively recent "arrivants"[37] to Arizona in possession of hybrid
religious and cultural practices rooted in Colonial encounters with the
Spanish and a language that had largely fallen into disuse in the United
States. In other words, Pascua Yaqui history and identity did not quite fit
the "American Indian Tribal" mold.

Presenting their case to the Senate Subcommittee on Indian Affairs
in 1977, representatives of the Pascua Yaqui worked to reframe the community in a more recognizably "Indian" light. Raymond Cross, the tribe's
lawyer, hedged their bets and insisted that the tribe was not in pursuit of
"full recognition," which would entail the exercise of civil or criminal
jurisdiction on the reservation, but "limited recognition," which would
enable them to organize under a constitution and secure federal services.[38]
For his part, the Pascua Yaqui spiritual leader and driving force behind the
recognition campaign, Anselmo Valencia presented linguistic and cultural
practices as enduring markers of the group's "Indianness":

> The Yaquis are Indians in every sense of the word. We have our own
> language, our own culture, such as the Pascola Dancing, the deer dancing
> and the coyote dancing. These dances are Indian in origin. In the deer
> dance, we sing to honor the great mountains, the springs, the lakes. We
> sing of our father the Sun, and of creatures living and dead. We sing of
> trees and leaves and twigs. ... All of the songs sung and played are to
> the olden times—ancient Yaqui Indian stories.[39]

Valencia's narrative went on to imply that "Yaquiness," as indexed by
these linguistic and cultural practices, predates colonial encounters. "The

---

[37] Jodi Byrd, *The Transit of Empire: Indigenous Critiques of Colonialism* (Minneapolis: University of Minnesota Press, 2011); Shona N. Jackson, *Creole Indigeneity: Between Myth and Nation in the Caribbean*
(Minneapolis: University of Minnesota Press, 2012).
[38] US Congress. Senate, "Trust Status for the Pascua Yaqui Indians of Arizona," § Select Committee on
Indian Affairs (1977).
[39] Ibid.

Catholic faith and the various governments under which the Yaquis have had to suffer have tried for centuries to undermine our 'Yaquiness,' but after 400 years they have not succeeded. We have retained our language, our culture, and our Indianness."[40] Such an articulation of Yaqui history necessarily negates historical evidence of engagement with dominant societies and cultural hybridity.[41] However, this negation enabled the Yaqui to better fit the primordialist dictates of recognition.

Valencia also reconfigured the narrative to establish a precolonial connection to US soil, which would in turn undermine any accusations that the Yaqui were more Mexican immigrants than American Indians:

> Yaqui Indians are, and have been, from the southwest since before the establishment of the international boundaries which divide this continent. ... This continent which, since its creation, has belonged to the Indians from one end to the other. After such boundaries were established[,] Yaquis were still here[.] Yes, the majority of the Yaquis stayed in Mexico after the Gadsden Purchase of Arizona Territory and other lands. But they traveled back and forth across the internal line until the 1920s.[42]

On the surface, this is not a particularly radical narrative. Documentary evidence indicates that Yaqui Indians were present in the region that would become southern Arizona as early as 1796—well before the region came under US control. According to Spanish colonial records, Jesuit missionaries brought a group of Yaquis to the Tumacacori Mission to help facilitate the conversion of local Indians.[43] However, Valencia's presentation went a step further when he stated that the Yaqui remained in the region up to and after the time when it became US territory in 1854. As far as I know, there is no concrete evidence (documentary or oral historical) to suggest that these individuals remained as a distinct community.[44] Rather, it would appear that Yaquis did not start moving "back and forth" in significant numbers until the late nineteenth century.[45] Moreover, the seemingly out-of-place invocation that "this continent which, since its creation, has belonged to the Indians" did more rhetorical than empirical work. If the Yaqui are Indians and the continent is Indian, transitive logic suggests

---

[40] Ibid.

[41] Folsom, *The Yaquis and the Empire*; Hu-DeHart, *Yaqui Resistance and Survival*; Edward H. Spicer, *The Yaquis: A Cultural History* (Tucson: University of Arizona Press, 1980).

[42] US Congress. Senate, Trust Status for the Pascua Yaqui Indians of Arizona.

[43] Alfred F. Whiting, "The Tumacacori Census of 1796," *Kiva* 19, no. 1 (1953): 6.

[44] James E. Officer, *Hispanic Arizona, 1536–1856* (Tucson: University of Arizona Press, 1987), 88, 380.

[45] Spicer, *The Yaquis: A Cultural History*, 158.

that the Yaqui can claim a temporally deep connection to virtually any part of the continent, including southern Arizona.

Anticipating challenges to their campaign, Valencia and Cross did not rely on the spiritual leader's testimony alone. When it came to reframing the community as an American Indian Tribe, the petitioners called on their longtime anthropologist ally.[46] With prompting from the tribe's lawyers, Spicer submitted a succinct testimony in which he concluded based on "[his] long and extensive study of the Yaqui peoples ... that they form a distinct Indian group or tribe."[47] Without ruminating too deeply on the precise meaning of terms such as "Indian group or tribe," Spicer asserted that "there is no question about [their] being Indians in the same sense that the [Navajo], the Papagos [now Tohono O'odham], the Apaches, and other people of Arizona are Indians."[48] The campaign for federal recognition, Spicer argued, was simply the latest in a long-standing "active initiative for developing their community."[49]

Despite the somewhat tenuous nature of Valencia's re-narrativizations and the general nature of Spicer's written testimony, Valencia and company successfully persuaded politicians like Arizona Senator Dennis DeConcini to conclude that the Yaqui had long been a "major and unique American Indian tribe" whose "ancestors ... have lived in what we call the Southwest ... from time immemorial."[50] Enough politicians agreed with DeConcini, and the Yaqui were officially granted recognition in 1978. Thus, by framing the Yaqui experience as being that of an "American Indian tribe," Valencia, with the assistance of Spicer, simultaneously reconstructed Yaqui history and political status vis-à-vis the United States.

A "HISTORIC TRIBE"?

The benefits of recognition would not materialize instantaneously. It would take a full ten years until the Pascua Yaqui were able to adopt a constitution with the approval of the BIA. However, in 1991, the tribe moved to revise this document. The proposed revisions would enable the Pascua Yaqui to enroll additional members. Although the prospect of opening the rolls was

---

[46] Nicholas Barron, "Assembling 'Enduring Peoples,' Mediating Recognition: Anthropology, the Pascua Yaqui Indians, and the Co-Construction of Ideas and Politics," *History and Anthropology*, 2019, https://doi.org/10.1080/02757206.2019.1695203.

[47] US Congress. Senate, Trust Status for the Pascua Yaqui Indians of Arizona, 11.

[48] Edward H. Spicer, "Edward H. Spicer to Senator Paul Fannin," January 9, 1976, Box 165, Folder 13, Morris K. Udall Papers.

[49] Ibid.

[50] US Congress. Senate, Trust Status for the Pascua Yaqui Indians of Arizona, 2

no doubt a concern to the BIA, the office narrowed in on other aspects of the proposed amendments. Namely, federal officials protested "revising the preamble and the powers article" by "inserting words like 'being a sovereign nation' and 'in addition to its inherent sovereign powers.'"[51] Carol Bacon, the acting director of Tribal Government Services, asserted that such language would suggest that the federal government considered the Pascua Yaqui to be a "historic tribe." As Bacon explained in her legal and technical review of the revised constitution, the BIA was of a different opinion. "The origin of the Pascua Yaqui Tribe is somewhat different from that of a historic tribe," Bacon explained. "The term 'tribe' as used in Federal Indian affairs generally refers to a community of people who have continued as a body politic without interruption since time immemorial and retain powers of inherent sovereignty."[52] Following this logic, Bacon reasoned, the Pascua Yaqui constituted what the BIA termed an "adult Indian community" or "created tribe"—not a "historic tribe." According to Bacon, this distinction was a matter of well-established precedent:

> Since the enactment of the Indian Reorganization Act [IRA] of June 18, 1934, the Department has held that Adult Indian Communities may not possess all of the same attributes of sovereignty as a historic Tribe. A historic Tribe has existed since time immemorial, and its powers are derived from its inextinguishable and inherent sovereignty.

> A historic Tribe has the full range of governmental powers except where it has been removed by Congress in favor of either the United States or the state in which the Tribe is located. By contrast, a community of adult Indians is made up of individual Indian people who reside together on trust land.[53]

Thus, as described by Bacon, recognizable tribes could be further subdivided into two distinct kinds: adult Indian communities (also referred to as *created tribes*) and historic tribes. Each kind came with its own set of rights and privileges. Although terms like these were presented as a matter

---

[51] US Congress. House of Representatives., "Pascua Yaqui Status Clarification Act," § Subcommittee on Native American Affairs of the Committee on Natural Resources (1993).

[52] Ibid.

[53] Ibid. Contrary to Bacon's statement, the IRA makes no mention of a distinction between "historic tribes" and "adult Indian communities," which Bacon alternatively referred to as *created tribes*. More precisely, Bacon was referring to a 1936 Solicitor's Opinion regarding Section 16 of the IRA, which describes the right of tribes to adopt a constitution. But the opinion in question never uses the term *adult Indian community* (or *created tribe* for that matter). Moreover, it never explains what is meant by a "historic tribe." Rather, it simply states that "a group of Indians which is organized on the basis of a reservation and which is not an [historic] tribe may not have all of the powers enumerated in the Solicitor' opinion on the Powers of Indian Tribes dated October 25, 1934." There is no explanation for what constitutes a historic tribe.

of past congressional legislation (i.e., the IRA) and not the whims of individual bureaucrats, they remained what Annemarie Mol has termed *political ontologies* for adult Indian communities and historic tribes were not and are not biological realities but social constructions forged in the fires of New Deal-era federal Indian policy.[54]

To substantiate the office's opinion that the Pascua Yaqui did not meet the necessary criteria for a "historic tribe," thereby justifying the legitimacy of what might appear to be problematic if not arbitrary political ontologies, Bacon invoked the "available historical evidence." More specific, she quoted passages from a little-known article from Edward Spicer titled "Highlights of Yaqui History."[55] Published in 1974 in the journal *The Indian Historian*, "Highlights of Yaqui History" surveyed nearly 400 years of Yaqui experiences throughout the Southwest. However, Bacon homed in on Spicer's use of the term *political refugees* to refer to Yaquis who migrated from Sonora to Arizona at the turn of the century. Bacon took this label to mean that "the Pascua Yaqui did not enter the country as a historical tribal unit," and therefore, could not be classified as a "historic tribe." In reading Spicer's work into the record, Bacon was not simply describing history, she was, in a highly co-productive manner, constructing a new political reality for the Pascua Yaqui Tribe.

The tribe quickly countered Bacon's classification of them as what she called a "created tribe" and her portrayal of Spicer's works. Albert V. Garcia, chairman of the Pascua Yaqui Tribe during this period, insisted that "officials have misquoted or taken entirely out of context the testimony of Dr. Spicer."[56] Garcia proceeded to quote passages not from "Highlights of Yaqui History," but from Spicer's 1977 written testimony in support of federal acknowledgment. There seems to have been miscommunication between the BIA and the tribe over what exact piece of writing they were both discussing. "If one reads Professor Spicer's letter in its entirety," Garcia insisted, "we can see that the Bureau of Indian Affairs has simply excised the part about 'political refugees' and used it to support its flimsy argument that the Yaquis are not an historical tribe."[57] Despite the confusion regarding the exact source (was it the article or the testimony?), Garcia keenly observed a difference of opinion between himself and Bacon regarding the significance of Spicer's use of the term *political refugees*,

---

[54] Annemarie Mol, "Ontological Politics. A Word and Some Questions," in *Actor Network Theory and After*, eds. John Law and John Hassard (Oxford: Blackwell Publishing, 1999), 75–89.

[55] Edward H. Spicer, "Highlights of Yaqui History," *The Indian Historian* 7, no. 2 (1974): 2–9.

[56] US Congress. House of Representatives., Pascua Yaqui Status Clarification Act.

[57] Ibid.

which appears in both documents. Quoting from Spicer's written testimony, Garcia explained:

> But even the quote attributed to Professor Spicer states that the Yaquis "made it clear to churches and other agencies that they will continue to guide their religious and community life in their own way. …" He then states that "their status is simply that of immigrants from Mexico or citizens by virtue of birth in the United States." This does not mean and cannot be interpreted to mean that the Yaqui are not a historical tribe.[58]

Informed by his own reading of the "available historical evidence," Garcia concluded, "a tribe as well as an individual can be a political refugee."[59]

In 1993, this debate over Spicer's characterization of the Pascua Yaqui as political refugees and the status of the tribe would move from Bacon and Garcia's letters to the hearings of the House Subcommittee on Native American Affairs. It was here that Bacon and Garcia would need to defend their competing views on Spicer and his historical highlights. In doing so, both sides found themselves operating at the productive intersections of science and politics. By debating the meaning of ethnohistorical representations, the Yaqui and BIA used Spicer's scholarship as a means to reshape the relationship between two polities. In this instance, ethnohistory became politics by other means.

MAKING HIGHLIGHTS

It is often difficult to pinpoint the motivations behind a given intellectual production. However, the archive leaves little confusion about "Highlights of Yaqui History." Spicer began writing this article in January of 1974 as an unsolicited response to another account of Yaqui history and culture. In the fall of 1971, *The Indian Historian*, a fledgling ethnohistorical journal, presented an article by Marguerite Jensen titled "The Yaqui." A brisk three-pages, Jensen relied on histrionic tropes to characterize Yaqui history and culture as "a mosaic of strife, desert sand and towering mountains, color, pageantry, isolation and poverty."[60] In the following text, I quote a long passage from Jensen's article to illustrate how her depiction of the Arizona Yaqui and Pascua Village was particularly reductive, freezing the community in a kind of suspended ethnohistorical animation divorced from their modern surroundings:

---

[58] Ibid.
[59] Ibid.
[60] Marguerite Jensen, "The Yaqui," *Indian Historian* 4, no. 3 (1971): 41.

Those Yaqui who crossed the Rio Grande moved from one kind of persecution to another. They escaped from active persecution in their homeland, only to be caught up in the passive persecution of isolation and poverty in places like Tucson, Marana, Nogales, Phoenix, and Scottsdale. They were political refugees without citizenship who sought asylum. They were expatriates, numbering 3000 to 4000, who welcomed anonymity, glad to hide in places like Tucson's Pascua Pueblo. To a great extent, their exclusion and isolation has been self-generated, reinforced by fear of disclosure and possible deportation.

So the pueblo of Pascua hasn't changed much since 1919 when the first Yaqui took up residence in the heart of the city, hidden from view by the large industrial plants surrounding the village. ... In 1970, it is still described as a collection of little tin, scrap-wood, cardboard and adobe shacks, their drabness relieved only by the invariable gardens of gay flowers. There are no indoor toilets, sidewalks or paved streets; there is no running water or electricity. Wishing to remain hidden, the Yaqui have not complained about inadequate housing, frequent lack of food, and the spector [sic] of persistent unemployment, except for those who work as gardeners and garbage collectors.[61]

Change, as presented in Jensen's article, was a relatively novel phenomenon for the people of Pascua:

The young are beginning to rebel against this kind of life, beginning to come out of hiding. ... For over 50 years, the Yaqui were silent; now they too add their voices to those of other deprived groups. At last, the refugees are breaking out of their self-imposed exile.[62]

The article likely went unnoticed by the majority of the journal's readers. However, for Spicer, the leading anthropological and ethnohistorical authority on all things Yaqui, Jensen's account was something of an academic eyesore. As Spicer conveyed to Jeannette Henry, the journal's editor:

When you published "The Yaqui" by Marguerite Jensen in your fall 1971 issue, I was dismayed. It was a well-meaning article, but so full of confusion regarding Yaqui history and tending so much towards making the Yaqui seem like shy and backward people *at the edge of everything*, who "travel the Sonoran Desert exactly as their hunting and gathering ancestors did in centuries past." (The quote is so far from any reality that I wonder how it could have been written by anyone with the least acquaintance with Yaquis.)[63]

---

[61] Jensen, "The Yaqui," 43.

[62] Ibid.

[63] Edward H. Spicer, "Edward Spicer to Jeannette Henry," January 21, 1974, Edward H. and Rosamond B. Spicer Papers, Arizona State Museum. Emphasis added.

So concerned was Spicer with Jensen's depiction that he felt compelled to compose a "brief summary of Yaqui history, such as is not available anywhere in either Spanish or English." It was a conscious effort to distinguish his account from Jensen's sensationalism. As Spicer conveyed to Henry, "I have refrained from putting something into the highly dramatic form which Yaqui experience and action through the centuries deserves. It seemed to me that the simple facts should come first. Maybe the dramatic narrative will come next."[64] The implication being that Jensen (and the journal) had led with the dramatic, ignoring the "simple facts" of Yaqui experiences.

That being said, Spicer's "highlights" were anything but "simple." Although Jensen traded in primitivist and primordialized tropes, Spicer embraced a more modernist[65] view of Yaquiness—one in which interactions with others and transformations in practices and beliefs were the very grist of distinctive peoplehood. For decades, Spicer worked with Yaquis in Arizona and Sonora who had themselves worked for transnational railroad companies, mining corporations, and intensive agriculturalists. Many of these same individuals and their relatives had fought in the Mexican Revolution and World War II. In other words, Spicer knew full well that the Yaqui were hardly a people at the edge of anything. Although they had most definitely known struggle, the Yaqui were never isolated. If anything, their struggle implied persistent, complex, and often calculated interactions with internally diverse groups of Spanish, Mexican, and American communities. Spicer consciously chose to highlight these interactions in his article. The very first paragraph stands as a declaration of Yaqui historical ingenuity and self-awareness:

> Astride an international boundary for nearly a century, Yaquis have made themselves felt in important ways in both Mexico and the United States. Despite all-out efforts by the Diaz government of Mexico to dominate their communities before 1910, Yaquis fought for self-determination in their own country. They outlasted the landlord government of Mexico and made their cause an important theme of the 1910 Revolution. In the United States, where many Yaqui sought political refuge during the long years of persecution in Mexico, they have also asserted their spirit of independence and made it clear to churches and other agencies that they will

---

[64] Ibid.

[65] My use of the label *modernist* follows Anthony D. Smith's taxonomy of theories of the nation and nationalism. Modernist views of the nation, as described by Smith, contend that: "nationalist ideologies, as well as the system of nation-states are modern, that is, both recent in date and novel in character; nations and national identities are also recent and novel; and most important, nations and nationalism are the produce of modernization and modernity." Anthony D. Smith, *The Nation in History: Historiographical Debates about Ethnicity and Nationalism* (Lebanon, NH: University Press of New England, 2000).

continue to guide their religious and community life in their own ways. At present, a constant struggle goes on in both countries between independence-minded Yaquis and assimilation-minded church and state agencies.[66]

Whereas Jensen spoke of isolation, Spicer spoke of "self-determination," a "spirit of independence," and a "constant struggle." This was not a people "wishing to remain hidden." Rather, here was a people who had "made themselves felt in important ways." Thus, by writing "Highlights," Spicer countered a simplified and exoticizing narrative and affirmed the historical agency of the Yaqui.

IRONIC IMPLICATIONS

Obviously, this context was absent from the BIA's reading of Spicer's article. Rather, Bacon focused on the use of the term *political refugee* to describe the Yaqui of Arizona. In a sense, Bacon's interpretation was accurate. Throughout his career, Spicer underscored the diasporic nature of Yaqui culture and history. Though he never explicitly rejected Valencia's depiction, Spicer also never presented the Pascua Yaqui as having an autochthonous connection to what is now the United States. However, there is a deep and unavoidable irony in the BIA's deployment of Spicer's article. Spicer devoted his professional life to supporting Pascua Yaqui self-determination. And yet, the federal government attempted to use his scholarship (albeit a fraction of it) to undermine claims to tribal sovereignty and the group's conception of their own history. Spicer's use of phrases like *political refugee* was never intended to substantiate or challenge the political reclassification of the Yaqui, let alone speak to an obscure bureaucratic distinction between "historic" and "created" tribes.

Ultimately, Bacon's interpretation of the "available historical evidence" and Spicer's article in particular proved futile. Congress sided with the Pascua Yaqui, and the bill to amend the tribal constitution passed both chambers in 1994. For all intents and purposes, the Pascua Yaqui became a "historic tribe." Thinking back to Lurie's warning regarding the incongruent nature of the scholastic and the juridical, we can see that the law was not set up to discern the technical merits and nuances of Spicer's portrayal of the Yaqui. Thus, this case highlights the chasm between the law and the academy with respect to the depiction of Indian culture and

---

[66] Spicer, "Highlights of Yaqui History," 2.

history as well the paradoxical consequences of ignoring this disjuncture. For although the histories of science and politics may operate on a shared terrain as Shapin and Schaffer suggest, this does not mean that the process of instrumentalizing scientific representations for governmental ends is without complication.

CONCLUSIONS

As this case has shown, the Pascua Yaqui and federal officials have long called on and (occasionally) debated the meaning of Edward Spicer's depictions of this borderlands people. By reconstructing the conditions under which Spicer's portrayals were constituted, my goal has not been to resolve disputes between Yaqui representatives and their counterparts in the federal government. That is to say, I have tried to avoid naturalizing the logics of recognition by treating *historic tribe* and *created tribe* as universally valid categories. Rather, my goal has been to highlight the implications of transporting scholarly consideration of Native culture and history into new arenas such as congressional committees. By historicizing the conditions under which Spicer developed his portrayals of the Yaqui, I have illustrated how an attempt to oppose reductive depictions of Indian history during the 1970s was, ironically, adopted by the federal government in the 1990s to undermine the Pascua Yaqui Tribe's sense of self-determination.

The purpose of exploring such cases, I believe, is not to discourage the operationalizing of extant anthropological and ethnohistorical knowledge. Rather, my objective has been to illustrate the limits of control that scholars of Indigenous culture and history have over their ideas and the potential for those ideas to be put toward unforeseen ends. Obviously, Spicer could not predict nor control how his use of a term like *political refugee* would be instrumentalized against the Yaqui. He had been deceased for nearly a decade when the BIA adopted "Highlights" for its own purposes. However, it is difficult to say how his physical presence may or may not have changed the outcome. Spicer would have been tasked with translating his use of political refugee as a scholastic-historical category into the government's use of political refugee as a bureaucratic-legal category. Scholars, such as Arthur Ray, who have offered their ethnohistorical expertise to tribal claims, have written about the difficulty of, as he phrases it, "telling it to the judge"—teaching the judiciary about the intricacies of Indigenous and colonial history while on the stand.[67] Underscoring the more pernicious and cunning dimensions of acting as expert and educator, David Dinwoodie has observed firsthand in the context of First Nations land claims in Canada how the testimony of expert witnesses, even those aligned with tribal interests, can be coerced in subtle but highly consequential ways once on the stand.[68] The experiences of Ray and Dinwoodie, not unlike Lurie before them, suggest that a court is no place for the nuanced exploration of ethnohistorical differences, and yet, courts continue to be sites for such explorations. The Yaqui case shows how other highly bureaucratized, court-like settings, such as congressional hearings, entail similar limitations.

But again, my objective is not to suggest that ethnohistorical writings are to be excised from Indigenous claims proceedings altogether. The application of such works, however, needs to be carefully considered. For those who still think anthropologists, historians, ethnohistorians, and their respective oeuvres are well positioned to guide state policy by representing a preexisting Indigenous reality, this micro history of the construction and implementation of Spicer's work should engender a reflexive pause. Perhaps such written works, *when understood as socially situated historical objects in their own right*, are better suited to question unexamined assumptions of prevailing political institutions. As I hope is now clear, when one considers the process by which Spicer's article came to fruition (i.e., within an academic debate regarding the representation of Indigenous identity and colonial history), the BIA's use of the terms *political refugee* and *historic/ created tribe* can, rather than being reified, be thrown into examinable relief. Thus, histories of the mobilization and the implementation of ethnohistorical representations offer practical application in contemporary sociopolitical life as they embolden grounded and reflexive analyses of the uses of science.

---

[67] Arthur J. Ray, *Telling It to the Judge: Taking Native History to Court* (Montreal: McGill Queen's University Press, 2011).

[68] David W. Dinwoodie, "Recognizing Aboriginal Perspectives in Land Claims Litigation" (American Anthropological Association, San Jose, California, November 15, 2018).

Chapter 8

The Use and Misuse of Anthropological Evidence: Digital Himalaya as Ethnographic Knowledge (Re)Production

Mark Turin

COLLECT, PROTECT, CONNECT: THE BIRTH OF DIGITAL HIMALAYA

Almost twenty-three years ago, in December 2000, a group of four anthropologists and historians at the University of Cambridge (of which I was one) set out to explore new methods for collecting, protecting, and connecting historical anthropological collections in a range of media formats relating to the Himalayan region in ways that would widen access to the materials through emerging digital platforms. Motivating us was what Natalie M. Underberg and Elayne Zorn have described as the desire to "investigate the social impact of new technologies, with the goal of responsibly integrating technology into cultural representations."[1] Structured through the emerging "participatory culture of the twenty-first century,"[2] we were eager to explore whether an opportunity existed to challenge traditional hierarchies of anthropological data, evidence, authority, value, and voice.

Sarah Harrison, Alan Macfarlane, Sara Shneiderman, and I named this pilot project "Digital Himalaya," a placeholder title that has since come to stick. We began by digitizing older sets of ethnographic data held in university and personal collections across Europe to protect them from

---

[1] Natalie M. Underberg and Elayne Zorn, *Digital Ethnography: Anthropology, Narrative, and New Media* (Austin: University of Texas Press, 2013), 4.
[2] Ibid., 41.

obsolescence and decay, forward migrate them as new standards emerged, and share them back with originating communities in the Himalayan region and with scholars everywhere through the Web and other digital media as appropriate.

The process, challenges, early successes, and ethical quandaries— not to mention the more technical steps involved in selecting the original collections for digitization, the process of curation, the frequency of updates, and the necessary international collaboration that ensued—have been the topic of many academic and popular articles[3] and are beyond the scope of this current contribution. In this chapter, I rather address thorny questions about data and evidence, both visual and textual, through the experience of establishing and then directing Digital Himalaya. In the process, I explore the past, present, and future of ethnographic data and anthropological evidence through the work of the Digital Himalaya Project, and I ask: Is knowledge always, and by definition, information that has somehow been organized, and is knowledge organization therefore necessarily reductive and selective?

ETHNOGRAPHIC DATA AND THE PRODUCTION OF ANTHROPOLOGICAL EVIDENCE

Lurking behind understandings of "evidence" and "data" are entrenched assumptions about the nature of knowledge in different disciplines. Writing about history, Joan W. Scott acknowledges that the status of evidence is at best "ambiguous," and that a "narrative can be said to determine the evidence as much as the evidence determines the narrative."[4] As an area of study, anthropology has long positioned fieldwork as an almost sacred process—"diacritical"[5] as Kirsten Hastrup has described it—a *rite de passage* through which the ethnographer passes in order to generate prized

---

[3] See Sara Shneiderman and Mark Turin, "Digital Himalaya: An Ethnographic Archive in the Digital Age," in *Interarchive: Archival Practices and Sites in the Contemporary Art Field*, eds. Beatrice von Bismarck et al. (Cologne: Verlag der Buchhandlung Walter König, 2002), 359–61; Mark Turin, "Born Archival: The Ebb and Flow of Digital Documents from the Field," *History and Anthropology* 22 (December 2011): 445–60; Mark Turin, "Salvaging the Records of Salvage Ethnography: The Story of the Digital Himalaya Project," *Book 2.0* 1, no. 1 (2012): 39–46; Mark Turin, "The Unexpected Afterlives of Himalayan Collections: From Data Cemetery to Web Portal," in *The Anthropology of Expeditions: Travel, Visualities, Afterlives*, eds. Joshua A. Bell and Erin L. Hasinoff (New York: Bard Graduate Center, 2015), 242–68.

[4] Lionel Gossman, "Towards a Rational Historiography," in Transactions of the American Philosophical Society 79, pt. 3 (Philadelphia: American Philosophical Society, 1998), 26, quoted in Joan W. Scott, "The Evidence of Experience," *Critical Inquiry* 17 (Summer 1991): 776.

[5] Kirsten Hastrup, "The Ethnographic Present: A Reinvention," *Cultural Anthropology* 5 (February 1990): 45.

and potentially verifiable anthropological knowledge. In addition, and unlike other disciplines, there is widespread agreement and understanding among practitioners that in ethnography, research materials are co-produced by the researcher and the researched, "before they become commoditised into 'data.'"[6]

Co-production, as Sheila Jasanoff argues, is "shorthand for the proposition that the ways in which we know and represent the world (both nature and society) are inseparable from the ways in which we choose to live in it."[7] In other words, we co-produce, just as we are ourselves co-produced. Although contemporary anthropology takes pride in a strategic marshalling of co-production that is positioned as an ethical innovation or rebalancing of expertise, Jasanoff's argument runs deeper. To anthropologists, she suggests, the very idiom of co-production "offers further tools for analyzing problems of essentialism and stereotypic reproduction, showing how the cultural capacity to produce and validate knowledges and artifacts can account for long-term stability, as well as creativity and change."[8] And yet, as those who have studied the history of the discipline have shown, anthropological knowledge tends to have an intrinsically "elusive quality,"[9] meaning that "if what is reported is not to be dismissed as mere recording or description, it must be recognised as understanding."[10]

From its very beginnings, anthropology has had an ambivalent relationship regarding its location on that rather unrefined scale outlined by C. P. Snow in his *The Two Cultures and the Scientific Revolution.*[11] Some practitioners situate the discipline firmly within the humanities, whereas others were—and still are—lured toward the scientific end of the continuum. The bedrock of much anthropological thinking still aligns with a broadly conceived "positivist view stipulating that a theory needs to be tested against data; if theory is the text, data become the corrective context."[12] But if we admit that anthropological knowledge is usually derived from ethnographic data—gathered and collected through fieldwork which is an inherently communicative, subjective, historically contingent,

---

[6] Peter Pels et al., "Data Management in Anthropology: The Next Phase in Ethics Governance?" *Social Anthropology* 26, no. 3 (2018): 391, doi: 10.1111/1469-8676.12526.

[7] Sheila Jasanoff, ed., *States of Knowledge: The Co-production of Science and Social Order* (London: Routledge, 2004), 2.

[8] Ibid., 4.

[9] Timothy Jenkins, "Fieldwork and the Perception of Everyday Life," *Man* 29 (June 1994): 444.

[10] Johannes Fabian, "Ethnographic Misunderstanding and the Perils of Context," in *The Problem of Context: Perspectives from Social Anthropology and Elsewhere*, ed. R. M. Dilley (New York: Berghahn Books, 1999), 85.

[11] C. P. Snow, *The Two Cultures: And a Second Look: An Expanded Version of The Two Cultures and the Scientific Revolution* (New York: New American Library, 1963).

[12] Fabian, "Ethnographic Misunderstanding," 91.

and necessarily imperfect event—what is the evidentiary basis for anthropological knowledge? Moreover, underlying the anthropological endeavor lies
lingering discomfort with the very idea that knowledge is essentially data
"that are *already commodified*,"[13] or put another way, data that have been
"alienated from the social relations of research by contractual forms of
informed consent and anonymisation."[14]

Along the way, anthropology has on occasion fallen prey to the same
self-important weakness as Narcissus, that impossibly handsome hunter
from Greek mythology who fell in love with his own image reflected in a
pool of water. "That we must go to extreme lengths to allow the field of
study to *actually exert* the desired constraints on the information construed,"
writes Karin D. Knorr-Cetina, witheringly, "is demonstrated by the development of anthropology, which long ago denounced societal ethnocentrism,
only to find itself continuously engaged in its own professional ethnocentrism."[15]

Many have asked whether it is useful or even "possible to distinguish
the collection of information from interpretation or analysis,"[16] given that
ethnographic understanding "happens always after the fact,"[17] rather than
in the moment itself. Hastrup has more recently noted that "the question
of evidence is acute if anthropology shall aspire to anything but reporting
quaint stories from strange places."[18] Thinking in this vein, and echoing
Hastrup, the Digital Himalaya Project team approached knowledge as a
"social phenomenon rather than simply a substance."[19] We challenged
ourselves to think through by what process analogue data can become
digital evidence, what is lost when certain data points are excluded and
others are amplified, and—perhaps most fundamental—what it means to
edit and publish data in the digital age. In this, we were preparing to
enter an ethically fraught space in which ethnographic data were being
increasingly "gathered, produced, stored, circulated and shared digitally
through online third-party services,"[20] as stated by Igor Boog, in ways that
could never have been anticipated by either the original researchers or
the ethnographic subjects.

---

[13] Pels et al., "Data Management in Anthropology," 393 (italics in the original).

[14] Ibid., 391.

[15] Karin D. Knorr-Cetina, *The Manufacture of Knowledge: An Essay on the Constructivist and Contextual Nature of Science* (Oxford: Pergamon, 1981), 19.

[16] Fabian, "Ethnographic Misunderstanding," 91.

[17] Ibid.

[18] Kirsten Hastrup, "Getting it Right: Knowledge and Evidence in Anthropology," *Anthropological Theory* 4, no. 4 (2004): 455.

[19] Ibid., 456.

[20] Pels et al., "Data Management in Anthropology," 399.

Hastrup describes the transformative sleight-of-hand and intellectual conceit of ethnographic fieldwork with forensic precision: "While it lasts, it is a radical experience of estrangement and relativism. Afterward, it becomes memory and the backbone of objectivism."[21] Frederick Barth gets at this same point, albeit through less lyrical language: "Actions become knowledge to others only after the fact."[22] Exploring how that "magic" is affected and how the transformation is produced involves unpicking the threads of anthropological knowledge creation. One of the elephants in the room is that at the very center of anthropological evidence lies the unassailable monograph or academic article—"before fieldwork becomes science, it has to be transformed into text."[23] Where does that leave the rich audiovisual materials that ethnographers have collected—and continue to collect—in the field, including 16-mm film, reel-to-reel audio, and later, analogue and then digital video that we were planning to digitize and share through the Web? Or, more simply put, is film data or knowledge?

THE (DE)VALUING OF ETHNOGRAPHIC FILM

Matthew Durington and Jay Ruby come to the rather depressing if inescapable conclusion that for the first half of the twentieth century at least, while the ostensible purpose of ethnographic film was educational, "there is no evidence that they were ever used in teaching."[24] Marcus Banks and Ruby show how the "claims made for the value of ethnographic film in the broader anthropological project are just that—claims. It is significant that ... films are very rarely cited as data sources in written ethnography."[25] Faced with the potential for sharing hundreds of hours of ethnographic moving images and thousands of photographs through new online and offline technologies, Digital Himalaya would have to make a strong case for spending precious time and limited resources digitizing and mobilizing historical visual media, an aspect of the ethnographic endeavor that had been systematically undervalued by the academy and consistently referred to in most disparaging terms.

By way of illustration, when Christoph von Fürer-Haimendorf, whose exceptional film collection would become the core of the Digital Himalaya

---

[21] Hastrup, "Ethnographic Present," 45.

[22] Fredrik Barth, "An Anthropology of Knowledge," *Current Anthropology* 43, no. 1 (2002): 1.

[23] Hastrup, "Ethnographic Present," 47.

[24] Marcus Banks and Jay Ruby, eds., *Made to Be Seen: Perspectives on the History of Visual Anthropology* (Chicago: University of Chicago Press, 2011), 6.

[25] Ibid., 10.

moving image collection, mentioned to anthropological founding father Bronislaw Malinowski in 1935 that he intended to photograph in the field, the grandfather of ethnography dismissed this as "Thomas Cook-ism," a form of "tourist activity, below the dignity of an anthropologist and of only decorative use."[26] In his autobiography, written many years later, von Fürer-Haimendorf describes this trivialization with characteristic tact but expressed that it "widened the range of those who held such a view."[27] "Apart from his brilliance Malinowski had surprising prejudices," writes von Fürer-Haimendorf, "he and his followers looked down on anthropological photography and considered any visual documentation unnecessary and not worthy of serious academics."[28] Film was simply not considered an effective and appropriate tool for that generation of ethnographic knowledge.

Cost was an issue. It's interesting to note that in the 1940s, von Fürer-Haimendorf had struck up a relationship with Osman Ali Khan Siddiqi, Asaf Jah VII, the Nizam of Hyderabad in India, who supplied the expensive film stock that von Fürer-Haimendorf used to document the Chenchu and other communities. After the war, the British Broadcasting Corporation, along with Austrian and Bavarian television, were looking to commission ethnographic films to quench the seemingly inexhaustible appetite of television audiences for romantic ethnographic travelogues, but they lacked the experience and networks to make such films themselves. The solution was a creative and mutually beneficial arrangement: television companies would provide the film stock and cover some of the costs of travel and fieldwork, while von Fürer-Haimendorf would act as their contracted filmmaker, shooting 16mm with the steady hand and good eye for which he was already known. On his return to Europe, he delivered the reels to the commissioning body, which then, through a process of cutting and editing, would composite the raw footage into dramatic-sounding documentaries with titles such as *The Men Who Hunted Heads*[29] and *The Land of the Gurkhas*.[30]

Through the editing process, television producers would regularly intermix ethnic groups from different districts (and even countries), lay down a classical European orchestral score as the soundtrack over footage of Himalayan rice paddies, and add a commanding voiceover by David

[26] Alan Macfarlane, "Early Ethnographic Film in Britain: A Reflection on the Work of Christoph von Fürer-Haimendorf," *Visual Anthropology* 23, no. 5 (2010): 379.

[27] Ibid.

[28] Christoph von Fürer-Haimendorf, *Life Among Indian Tribes: The Autobiography of an Anthropologist* (Delhi: Oxford University Press, 1990), 9.

[29] Christoph von Fürer-Haimendorf, *The Men Who Hunted Heads—The Nagas of Assam* (London: British Broadcasting Corporation, 1971), filmstrip, 50 min.

[30] Christoph von Fürer-Haimendorf, *Travellers' Tales: The Land of the Gurkhas* (London: British Broadcasting Corporation, 1957), filmstrip, 1200 ft.

Attenborough or a similarly authoritative narrator, airing the finished "documentary" to public acclaim. What little evidential authority these films might have had at the outset was shredded in the process, making the edited films far less historically and ethnographically interesting than the raw footage and "rushes" to which we had been given access through the Digital Himalaya Project's growing network. At the same time that these films were being produced for public consumption, "trustyworthy agents"—such as Attenborough and von Fürer-Haimendorf—"necessary to the constitution of any body of knowledge" were being identified and promoted.[31] In Shapin's analysis, gentlemen such as these—in our case, one English, the other Austrian—embodied authority and were seen to be conveyors of ethnographic evidence. They fit the dominant cultural paradigm "of the type of individual one could trust to speak the truth"[32] and could thus serve as a "reliable spokesman for reality."[33]

IN DEFENSE OF THE RAW (OVER THE COOKED OR PROCESSED)

Although raw data and processed data are not categorical opposites in the way that high priest of structuralism, Claude Lévi-Strauss, positioned "raw" and "cooked" in his 1964 publication that launched his four-part *Mythologiques*,[34] it is useful to explore the distinction, certainly in the context of ethnographic film. Peter Pels et al. argue that anthropologists should "insist on making an epistemological distinction between 'raw' and 'processed data', even if such classifications only remain stable within specific, contingent contexts."[35] In the same series of essays, Heather Richards-Rissetto offers some pointers about how we might make sense of the difference: "What are data? Are they only the initial observations we record? What about post-processed data—are these simply data or have they become knowledge?"[36] Through the Digital Himalaya Project, we were learning how ethnographic film—as data—was being "cooked" and "processed," and not just through appropriate and judicious editing, but more troubling, through ethically questionable repurposing for consumption by television

---

[31] Steven Shapin, *A Social History of Truth: Civility and Science in Seventeenth-Century England* (Chicago: University of Chicago Press, 1994), xxvi.

[32] Ibid., xxvi.

[33] Ibid., xxviii.

[34] Claude Lévi-Strauss, *Mythologiques*, vol. 1, *Le Cru et le cuit* (Paris: Plon, 1964).

[35] Pels et al., "Data Management in Anthropology," 394.

[36] Ibid., 410.

companies. As the "cooking" had involved creating cultural impossibilities that had never existed, and could never exist, it was imperative that if we were to make any use of these ethnographic films, we would have to return to the rushes and work from the raw footage itself.

REVALUING ETHNOGRAPHIC FILM THROUGH DIGITAL RETURN

Through the von Fürer-Haimendorf collection and others, previously unanticipated collaborations began to emerge. The custodians of such collections in European holding institutions often had only limited knowledge about the footage that they curated, based on a few quickly scribbled notes on a film canister or on an ancient accession form. Back in the Himalayan region, descendants of the individuals who were featured in the films often had no way of knowing that such footage even existed in European collections. When we approached communities in Nepal, Bhutan, Tibet, and northern India about the existence of these unique visual records, all were eager to view them and then have permanent copies of the films and photographs of their ancestors. Relationships of trust began to develop out of a process that has since come to be referred to as *digital return*.[37]

Context is all. We know that there is no single anthropological knowledge, and that it cannot be "totalized," but is rather "constructed in the construal of specific encounters. This is as true for the anthropologist as for the informant."[38] The issue, until recently, has been that the "informant," of whom Jenkins writes, had little access and ever fewer rights to the tools of anthropological knowledge construction. Although context mattered enormously, the context was overwhelmingly shaped by the research goals and intellectual agendas of the powerful ethnographer. In his conversation with Nandi Dill, Fred Ritchin reminds us that "the history of photography is almost never told from the point of view of the subject. It is usually told from the point of view of the creator of the image, and we celebrate the photographer's vision."[39] Digital Himalaya had an opportunity to invert some of that authority and voice by consulting with community members

---

[37] See Joshua A. Bell, Kimberly Christen, and Mark Turin, "Introduction: After the Return," *Museum Anthropology Review* 7 (Spring–Fall 2013): 1–21.

[38] Jenkins, "Fieldwork and the Perception," 452.

[39] Nandi Dill, "Notes from the Field: An Interview with Fred Ritchin," *Humanity: An International Journal of Human Rights, Humanitarianism, and Development* 4 (Winter 2013): 401.

and seeking their input on if, how, where, and when the images of their ancestors could and should be shared.

Through partnerships, such as Digital Himalaya, members of historically marginalized and ethnographically scrutinized communities can become revalued as knowledge holders and experts in collaborations that are mediated through visual records. The insights offered by community members are of immense value, contributing essential context to historically under-documented collections.[40] For Digital Himalaya, the process of engaging with source communities through DVDs and hard disks packed with histori-cal footage, and later through online interactions, was more than a routine or mechanical process of cultural return in digital form. Instead, it became an exciting opportunity for collaboration through which collections were enriched and better understood. I am reminded of the inspiring work of Willow Cree writer, journalist, cultural advocate, and commentator—Paul Seesequasis—who writes about the collaborative social media project he started to collect archival photographs of everyday life in First Nations, Métis, and Inuit communities from across Canada from the 1920s to the 1970s and harnesses the connective and communicative power of the Internet to "assemble, digitize and distribute"[41] them back to communities who recognized themselves and their ancestors. "This act of naming," writes Seesequasis, "brought another layer to the photographs: reclamation."[42]

Such recalibrations can be read in two ways, either as exercises in mediated "decolonization" or as a form of reciprocity that "strives to enable communities to have an equal say in how their culture is portrayed by bringing them into discussion";[43] although we should be skeptical of what level of representational "equality" is actually reached in such remedia-tions. Even with equality remaining elusive, working to flatten hierarchies of authority, and seeking to broaden access to content can be effective in pushing back against entrenched colonial models of knowledge production. As Ritchin notes for social media, but is equally true of other forms of digital remediation, "the forming of hierarchies may be seen as a form of paternalism, as taking the decision-making power away from people."[44]

---

[40] For a discussion of the forms that relationships between museums and source communities can take, see Laura L. Peers and Alison K. Brown, eds., *Museums and Source Communities: A Routledge Reader* (London: Routledge, 2003).

[41] Paul Seesequasis, *Blanket Toss under Midnight Sun: Portraits of Everyday Life in Eight Indigenous Communities* (Toronto: Knopf Canada, 2019), 165.

[42] Ibid., 2.

[43] Underberg and Zorn, *Digital Ethnography*, 26.

[44] Dill, "Notes from the Field," 398.

ACCESS AND AUDIENCE: CHANGING
EXPECTATIONS

When we established the Digital Himalaya Project in 2000, we naively imagined that we were building a Web portal primarily for academic users in the Global North who would have unfettered access to the Internet through fast broadband networks, and that communities in the Himalayas would be better served by having us burn the digitized collections onto DVDs and for us to deposit hard disks to institutes, colleges, and universities across Asia. This certainly meshed with the prevailing dogma of the time, neatly encapsulated in Underberg and Zorn's description of projects that seek to "make collections of objects, texts, and audio and visual recordings available to the world—or more properly, that part of the world with Internet access. Those without access, primarily in the Global South, face a serious problem that scholars need to address."[45] As we quickly learned, however, Global North and Global South are insufficiently nuanced categories for understanding that had easy access to our collections. The terms say nothing about class and resources, perhaps the most important consideration in understanding the changing demographics of our users.

Ever since we started tracking visits to and downloads from our website in 2005, a strikingly different pattern has emerged. Of the 500,000+ unique "sessions" that Google Analytics has recorded, 19 percent have been from Nepal, 16 percent from the United States, 10 percent from India, and 8 percent from the United Kingdom. It is particularly satisfying that so many Web users in Nepal and India have accessed our content, offering a comprehensive challenge to our early and quite erroneous assumption in 2000 that the "West" would have the Web and the "Rest" would have hard disks and DVDs. Similarly arresting is the data provided by Google about device category. Of the half a million sessions (noting, of course, that a session may include many page views) that the site has received since we started to track in 2005, only 9 percent have been on mobile devices, and 2 percent on tablets, with the remainder from desktop or laptop computers. Yet the use of handheld devices to access Digital Himalaya content has increased dramatically over time: in the last year alone, mobile devices accounted for 20 percent of all visits and tablets for 4 percent. Given the increasing penetration of 3G mobile services across the Himalayan region, we can only expect this trend to increase in the coming years. At the same time, we receive as many requests from institutions in

---

[45] Underberg and Zorn, *Digital Ethnography*, 5.

the Global North for offline copies of our collections on hard discs as we do from scholarly institutes in the Himalayan region. Some of our heaviest users download PDF files and films from our website using solar or hydro-powered satellite broadband Internet connections in Himalayan locations that would traditionally be described as "remote," as they have no vehicular access and are not connected to the national electricity grid.

WHAT IS DIGITAL HIMALAYA? CHANGING EXPECTATIONS

As the project has aged and the Internet has matured, I have been interested to observe a slowly changing perception of what Digital Himalaya is and how it works. Is it an "archive" of fieldwork data? If so, by whom is it curated and by what standards and selection process are materials included or excluded for dissemination? Or is Digital Himalaya more of an *archive of an archive*: a constantly mutating, transmigratory, and postmodern "collection of collections"[46] that could never have been brought into conversation other than through a Web interface. What counts as evidence in such a collection? Those of us working in these spaces know, in quite embodied ways, that the form and structure of newer digital media impacts both the subject and the tools of archival practice.[47]

By Web standards, we are now an old project, designed and built before Google was a household name, when 4-megabyte (MB) downloads were still large, and our project team accessed a shared file folder through dial-up modems. Although we have redesigned the website more than once and have increased the size of our media collections as bandwidth has increased, I cannot escape the awkward feeling that our entire collection and approach is still rooted in an earlier, less interactive, and more traditional era of Web technology. A large amount of the correspondence that we receive in the project email inbox comes from scholars looking to publish in one of the many journals that we host online, even though we make it quite clear on our website that we are simply the online hosts, not editors or publishers. But as digital publishing has become the norm, and the front-end delivery of academic content becomes more widespread through open-access initiatives, perhaps we are fulfilling part of the role

---

[46] Bart Harloe and John M. Budd, "Collection Development and Scholarly Communication in the Era of Electronic Access," *The Journal of Academic Librarianship* 20 (May 1994): 83.

[47] Richard Rinehart and Jon Ippolito, *Re-Collection: Art, New Media, and Social Memory* (Cambridge, MA: MIT Press, 2014.), 232.

of publisher, if only through dissemination, so this conflation of roles is to be expected.

As search tools have become more effective and more pervasive, we find that our collections are located, accessed, and downloaded without the user ever visiting or even knowing about our website. A simple search for a map, some census data, or a publication from the Himalayan region may send a prospective user to one of our file servers, bypassing the loose architecture of our website altogether. Although some technologists would perceive this as a problem, we rather view it as an asset: the visibility and discoverability of the data collections hosted by Digital Himalaya have now reached the point that they no longer require the fabric of our original website to facilitate access.

Similarly, we have opted for a redundancy approach to our multimedia collections, which are now housed on University of Cambridge streaming servers, in the University of Virginia's Tibetan and Himalayan Library (THL), and on YouTube. Not only is YouTube a very popular site for streaming videos, but it facilitates the very interaction, feedback, and commentary (in any number of languages) to which we originally aspired and which our own basic website does not permit. Our thinking about the importance of our own interface has changed as standards have emerged over time, and as media sharing sites have come to dominate the market. No longer are we allocating resources to developing sophisticated search-and-retrieval systems or static pages that house image, audio, and video collections. Rather, we are focusing on pushing our content and its associated metadata to the places and platforms where it is most visible and best utilized. This is indicative of a wider reorientation in some digital projects to move away from developing customized and curated interfaces of content collections to a "broadcasting" approach that makes use of free, albeit commercial, platforms to reach the widest possible audience.

THE DIGITAL FUTURE: FROM VULNERABILITY TOWARD SUSTAINABILITY

In the back of my mind, as I finalize this chapter, is my growing sense of unease about the sustainability of digital projects, an unease shared by other commentators working with new media in the digital realm. Serge Abiteboul describes digital "recording formats as more ephemeral than

Sumerian tablets or paper,"[48] while also suggesting that "digitization offers a particular form of immortality."[49] In their 2014 volume *Re-Collection: Art, New Media, and Social Memory*, Richard Rinehart and Jon Ippolito ask readers to reflect on how increasingly digital forms of civilization—in which we would do well to include digital data and evidence—will persist beyond our lifetimes, and argue that the vulnerability of new media art illustrates a larger crisis for social memory. Rinehart and Ippolito's proposed "variable media approach" to new media, with responsibilities distributed between producers and consumers, "encourages creators to define a work in medium-independent terms so that it can be translated into a new medium once its original format is obsolete."[50]

Over Digital Himalaya's twenty-three years, as new standards and possibilities have emerged, I have come to the conclusion that *if* the data and material collections with which we have worked are "safe," however we might define that, then the structure that holds them together should be permitted to decay as new platforms take their place. In this, then, Digital Himalaya may be a simple Buddhist lesson in impermanence and nonattachment to form and structure, letting go of our now quite-dated website so that the collections may live on through a generative process of rebirth and renewal.

Although our current website will in time be retired, the collections that we have helped to digitize have secured a new and permanent (to whatever degree we may use that word in this context) online home within the digital library at the University of British Columbia where I work, through what my colleagues in the library are calling the *Open Collections portal*. As Rinehart and Ippolito note, "new media works are going to need to be managed and migrated on a continual basis."[51] Rather like the phoenix of ancient Greek mythology, I have now come to see—and even appreciate—how, if successful, Digital Himalaya will be cyclically regenerated and reborn, gaining new life by mutating and rising from the ashes of its earlier incarnations. The collections should and, I hope, will endure, while the form in which they are encoded will metamorphose over time and the social work that they do will also likely change. I have had to accept that the digital is just as transient, evanescent, and inconstant as other forms of existence.

---

[48] Serge Abiteboul, "The Digital Shoebox," in *Memory*, eds. Philippe Tortell, Mark Turin, and Margot Young (Vancouver, BC: Peter Wall Institute for Advanced Studies, 2018), 225, www.jstor.org/stable/j.ctvbtzpfm.29.

[49] Ibid., 228.

[50] Rinehart and Ippolito, *Re-Collection*, 11.

[51] Ibid., 233.

CONCLUDING THOUGHTS ON DATA AND
EVIDENCE IN ANTHROPOLOGY

"Events are happenings of social significance,"[52] contends Hastrup. As a corollary, might we then ask whether evidence is data of social significance? Now that the pool of users, consumers, and creators of anthropological content is finally widening to include the descendants of the historical subjects of anthropological scrutiny—the observed and enumerated citizens so problematically referred to as *informants* by our disciplinary ancestors— the very fabric of what constitutes social significance necessarily changes and offers the potential to be more inclusive of previously marginalized and devoiced perspectives.

It is through a similar process of revaluing and broadening, that ethnographic films—previously consigned to the classroom as a babysitting tool for tired or ill instructors—can assume new life. To accomplish this, as Ritchin has said of photographs, one must stop thinking of the visual as objective, authoritative, fixed in frame, or "definitive 'proof.'"[53] Rather, we need to become comfortable in the knowledge that "making images, or being in media, is mediating,"[54] and that digitizing and disseminating images—whether static photographs or moving film—is an incredibly powerful form of remediation that itself can generate a form of "visual citizenship."[55] Seesequasis reminds us that "the story is only a small part of the picture and the picture is only a small part of the story."[56] Such work is also inherently humanistic, "a conversation between what is out there, ourselves, ourselves and other people, ourselves and the past, the future, and so on,"[57] and will always be an endeavor, more than simply "a dialogue among images."[58]

In their very readable *Digital Ethnography: Anthropology, Narrative, and New Media,* Underberg and Zorn outline how anthropologists were "relatively slow to adopt the use of computers as well as to consider the effects of digital technology generally on their field."[59] In the early days of interdisciplinary collaboration, they identify the main question as being: "How much computer science do anthropologists need to know?"[60] What

---

[52] Hastrup, "Ethnographic Present," 49.
[53] Fred Ritchin, "The Web Waits for the Photographer, Too," *Nieman Reports* 52 (Summer 1998): 39.
[54] Dill, "Notes from the Field," 400.
[55] Ibid., 401.
[56] Seesequasis, *Blanket Toss Under Midnight Sun*, 3.
[57] Dill, "Notes from the Field," 400.
[58] Ibid.
[59] Underberg and Zorn, *Digital Ethnography*, 6.
[60] Ibid., 7.

they don't go on to say, but would certainly be what I would ask next, is this: How much anthropology do computer scientists need to know?

ACKNOWLEDGMENTS

I am grateful to Ben Shneiderman for a supportive and critical reading of an early draft of this essay, and to Adrianna Link and Kyle Roberts at the American Philosophical Society for the invitation to participate in the stimulating conference for which this chapter was written and for helping to shepherd it through to publication. My thanks to Michael Eng, Susan Laquer, and Rena Lederman, all of whom asked probing and welcome questions during my Zoom presentation, which helped me in the further development of this contribution, and to the external reviewers of this manuscript whose comments and suggestions have helped flesh out my analysis. I am very grateful to Julia Schillo, who assisted with copy editing and helped prepare the manuscript for submission. Needless to say, all remaining errors and infelicities are my own.

BIBLIOGRAPHY

Abiteboul, Serge. "The Digital Shoebox." In *Memory*, edited by Philippe Tortell, Mark Turin, and Margot Young, 225–32. Vancouver, BC: Peter Wall Institute for Advanced Studies, 2018. www.jstor.org/stable/j.ctvbtzpfm.29.

Banks, Marcus, and Jay Ruby, eds. *Made to be Seen: Perspectives on the History of Visual Anthropology*. Chicago: University of Chicago Press, 2011.

Barth, Fredrik. "An Anthropology of Knowledge." *Current Anthropology* 43, no. 1 (2002): 1–18.

Bell, Joshua A., Kimberly Christen, and Mark Turin. "Introduction: After the Return." *Museum Anthropology Review* 7 (Spring–Fall 2013): 1–21.

Dill, Nandi. "Notes from the Field: An Interview with Fred Ritchin." *Humanity: An International Journal of Human Rights, Humanitarianism, and Development* 4 (Winter 2013): 393–402.

Fabian, Johannes. "Ethnographic Misunderstanding and the Perils of Context." In *The Problem of Context: Perspectives from Social Anthropology and Elsewhere*, edited by R. M. Dilley, 85–104. New York: Berghahn Books, 1999.

Fürer-Haimendorf, Christoph von. *Life Among Indian Tribes: The Autobiography of an Anthropologist*. Delhi: Oxford University Press, 1990.

———. *The Men Who Hunted Heads—The Nagas of Assam*. London: British Broadcasting Corporation, 1971. Filmstrip, 50 min.

———. *Travellers' Tales: The Land of the Gurkhas*. London: British Broadcasting Corporation, 1957. Filmstrip, 1200 ft.

Harloe, Bart, and John M. Budd. "Collection Development and Scholarly Communication in the Era of Electronic Access." *The Journal of Academic Librarianship* 20 (May 1994): 83–87.

Hastrup, Kirsten. "The Ethnographic Present: A Reinvention." *Cultural Anthropology* 5 (February 1990): 45–61.

———. "Getting It Right: Knowledge and Evidence in Anthropology." *Anthropological Theory* 4, no. 4 (2004): 455–72.

Jasanoff, Sheila, ed. *States of Knowledge: The Co-production of Science and Social Order*. London: Routledge, 2004.

Jenkins, Timothy. "Fieldwork and the Perception of Everyday Life." *Man* 29 (June 1994): 433–55.

Knorr-Cetina, Karin D. *The Manufacture of Knowledge: An Essay on the Constructivist and Contextual Nature of Science*. Oxford: Pergamon, 1981.

Lévi-Strauss, Claude. *Le Cru et le cuit*. Vol. 1 of *Mythologiques*. Paris: Plon, 1964.

Macfarlane, Alan. "Early Ethnographic Film in Britain: A Reflection on the Work of Christoph von Fürer-Haimendorf." *Visual Anthropology* 23, no. 5 (2010): 375–97.

Peers, Laura L., and Alison K. Brown, eds. *Museums and Source Communities: A Routledge Reader*. London: Routledge, 2003.

Pels, Peter, Igor Boog, J. Henrike Florusbosch, Zane Kripe, Tessa Minter, Metje Postma, Margaret Sleeboom-Faulkner, Bob Simpson, Hansjörg Dilger, Michael Schönhuth, Anita von Poser, Rosa Cordillera A. Castillo, Rena Lederman, and Heather Richards-Rissetto. "Data Management in Anthropology: The Next Phase in Ethics Governance?" *Social Anthropology* 26, no. 3 (2018): 391–413. doi: 10.1111/1469-8676.12526.

Rinehart, Richard, and Jon Ippolito. *Re-Collection: Art, New Media, and Social Memory*. Cambridge, MA: MIT Press, 2014.

Ritchin, Fred. "The Web Waits for the Photographer, Too." *Nieman Reports* 52 (Summer 1998): 38–39.

Scott, Joan W. "The Evidence of Experience." *Critical Inquiry* 17 (Summer 1991): 773–97.

Seesequasis, Paul. *Blanket Toss under Midnight Sun: Portraits of Everyday Life in Eight Indigenous Communities*. Toronto: Knopf Canada, 2019.

Shapin, Steven. *A Social History of Truth: Civility and Science in Seventeenth-Century England*. Chicago: University of Chicago Press, 1994.

Shneiderman, Sara, and Mark Turin. "Digital Himalaya: An Ethnographic Archive in the Digital Age." In *Interarchive: Archival Practices and Sites in the Contemporary Art Field*, edited by Beatrice von Bismarck, Hans-Peter Feldmann, Hans Ulrich Obrist, Diethelm Stoller, and Ulf Wuggenig, 359–61. Cologne: Verlag der Buchhandlung Walter König, 2002.

Snow, C. P. *The Two Cultures: And a Second Look: An Expanded Version of The Two Cultures and the Scientific Revolution*. New York: New American Library, 1963.

Turin, Mark. "Born Archival: The Ebb and Flow of Digital Documents from the Field." *History and Anthropology* 22 (December 2011): 445–60.

———. "Salvaging the Records of Salvage Ethnography: The Story of the Digital Himalaya Project." *Book 2.0* 1, no. 1 (2012): 39–46.

———. "The Unexpected Afterlives of Himalayan Collections: From Data Cemetery to Web Portal." In *The Anthropology of Expeditions: Travel, Visualities, Afterlives*, edited by Joshua A. Bell and Erin L. Hasinoff, 242–68. New York: Bard Graduate Center, 2015.

Underberg, Natalie M., and Elayne Zorn. *Digital Ethnography: Anthropology, Narrative, and New Media*. Austin: University of Texas Press, 2013.

Chapter 9

Historical Evidence, Artificial Intelligence, and the Black Box Effect

Joshua Sternfeld

> First, I conclude that in considering COMPAS (or other risk assessment tools) in sentencing, a circuit court must set forth on the record a meaningful process of reasoning addressing the relevance, strengths, and weaknesses of the risk assessment tool.
>
> Second, this court's lack of understanding of COMPAS was a significant problem in the instant case. At oral argument, the court repeatedly questioned both the State's and defendant's counsel about how COMPAS works. Few answers were available.[1]

On July 13, 2016, the Supreme Court of Wisconsin issued its decision for *State v. Loomis*, a case that placed an algorithmic risk assessment tool called *COMPAS (Correctional Offender Management Profiling for Alternative Sanctions)* in the spotlight. COMPAS had been used to assess the defendant's recidivism risk, and the trial raised questions about the algorithmic methods the tool employed to reach its determination. The specifics of the case are explored further in this chapter, but for the moment, it is worth noting the uncertainty expressed in the epigraph by one of the majority justices, Shirley S. Abrahamson. The court, tasked with evaluating the "relevance, strengths, and weaknesses" of COMPAS raised questions about how it functioned, only to receive "few answers." For reasons unexplained, the court also denied a request by the developer of COMPAS, Northpointe, to file an amicus brief "to discuss the history, accuracy, and

---

[1] *State v. Loomis*, 881 NW 2d 749 (2016).

efficacy of COMPAS, as well as the use of risk assessment tools like COMPAS throughout the criminal justice system." This amicus brief, according to Justice Abrahamson, could have gone a long way to alleviate confusion, misinformation, and misunderstanding.

The Justice's expression of frustration is but one example of a familiar exchange with artificial intelligence (AI) systems. AI systems work by seamlessly recommending products to purchase or articles to read, diagnosing cancerous tumors, or identifying criminal suspects through facial recognition. But trying to understand how these systems operate, why they seem to know just the right song to play next, or why they unexpectedly mistook a cat for a wolf, requires evidence that is typically elusive to obtain. The Wisconsin court confronted a black box, a term commonly applied to AI systems whose processes or data are rendered invisible to human observation. The malleable term denotes a system's inscrutability—that is, the system's actions or its underlying data, which are used for training and operational purposes, are either inaccessible or uninterpretable by humans.[2]

I propose that the court's experience with the COMPAS black box can serve as a proxy for the challenges historians will face in studying this age of artificial intelligence, an era marked by algorithmically fueled historical change at all levels of society. Researching any number of topics, whether in commerce, medicine, communication, criminal justice, the military, the arts, or a host of other sociopolitical and cultural concerns, will undoubtedly require historicizing one or more AI systems. But how should historians establish historical context when critical evidence depends on big data sets generated by systems that are often hidden from public scrutiny, or so massive as to inhibit reliable interpretation? Historicization will demand, to borrow language from the court's decision, analysis of the "relevance, strengths, and weaknesses" of the system. Often, however, historians—like the historical actors they are studying—will encounter the black box phenomenon, an epistemological void marked by the absence of evidence. Like the court, historians will face inaccessible evidence due to a combination of technical, social, cultural, and legal factors beyond one's direct control.

This chapter considers in four sections the historicization of AI systems as black boxes. The first section frames the issue as a problem identifying

---

[2] Zachary C. Lipton, "The Mythos of Model Interpretability. ArXiv Preprint ArXiv: 160603490," last modified March 6, 2017, https://doi.org/10.48550/arXiv.1606.03490; Mike Ananny and Kate Crawford, "Seeing without Knowing: Limitations of the Transparency Ideal and Its Application to Algorithmic Accountability," *New Media & Society* 20, no. 3 (2018): 973–89; and Dan McQuillan, "Data Science as Machinic Neoplatonism," *Philosophy & Technology* 31, no. 2 (2018): 253–72.

and interpreting historical evidence within algorithmic cultures. Unlike earlier scientific epistemic cultures, algorithmic cultures are defined by a deliberate attempt to obfuscate their knowability, which contributes to a crisis of epistemology. To date, researchers have attempted to overcome this epistemological gap via sociological studies that typically overlook longitudinal historical analysis. I address algorithmic black boxes as historical phenomena by accepting their opaqueness as a feature worthy of study. Historical actors, and the historians studying them, may lack access to the data and algorithmic source code fueling an AI system's operations. To compensate for this epistemological gap, we must study the evidentiary traces generated by the network of human and algorithmic agents alike, including experiences with the system's black box properties, what I define as the *black box effect*. The black box effect manifests itself during expressions of confusion, disorientation, or frustration by users or onlookers of algorithmic systems, followed by behavioral, material, policy, or other adaptive responses.

The next two sections apply the theoretical framework described in the first to the aforementioned *State v. Loomis*, a federal appeal of a 2013 Wisconsin criminal sentencing that challenged the efficacy of a controversial recidivism risk assessment tool. The authorities involved—judges, criminologists, lawyers, and municipal officers—confronted the algorithmic tool's interpretation of data derived from prior arrest records. Although perhaps not fully able to articulate their concerns at the time, their confusion stemmed from how criminal data had been severed from their original social context.

My historical analysis of *State v. Loomis*, which considers the circumstances of the trial, the data and functionality of COMPAS, and how the tool was implemented in the Wisconsin criminal justice system, demonstrates a sociotechnical approach to historicizing an AI system. The court case serves as a prime example of how AI systems *de*contextualize data upon input, and then *re*contextualize data through their outputs. In other words, via opaque machine-learning algorithms, these systems selectively appropriate data from the past and interpret them, much like an historian would interpret evidence. Those conducting the legal examination of the recidivism tool were unable to obtain access to critical data or core algorithms that, at least in theory, could have brought additional clarity to this contextualizing process. The frustration derived from a perceived lack of access, what I call the *black box effect*, influenced the judicial response and its reception. The black box effect introduces a paradox for historians: algorithmically produced data and outcomes are often beyond the ability of historical actors to interpret them, yet it is the circumstances surrounding their un-interpretability that warrants their consideration as historical evidence.

What is at stake with the historicization of AI systems as black boxes is defining historical agency for a class of technologies that, with varying degrees of autonomy, interprets reality distinct from its human counterparts. Those involved with the court case wanted to know the extent to which the sentencing decisions were plausibly influenced by the algorithmic tool's analysis of the defendant's criminal record. Did the tool merely reflect the sentencing judge's independent decision, or did it provide a nudge toward determining the severity of the sentence? Drawing that line between human and machinic agency is always fraught with underlying contexts, especially when accounting for potential algorithmic bias. Academic and media studies of algorithmic recidivism tools like COMPAS have focused on their troubling reinforcement of long-standing racism within the criminal justice system.[3] Often what is overlooked are the nonempirical sociocultural contexts associated with the tool's application by various users, such as correctional officers within the Wisconsin Department of Corrections.

In the concluding fourth section, I propose that comprehensive consideration of AI systems warrants a historical methodology capable of addressing the complex distribution of agency across a human–nonhuman network. Foremost, such a method must attend to epistemological gaps created by inaccessible evidence. A method for historicizing AI systems' characteristic black box features facilitates the representation of historical change over time and the extent to which in any given situation we can attribute causality to a system. To clarify, I am not advocating that we fill the evidential void created by an algorithmic black box by somehow "decoding" the black box, a task rendered nearly impossible by any number of social, computational, political, or commercial limitations. Rather, the historicization of AI systems must account for the experiential responses by historical agents who interact with these systems as black boxes. To overcome the problems created by the absence or inscrutability of algorithmic data as evidence, historians must approach the black box effect as a unique category of historical evidence.

---

[3] See, among many other examples, Sonja B. Starr, "Evidence-Based Sentencing and the Scientific Rationalization of Discrimination," *Stanford Law Review* 66, no. 4 (2014): 82; and Julia Angwin et al., "Machine Bias," *ProPublica* (2016), https://www.propublica.org/article/machine-bias-risk-assessments-in-criminal-sentencing.

THE PROBLEM IDENTIFYING AND INTERPRETING HISTORICAL EVIDENCE WITHIN ALGORITHMIC CULTURES

AI systems[4] represent a class of technological agents that see, model, and interpret the world distinct from humans. When a facial recognition system identifies a potential criminal, or a program diagnoses a patient with cancer, questions abound as to how the system generated its response, and whether those responses remain consistent across multiple-use contexts. Ideally, we should be able to evaluate AI systems' trustworthiness by interrogating their data and computational processes. Unfortunately, as AI technologies have developed at lightning speed, our ability to comprehend their knowledge production has lagged.[5] They possess their own idiosyncrasies fashioned as hermeneutic engines that selectively draw on data and arrive at decisions in ways that even elude their developers.[6]

How then do we resolve the hermeneutic inscrutability of AI systems? At first glance, Knorr-Cetina's work on epistemic cultures in the sciences offers a multifaceted methodology for examining scientific knowledge production as a "kaleidoscope" of empirical, technological, and social machineries with one significant difference: An assumption of trust and willingness to share knowledge outcomes accompanies the communities she studies. The ethnographic and historical study of artificial intelligence, on the other hand, poses a unique set of epistemic challenges distinct from the scientific cultures examined by Knorr-Cetina. Machine learning operates according to its own science—data science—which McQuillan characterizes as "not simply a method but an organising idea," one that "resonates with a belief

---

[4] According to Crawford, AI systems encompass the entirety of the material, technical, commercial, political, and cultural infrastructure network, everything from the hardware designed to process and transmit data, sensors to gather data, to the executives, lawyers, data curators, users, and a bevy of other actors who participate within the network. Seaver adds to these infrastructural matters by proposing a critical ethnographic approach that views algorithms as constructed heterogeneous sociotechnical systems that constantly change over time. Together, these definitions inform my approach to developing a methodology for historicizing AI systems. Kate Crawford, *The Atlas of AI: Power, Politics, and the Planetary Costs of Artificial Intelligence* (New Haven, CT: Yale University Press, 2021); Nick Seaver, "Knowing Algorithms," in *DigitalSTS: A Field Guide for Science & Technology Studies*, eds. Janet Vertesi and David Ribes (Princeton, NJ: Princeton University Press, 2019).

[5] Campolo and Crawford suggest that even some of AI's top scientists and researchers employ "enchanted determinism," which they define as a "discourse that presents deep learning techniques as magical, outside the scope of present scientific knowledge, yet also deterministic, in that deep learning systems can nonetheless detect patterns that give unprecedented access to people's identities, emotions and social character." Alexander Campolo and Kate Crawford, "Enchanted Determinism: Power without Responsibility in Artificial Intelligence," *Engaging Science, Technology, and Society* 6 (2020): 3.

[6] Gary Marcus, "Deep Learning: A Critical Appraisal," *arXiv preprint arXiv:1801.00631*, January 2, 2018, https://doi.org/10.48550/arXiv.1801.00631.

in a hidden mathematical order that is ontologically superior to the one available to our everyday senses."[7] AI systems replace the confined space of the laboratory for the disorderly real world, oftentimes enacting experiments without users' knowledge or conscious consent.[8] McQuillan suggests that "by providing actionable numbers with the aura of authority ... algorithmic predictions become forceful at a human level."[9] The more AI systems interpret data gathered from real-world circumstances, the more they obtain agency, that is, the ability to effect change. The result, as Mackenzie describes, is a romanticized notion that machine learning algorithms can achieve "epistemic order" from "unruly, messy, mixed or 'dirty' data."[10]

What distinguishes algorithmic cultures from other scientific epistemic cultures, is that algorithmic cultures *intentionally* obfuscate their methods and access to data, what is typically referred to as a *black box*. Carabantes suggests that corporations and governments hide their systems' methods in order to maintain security and competitiveness, which, according to Striphas, leads to "the gradual abandonment of culture's publicness and thus the emergence of a new breed of elite culture purporting to be its opposite."[11] Altogether, the inability to explain an AI system's interpretability, combined with the deliberate obfuscation of algorithmic techniques, create what Roberge and Castelle describe as a "crisis of epistemology and ontology."[12] In other words, the black box is a feature of AI, rather than a bug.

Although the term *black box* may have predated his work,[13] Latour nonetheless used the concept to great effect by integrating "non-human" innovations, such as the Kodak camera, within social relations.[14] His actor–network theory has provided a useful framework for scholars studying the

[7] McQuillan, "Data Science as Machinic Neoplatonism," 254.

[8] Seaver, "Knowing Algorithms," 415–16.

[9] McQuillan, "Data Science as Machinic Neoplatonism," 263.

[10] Adrian Mackenzie, "The Production of Prediction: What Does Machine Learning Want?" *European Journal of Cultural Studies* 18, nos. 4–5 (2015), 436.

[11] Manuel Carabantes, "Black-Box Artificial Intelligence: An Epistemological and Critical Analysis," *AI & Society* 35, no. 2 (2020): 309–17; Ted Striphas, "Algorithmic Culture," *European Journal of Cultural Studies* 18, nos. 4-5 (2015), 397.

[12] Jonathan Roberge and Michael Castelle, "Toward an End-to-End Sociology of 21st-Century Machine Learning," in *The Cultural Life of Machine Learning: An Incursion into Critical AI Studies*, eds. Jonathan Roberge and Michael Castelle (Cham, Switzerland; Palgrave Macmillan, 2020).

[13] Taina Bucher, "Neither Black Nor Box: Ways of Knowing Algorithms," in *Innovative Methods in Media and Communication Research*, eds. Sebastian Kubitschko and Anne Kaun (Cham, Switzerland: Springer International Publishing, 2016).

[14] Bruno Latour, "Technology Is Society Made Durable," in *The Sociological Review* 38, no. 1 Suppl. (1990): 103–31; *Reassembling the Social: An Introduction to Actor-Network-Theory* (Oxford: Oxford University Press, 2008).

sociological relations within algorithmic systems.[15] It is true that we may never have access to the underlying algorithms driving Facebook's News Feed, or Google's search algorithm, but scholars in emerging areas, such as critical data studies and critical algorithmic studies, profess that this should not inhibit their study.[16] Rauer argues that algorithms, even those that predate the digital turn, advance technological objects, such as those highlighted by Latour, in their agential potential by "mobilizing and activating objects," which introduces a type of autonomy "that is embedded in interaction and infrastructures."[17] Indeed, as the proceeding case study illuminates, the idea of an algorithmic system's (semi-) autonomy is one of the primary driving forces behind the anxiety and uncertainty expressed by the human actors. Bucher has further translated and updated Latour's work for algorithmic cultures, calling on us not to "fear" the black box but to face it head on by proposing a "technographic" methodology that considers sources external to the algorithm, such as technical specifications, press releases, conference papers, and other documents. My work builds on Bucher's call to disregard the "'impossibility of seeing inside the black box' as an epistemological limit" and to place black boxes within "a specific historical context," one in which "they evolve, have histories, change, affect, and are affected by what they are articulated to."[18]

The proliferation of work on algorithmic systems in the social sciences and increasingly the humanities, therefore, has assembled a methodological road map, but one that has not yet faced head on the epistemic issues tied to historical evidence. Current AI studies employing social science methodologies typically arrange experiments with contemporaneous versions of services such as YouTube, Facebook, or Netflix. But what happens when historians want to study an earlier iteration of an AI system, or trace the permutations of a system over time? What kinds of access to historical evidence will be available, assuming that the original algorithms and data

---

[15] Lucas D. Introna, "The Enframing of Code: Agency, Originality and the Plagiarist," *Theory, Culture & Society* 28, no. 6 (2011): 113–41; Oliver Leistert, "Social Bots as Algorithmic Pirates and Messengers of Techno-Environmental Agency," in *Algorithmic Cultures: Essays on Meaning, Performance and New Technologies* (London: Routledge, Taylor & Francis, 2016).

[16] The literature in these areas is too vast to summarize here. The following works were particularly influential in my thinking: Tarleton Gillespie, "The Relevance of Algorithms," in *Media Technologies: Essays on Communication, Materiality, and Society* (Cambridge, MA: MIT Press, 2014), 167–93; Andrew Iliadis and Federica Russo, "Critical Data Studies: An Introduction," *Big Data & Society* 3, no. 2 (2016): 1–7; Robert Seyfert and Jonathan Roberge, "What Are Algorithmic Cultures?" in *Algorithmic Cultures: Essays on Meaning, Performance and New Technologies*, eds. Robert Seyfert and Jonathan Roberge (London: Routledge, Taylor & Francis, 2016), 1–25.

[17] Valentin Rauer, "Drones," in *Algorithmic Cultures*, eds. Seyfert and Roberge, 153.

[18] Bucher, "Neither Black Nor Box."

are, and always have been, partially or entirely inaccessible? As the contemporary moment recedes into the past, historians need increasingly creative solutions for studying how a system functions within a human–nonhuman network. In the age of artificial intelligence, where secrecy and obfuscation reign, what even constitutes historical evidence? Where do we locate it, and how do we know we have found what we are looking for? From a historical perspective, the crisis of epistemology can be reframed as a crisis of evidence.

The path going forward begins by identifying evidentiary "traces," those elusive fragments that Ginzburg's body of work eloquently explores. "Historian's knowledge," wrote Ginzburg, "like the doctor's, is indirect, based on signs and scraps of evidence, conjectural."[19] AI systems may lack transparency to the finer points of their operation, yet at every point of an interaction between human and non-human agents, evidentiary traces are created, from the data fed into an AI system, to the system outputs, to the human responses that arise from those outputs.[20] Shaw proposes that the traces left behind by big data software systems represent more than "transactions" that can point to the scientific study of human behavior. Rather, he argues, they represent the "traces left by past engagements."[21] In some instances, the evidence of historical interest is generated by the systems themselves, whereas in other instances, the human interactions with the systems are of most interest. Evidentiary traces appear as an assortment of documentary and material formats historians are accustomed to handling—audiovisual content, government reports, court cases, and academic scholarship—although in other instances, they may appear in novel formats such as raw data sets, computational formulas, proprietary technologies, and technical articles written by data scientists. Much like the historical testimonies, or "any text," to which Ginzburg referred, the trace evidence left behind in the wake of an AI system creates "opaque zones," referents of a black box that are worthy of study.

There is still the question about how to analyze data used and generated by the AI system, such as its training data set, as historical evidence. The temptation would be to assemble as a starting point an analytic portrait of the underlying training data and source code of the system. Crawford's suggestive genealogy of ImageNet, the data set of millions of images attrib-

---

[19] Carlo Ginzburg and Anna Davin, "Morelli, Freud and Sherlock Holmes: Clues and Scientific Method," *History Workshop* 9 (1980): 16.

[20] The pragmatic, relativist approach that my work takes when considering the study of human–nonhuman networks is very much informed by Ananny and Crawford's framework to problematize algorithmic transparency. Ananny and Crawford, "Seeing Without Knowing."

[21] Ryan Shaw, "Big Data and Reality," *Big Data & Society* 2, no. 2 (2015). 3.

uted with revolutionizing AI image recognition in the 2010s, demonstrates that in some instances this may be possible and certainly preferable.[22] Gebru, Morgenstern, et al. propose that "datasheets" ought to accompany data sets employed by an algorithmic system that documents the data sets' "motivation, composition, collection process, [and] recommended uses."[23] In reality, most data sets—including the data set used to calibrate COMPAS—lack such information, or the information that is provided is insufficient to establishing proper sociocultural context.[24] Assembling some version of a datasheet for an AI system's training data set often poses a Sisyphean undertaking. The same interests protecting proprietary software and data also inhibit their systematic preservation,[25] and without long-term access to such information, a systematic historical analysis appears futile.

Given the absence of certain types of data that could be used as historical evidence, I propose historicizing the black box properties of AI systems. Such an approach follows McQuillan's suggestion to treat data science as "agential realism," that is, to "see it not as a description of a hidden layer of reality, but to understand it as part of the *production of reality*."[26] An AI system's black box nature, in other words, cannot be separated from its other relational and active features. When human agents interact and respond to algorithmic systems, they generally do not respond with knowledge of the system's underlying data or permutations. Rather, users of systems, whether consciously or not, engage with the systems as black boxes, as mysterious agents that seem to think and behave in predictable—or sometimes unpredictable— ways, not unlike the perceived "ghosts" within pre-twentieth-century automata identified by Jones-Imhotep.[27] The changes or results that arise from engagement with the black

---

[22] Crawford traces ImageNet's roots to the Brown Corpus of one million words published in 1961. Crawford, *Atlas of AI*, 98.

[23] Timnit Gebru et al., "Datasheets for Datasets," *Communications of the ACM* 64, no. 12 (2021): 86–92. See also Michelle Bao et al., "It's COMPASlicated: The Messy Relationship between RAI Datasets and Algorithmic Fairness Benchmarks," *arXiv preprint arXiv:2106.05498*, last modified April 28, 2022, https://doi.org/10.48550/arXiv.2106.05498.

[24] The following study examined data set annotations for facial recognition systems, but their findings, which concluded that the majority of systems lacked a nuanced sociohistorical understanding of key areas of identification such as race and gender, could easily apply to other algorithmic systems. Morgan Klaus Scheuerman et al., "How We've Taught Algorithms to See Identity: Constructing Race and Gender in Image Databases for Facial Analysis," *Proceedings of the ACM on Human–Computer Interaction* 4, no. CSCW1 (2020): 1–35.

[25] Clifford Lynch, "Stewardship in the 'Age of Algorithms,'" *First Monday* 22, no. 12. (2017), http://dx.doi.org/10.5210/fm.v22i12.8097.

[26] McQuillan, "Data Science as Machinic Neoplatonism," 268 (emphasis added).

[27] Edward Jones-Imhotep, "The Ghost Factories: Histories of Automata and Artificial Life," *History and Technology* 36, no. 1 (2020): 3–29.

box properties of an AI system constitute what I'm calling *the black box effect.*

The following case study presents a microhistory that lays out the pursuit and interpretation of AI-generated evidence by authorities in all their messiness, both in terms of obtaining data and interpreting a system's outputs. It presents a discrete, concrete event—a trial—that lends itself to considering the process of gathering and interpreting evidence, as well as the stumbling blocks that occurred along the way. The choice to frame the problem of evidence in algorithmic cultures using the microhistory format is done both out of pragmatism, but also as an acknowledgment that historians may not yet be prepared to tackle the multidimensional possibilities of AI systems that operate at vast, often global, scales.

STATE VERSUS LOOMIS

On July 23, 2013, after being convicted of participating in a drive-by shooting on February 11, Eric Loomis participated in an hour-long interview for a presentence investigation administered by the Wisconsin Department of Corrections. The interviewer asked Loomis a series of questions related to his criminal history, upbringing, and current living conditions. Many of the questions posed to Loomis were "static," that is, the information in-cluded factual statements, such as how many times Loomis had been returned to custody while on parole or how many times he had been arrested as a juvenile or adult. Other questions addressed "dynamic" factors—areas that could potentially be correctable with services or treatment—such as Loomis's criminal associates and history of substance abuse.[28]

The interview data, combined with Loomis's criminal file, contributed to a 137-question "core assessment"[29] fed into a risk and needs analysis (RNA) tool developed by the private company Northpointe, Inc. called *COMPAS.* COMPAS generated a report with an accompanying set of three

---

[28] *State v. Loomis.* A definition of static and dynamic factors was retrieved from National Center for State Courts and Center for Sentencing Initiatives, "NCSC Fact Sheet: Evidence-Based Sentencing," 2014, https://www.ncsc.org/__data/assets/pdf_file/0018/25290/ebs-fact-sheet-8-27-14.pdf. For a full breakdown of Wisconsin's presentence investigation process, including guidance on how to use COMPAS to conduct the investigation, see State of Wisconsin. "Presentence Investigations," *Electronic Case Reference Manual* (Madison, WI: Department of Corrections, 2020 accessed July 2022), https://doc.wi.gov/GuidanceDocumentsV2/Reentry/OOS_Electronic%20Case%20Reference%20Manual.pdf.

[29] As part of its investigation examining potential racial disparities in COMPAS risk assessments as applied to offenders in Broward County, Florida, ProPublica obtained a sample COMPAS Risk Assessment survey, which purportedly used as its scale set the "Wisconsin Core-Community Language." The authenticity or original source of the document could not be verified. The document was uploaded to the publicly accessible site Document Cloud: *https://www.documentcloud.org/documents/2702103-Sample-Risk-Assessment-COMPAS-CORE.html.* Angwin et al., "Machine Bias."

bar graphs that assisted the corrections officer in preparing an overall recidivism risk assessment. On a scale of one to ten, the three bars measured Loomis's pretrial recidivism risk, general recidivism risk, and violent recidivism risk, and all three rated Loomis as "high risk." On August 12, 2013, Loomis stood before a Wisconsin circuit court judge to receive his sentencing. After summarizing at length Loomis's troubled upbringing and recent arrest record, the judge added:

> You're identified, through the COMPAS assessment, as an individual who is at high risk to the community. In terms of weighing the various factors, I'm ruling out probation because of the seriousness of the crime and because your history, your history on supervision, *and the risk assessment tools that have been utilized*, suggest that your [sic] extremely high risk to re-offend.[30]

Shortly thereafter, the judge issued a severe sentence based on the risk he believed Loomis posed to the community: six years of initial confinement and five years of extended supervision for "fleeing and operating a vehicle without the owner's consent."[31]

Loomis filed an appeal for a resentencing, arguing that the judge appeared to rely on the COMPAS score to determine his sentence. Loomis contended that he had no basis for challenging the accuracy of the algorithmically generated risk score produced by COMPAS, which he argued "violates a defendant's right to due process, either because the proprietary nature of COMPAS prevents defendants from challenging the COMPAS assessment's scientific validity, or because COMPAS assessments take gender into account."[32] Loomis's appeals eventually reached the Wisconsin Supreme Court, which rejected the case on both counts. The U.S. Supreme Court declined to hear the case, thereby upholding the state supreme court's final motion. The series of decisions signaled that Loomis could not mount an evidentiary case to prove that COMPAS, and not the judge, was the determining factor in his sentencing.

COMPAS is classified as a fourth-generation actuarial tool based on its use of advanced algorithms to predict criminal outcomes.[33] The tool

---

[30] Brief filed in opposition. *Loomis v. Wisconsin*, 137 S. Ct. 2290 (2017). No. 16-6387 4 (Supreme Court 2017). https://www.scotusblog.com/case-files/cases/loomis-v-wisconsin/, 4 (emphasis added).

[31] Ibid.

[32] *State v. Loomis.*

[33] Correctional assessment dates to the 1920s, and the previous three generations marked the transition from reliance on clinical judgment to more empirical methods that assimilated additional criminogenic factors and social theories. By the mid-1990s, the fourth generation of tools, including COMPAS, incorporated a "broader selection of explanatory theories … [and] range of risk and need factors … [and] more advanced statistical modeling," among other elements. Tim Brennan, William Dieterich, and Beate Ehret. "Evaluating the Predictive Validity of the COMPAS Risk and Needs Assessment System," *Criminal Justice and Behavior* 36, no. 1 (2009): 22.

was originally designed to assist corrections departments' allocation of resources by forecasting which cases might pose higher risk, and the risk scores were not intended to "determine the severity of [a] sentence or whether an offender [ought to be] incarcerated."[34] Over time, however, local judicial systems turned to COMPAS to produce a general recidivism risk score, which was generated by isolating twenty-one questions of the core assessment focusing on an offender's criminal history, criminal associates, drug involvement, and early indicators of juvenile delinquency. The violent recidivism risk score used a different set of factors, including history of violence, history of noncompliance, vocational/educational problems, the person's age at intake, and the person's age at first arrest.[35] Loomis contended that by referencing COMPAS in his sentencing hearing, the judge had violated the tool's explicit intended use. He did not dispute the factuality of the data submitted to COMPAS, including his presentence investigation interview responses or the information in his criminal file. Rather, Loomis challenged his inability to assess how COMPAS interpreted his data and determined the risk he posed to the community.

In *State v. Loomis*, the Wisconsin Supreme Court reached an epistemic roadblock in its evaluation of the tool when Northpointe denied access to its proprietary algorithm and the training data used to calibrate the algorithm on the basis that the algorithm was a "trade secret"; as mentioned earlier, the company offered to provide an amicus brief outlining the history of COMPAS and its accuracy, which the court rejected.[36] Although full access to the algorithm is not available, we do know from public documents certain algorithmic features that convey in broad strokes how it functions. According to the COMPAS *Practitioner's Guide*, the algorithm employed regression modeling that assigned weights to data points collected in the core assessment.[37] However, those weightings are arguably less critical than having access to the training data on which the formula had been calibrated. This process of calibration—known as *fitting* the data—determined whether COMPAS functioned at an acceptable level of accuracy in predicting recidivism.[38] Loomis asserted that COMPAS generated a score based on an undefined normative group of criminals and therefore exposed

---

[34] *State v. Loomis.*

[35] "Brief of Plaintiff-Respondent." *State v. Loomis.*

[36] *State v. Loomis.*

[37] According to the Northpointe's *Practitioner's Guide*, "The methods used to develop both [the General Recidivism and Violent Recidivism Risk Scales] are described in various books on regression modeling and machine learning" (Northpointe Inc. 2015), http://www.northpointeinc.com/downloads/compas/Practitioners-Guide-COMPAS-Core-_031915.pdf.

[38] Jessica M. Eaglin, "Constructing Recidivism Risk," *Emory Law Journal* 67, no. 1 (2017): 59–122.

him to indeterminate biases. At the time, COMPAS had not yet been normed using Wisconsin data, and according to the Wisconsin Department of Corrections, was not normed until February 2016, nearly three years after his sentencing.[39]

An actuarial tool, such as COMPAS, relies on data compiled by police departments, courts, jails, and corrections departments, all of which potentially carry an assortment of biases, racial or otherwise. Even something as basic as defining *recidivism* can have substantial consequences for calculating risk scores.[40] Courts are constitutionally prohibited from basing their sentencing explicitly on race. The core assessment needn't ask directly for an offender's race, however, to be racially biased. For instance, an individual's vocational education, age at first arrest, criminal associates, drug involvement, or juvenile delinquency all contribute to what Benjamin characterizes as the "New Jim Code."[41] The societal biases are already baked into the data, which are then accentuated and objectified by COMPAS. A self-perpetuating data feedback loop is created in which minorities are disproportionately arrested, arrest data then informs the calibration of the actuarial tool, and the tool disproportionately classifies minorities as high risk.[42]

In Loomis's case, it should be noted, the charge of discrimination was directed toward gender, not race. Loomis claimed that in addition to denying an opportunity to challenge the COMPAS risk assessment's methodology, the instrument also violated his due process because it accounted for gender in formulating its risk assessment. In theory, if men

---

[39] "Appendix A: Assessment Considerations." Wisconsin, *Electronic Case Reference Manual*. Madison, WI: Department of Corrections, 2020, 169, https://doc.wi.gov/GuidanceDocumentsV2/DCC/DCC_ECRM%20Employment%20Verification12.09.2019.pdf. The Department of Corrections *Electronic Case Reference Manual* is periodically reviewed and updated. I have elected to use the version created November 2019 and approved by the DOC Reentry Director February 2020. Although the document is dated 2019/2020, the footer indicates the manual was copyrighted in 2012, which suggests most of the information was prepared prior to the Loomis case.

[40] Pamela M. Casey, Roger K. Warren, and Jennifer K. Elek, *Using Offender Risk and Needs Assessment Information at Sentencing: Guidance for Courts from a National Working Group* (Williamsburg, VA: Center for State Courts, 2011), https://www.ncsc.org/__data/assets/pdf_file/0019/25174/rna-guide-final.pdf.

[41] Noble makes a similar argument when she discusses how biases in algorithms form a new kind of "technological redlining." Ruha Benjamin, *Race after Technology: Abolitionist Tools for the New Jim Code* (Cambridge, UK: Polity Press, 2019); Safiya Umoja Noble, *Algorithms of Oppression: How Search Engines Reinforce Racism* (New York: NYU Press, 2018). See also Catherine D'Ignazio and Lauren F. Klein, *Data Feminism* (Cambridge, MA: MIT Press, 2020).

[42] In a succinct yet damning portrait of criminal justice tools, Eckhouse et al. argue that "[t]he problem of biased policing data…is much bigger than one vendor's model. The data used to build these models carry bias with it, and the models then learn and launder the bias. This is true for all criminal justice uses of data, as well as other algorithms that target ads, hire employees, and offer credit." Laurel Eckhouse et al., "Layers of Bias: A Unified Approach for Understanding Problems with Risk Assessment," *Criminal Justice and Behavior* 46, no. 2 (2019): 204.

tended to pose a higher recidivism risk than women, then the fact that Loomis was male could indeterminately inflate his overall score. The court dismissed Loomis's claim of gender bias, citing evidence that Northpointe developed a modified version of COMPAS for women, which, the company argued, reduced, rather than elevated, the potential for gender bias.[43] Regardless of the outcome, Loomis's bias charge alerted the state supreme court to the inaccessibility of the COMPAS algorithm and its data.

The Wisconsin Supreme Court's primary task was to ascertain whether Loomis's sentencing judge "relied" on, or merely "considered," the risk assessment score for his ruling. Did the COMPAS readout compel the judge to deliver a harsher sentence, or did it merely reflect what was already apparent from other pretrial information? In short, did the judge or the tool govern Loomis's sentence? The questions are indicative of the black box effect. Although the state supreme court ultimately ruled that the COMPAS score had no bearing on the sentence, the final motion conveyed the court's uncertainty. Justice Shirley S. Abrahamson's opinion, quoted at the opening of this chapter, admitted that the court's "lack of understanding of COMPAS was a significant problem in the instant case." The Wisconsin Supreme Court's analysis of COMPAS notably did not consider a direct explanation of the algorithm or its training data set. In the judges' opinion, the limited evidence they did consider, including academic studies and media investigations, presented a mixed record of COMPAS as a reliable tool that failed to clarify for the court their concerns that criminal sentencing was being handed over to an algorithm. Although there may have been little doubt that Loomis's high risk of recidivism was based on his prior criminal history, separate from the COMPAS assessment, the court heeded the admonition asserted by Klingele that the "paucity of reliable evidence" about COMPAS impeded its ability to determine the tool's limitations and its propensity for misuse.[44]

The inaccessible training data set contributed to the algorithmic tool's black box effect by denying the judges and others the capacity to trace the *source* of the tool's agency. Earlier studies of COMPAS, some of which the Wisconsin Supreme Court considered, expressed difficulty pinpointing which training data sets were used, beyond determining that COMPAS likely drew on a limited set of criminal records pulled from indeterminate jails and corrections departments in New York and Michigan. The 2015 COMPAS handbook, too, provides little clarity, indicating that the tool's "Core Norm Group" of 7,381 offenders (5,681 men, 1,700 women) was

---

[43] *State v. Loomis.*

[44] Cecelia Klingele, "The Promises and Perils of Evidence-Based Corrections," *Notre Dame L. Rev.* 91, no. 2 (2015): 576.

sampled from 30,000 COMPAS core assessments conducted between January 2004–November 2005.[45] The training data set, on which nearly all subsequent local variants of COMPAS were calibrated, encompassed a brief two-year window that spanned a limited subset of regional localities.

COMPAS may have produced a risk score for Loomis, but without presenting an analytic breakdown of the data set on which the tool had been normalized, it is unclear what the score represented. Instead, the lack of data transparency makes apparent how records from specific criminal justice systems were stripped of their local contexts and recontextualized under a series of social theories about criminality imposed by Northpointe.[46] The Northpointe developers periodically compared COMPAS scores with data from subsequent locales, including Wisconsin in 2012–13, to validate the system. What appears missing from these validation studies, however, is recognition that criminal behavior, policing, or rehabilitation strategies might vary across geographic locales and influence one another over time.[47] An apparent lack of appreciation of historical context runs the real risk that a tool, such as COMPAS, perpetuates certain biases and inhibits those reliant on the system from effecting lasting change in their communities. The black box effect, in other words, is expressed as a fear that the tool was operating according to indeterminate biases that could not be sourced or verified.

It is tempting to conclude this case study by affirming the presence of bias in COMPAS based purely on the algorithm and its underlying training data. For example, a widely cited ProPublica investigation of COMPAS's recidivism scores from Broward County, Florida, (cited by the Wisconsin Supreme Court in its ruling in the Loomis case) concluded that Black defendants were more likely than White defendants to receive a high-risk recidivism score.[48] But focusing purely on the scores themselves and not the entirety of how COMPAS is employed in the sentencing process

---

[45] Northpointe Inc., *Practitioner's Guide to COMPAS Core* (2015), http://www.northpointeinc.com/downloads/compas/Practitioners-Guide-COMPAS-Core-_031915.pdf. 11.

[46] The *Practitioner's Guide* outlines several criminological theories that "explain how people become involved in criminal behavior," which include "Sub-Culture Theory," "Sociopathic/Socialization Breakdown Theory," and "Criminal Opportunity Theory." Ibid., see Chapter 2.

[47] The study of COMPAS by Skeem and Louden (2007) conducted for the California Department of Corrections and Rehabilitation (CDCR), found "no evidence" that COMPAS "captures change in risk state over time." An April 2019 edition of the *Practitioner's Guide to COMPAS Core* would seem to confirm this early assessment. The Core norm group is the same 7,381-person sample cited in the 2015 version of the handbook discussed earlier. The company concedes that: "Agency-specific norm groups are developed for some clients." Jennifer L. Skeem and Jennifer Eno Louden, *Assessment of Evidence on the Quality of the Correctional Offender Management Profiling for Alternative Sanctions (COMPAS)* (Davis: Center for Public Policy Research, University of California, Davis, 2007).

[48] Angwin et al. and Bao et al. remain skeptical of ProPublica's findings, suggesting that studies of bias and fairness within risk assessment instruments, such as COMPAS, are themselves flawed by failing to account fully for the data set's contextual grounding. Bao et al., "It's COMPASlicated."

risks prioritizing the core algorithm and training data at the expense of a more nuanced historicization that balances the tool's potential biases with those of its users. What happens, as D'Ignazio and Klein advocate, when we move beyond the "inner workings of machine learning" and consider the "history, culture, and context that lead to discriminatory outputs in the first place."[49] A more comprehensive historicization of *State v. Loomis* ought to consider the application of COMPAS within the Wisconsin Department of Corrections (DOC).

HISTORICIZING THE WISCONSIN DEPARTMENT OF CORRECTIONS

An analysis of the publicly available instructions in the Wisconsin DOC *Electronic Case Reference Manual* on how to complete a presentence investigation (PSI) using COMPAS reveals a complex entanglement between COMPAS and Wisconsin's criminal justice system. A PSI report includes a combination of the risk assessment scores and criminogenic need scales generated by COMPAS algorithms and narrative text written by the corrections officer. The report presents static data, such as the defendant's prior record, alongside the officer's summary of "relevant" information such as family stability, attitudes, and values; mental ability; and the defendant's attitudes and beliefs.[50] The twenty or so criminogenic factors, based on "several important criminological theories" according to the COMPAS *Practitioner's Guide*, included areas such as criminal personality, criminal thinking, leisure/boredom, socialization failure, and social environment.[51] Such dynamic factors are difficult to measure empirically because they tend to ignore cross-cultural contingencies.[52] Nevertheless COMPAS reduces complex areas of a defendant's history and psyche as a set of criminogenic need scale scores. It represents these areas in the PSI report as both bar graphs and nonnumerical ratings such as low, medium, high, probable, unlikely, and highly probable. Figure 9.1, a fake sample PSI provided by the Wisconsin State Public Defenders' Office, shows how a COMPAS score is paired with a correctional officer's analysis, for example, classifying the fictitious defendant's criminal involvement as "low," social isolation as "probable," criminal personality as "highly probable," and family criminal-

---

[49] D'Ignazio and Klein, *Data Feminism*, 20.
[50] State of Wisconsin, "Presentence Investigations."
[51] For a full breakdown of the criminogenic needs, see Northpointe Inc., *Practitioner's Guide* (2015).
[52] Stefanie Schmidt, Roxanne Heffernan, and Tony Ward, "Why We Cannot Explain Cross-Cultural Differences in Risk Assessment," *Aggression and Violent Behavior* 50 (2020).

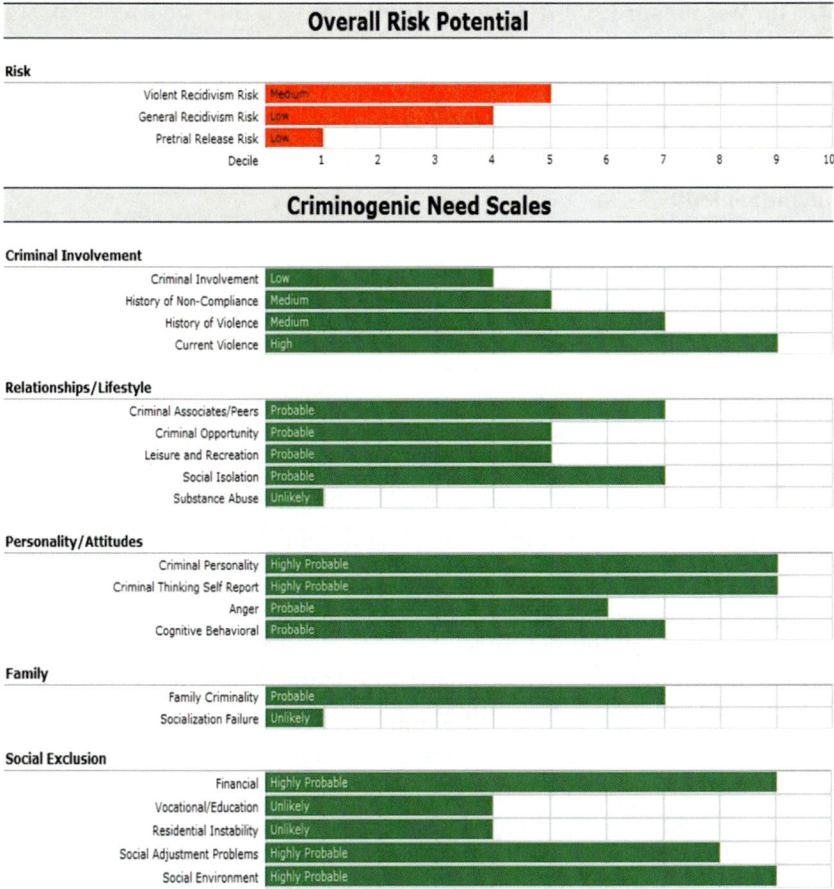

Figure 9.1. COMPAS recidivism risk scores and criminogenic need scales from a sample fake Wisconsin presentence investigation report.

Wisconsin State Public Defender's Office. "Pre-Sentence Investigation." 2014. Accessed July 14, 2021, from http://www.wispd.org/attachments/article/272/COMPAS%20PSI%20Presentation%20by%20 DOC.pdf.

ity as "probable."[53] Commentary by the officer accompanies each COMPAS score and is based on answers provided by the offender during the presentence interview along with the officer's observations.

The report's presentation of the score combined with the officer's explanatory text creates an aura of objectivity. But this information is highly

---

[53] Wisconsin State Public Defender's Office, *Pre-Sentence Investigation*, http://www.wispd.org/attachments/ article/272/COMPAS%20PSI%20Presentation%20by%20DOC.pdf.

interpretative and prone to biases beyond those tied solely to the algorithmic tool. The Wisconsin *Case Reference Manual*, which trains corrections staff on the use of COMPAS, contains instructions on how to produce a PSI in which COMPAS and officer bias could potentially entwine. For example, the following instructions to complete the Attitudes and Beliefs section suggests how the COMPAS Need Score ought to influence the officer's final judgement:

> Considerations should include the defendant's patterns of problem solving, thinking errors (cognitive distortions), coping skills, rationalization/justification for his/her behavior and how they view the world around them in general. COMPAS Criminogenic need scales of Criminal Personality, Criminal Thinking Self Report, Anger, Cognitive Behavior, and Social Adjustment Problems will provide insight into the defendant's attitudes and beliefs. Remember to keep comments factual, based on the defendant's demonstrated behavior or comments. Include report of inconsistent response pattern or potential faking concern as identified in the assessment.[54]

What may be intended as an officer's "factual" assessment is something far more idiosyncratic and prone to subjective interpretation. The officer is tasked with interpreting algorithmically generated scores for otherwise complex, highly relativized sociocultural constructs such as "social adjustment problems" (Figure 9.2). The instructions reveal the underlying contradictions at play: subjective criminogenic scores based on faulty, inaccessible data are treated as objective, which are then supported by additional "facts" gathered via an officer's observations. In addition, that information may have been collected from defendants prone to "potential faking," which itself is supposed to be flagged by the algorithm based on its criminological model and confirmed by the officer. All this data culminates with the "Agent's Impressions," a summary section intended to include "a professional analysis of the defendant, not personal opinion." The conclusions must, according to the manual, "integrate the COMPAS assessment information ... with [the agent's] professional judgment in a narrative format."[55]

The unavailable context of the original COMPAS training data set from New York and Michigan localities, combined with the discretion corrections officers possess in completing a PSI using the COMPAS system, indicate a much more intertwined portrait of this human–AI network than

---

[54] State of Wisconsin, "Presentence Investigations."
[55] Ibid.

◇ **Social Adjustment Problems**

Social Adjustment Problems Scale Score: Highly Probable

A highly probable score on this scale suggests that Mr. ROBERT NONAME is likely to have problematic relationships in multiple social contexts such as family, school and work. He would likely benefit from classes that can improve his social skills that may help build his social supports, particularly prosocial supports. A cognitive program aimed at improving his success in social contexts may be appropriate.

Agent Comments:

Mr. Noname told this writer that he is very sorry for what happened and he knows now that his behavior was wrong. He states at the time that he forgot he could not carry a weapon. Due to these statements he seems able to take partial, but not full responsibility. He does appear to be rationalizing and minimizing his behavior to a degree by commenting "...but it really wasn't that big of a deal, no one got hurt." Mr. Nomane's assessment indicates low impulse control. This is exhibited in his behavior of possessing the gun despite knowing he should not have one in his possession.

Mr. Noname stated he is trying to make positive changes in his life and believes he can be successful in staying out of trouble in the future. He believes everyone has the ability to succeed if they just put their mind to it. He maintains barbering has given him a second chance on life. His passion and motivation in this line of work will pull him through these hard times.

13   NONAME, ROBERT

Figure 9.2. COMPAS criminogenic need score for "Social Adjustment Problems" paired with Department of Corrections agent's commentary.

Wisconsin State Public Defender's Office. "Pre-Sentence Investigation." 2014. Accessed July 14, 2021, from http://www.wispd.org/attachments/article/272/COMPAS%20PSI%20Presentation%20by%20 DOC.pdf.

suggested by previous studies focusing almost solely on the COMPAS algorithm. COMPAS may bake racial bias into its algorithms; however, the officers determine just as much, if not more, of the data entered into a criminal's record. Moreover, officers determine how that data is presented in the report, and such decisions inevitably heighten, mute, or further distort the algorithmic bias. The black box effect in this case study thus stems from the court's inability to not only pinpoint the source and nature of bias within COMPAS, but also its employment within the Wisconsin Department of Corrections. The concern might be summarized as follows: To what degree, and in what fashion, is COMPAS perpetuating a criminal justice system historically stacked against persons of color and other under-privileged socioeconomic communities?

Expressed in historical terms, the problem captured in this black box effect is one of *interpretation*. COMPAS interprets criminogenic behavior using a set of social theories that it applies to an unsourced training data set of prior criminal records. The DOC agent interprets the core assessment and the criminogenic need scale scores when preparing the PSI final report. A flowchart from the Wisconsin Department of Corrections, in fact, shows

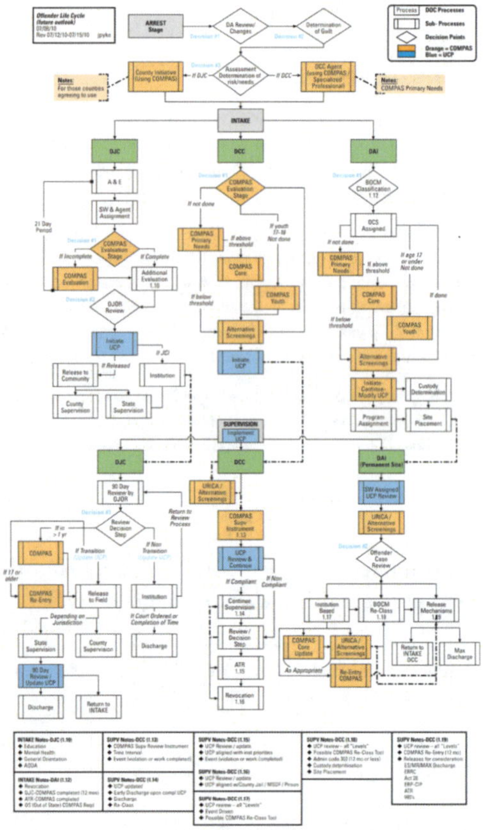

Figure 9.3. Flowchart of the Offender Life Cycle within the Wisconsin Department of Corrections. Shapes marked in orange indicate the use of COMPAS.

State of Wisconsin, "Offender Life Cycle." (2010), https://doc.wi.gov/Documents/AboutDOC/Reentry/offend erlifecycle.pdf.

how COMPAS helps inform not just PSIs, but nearly every major decision point in the lifecycle of an offender. The chart presents a striking visualization of how embedded COMPAS has become in the state's criminal justice system, revealing that COMPAS assessments contribute to no less than twenty-one critical decision points and processes, including the probation sentencing process, prison sentences, jail programming, and community referrals (Figure 9.3).[56] Each orange shape, which marks the use of COMPAS, represents an exchange between the offender and corrections officers

---

[56] State of Wisconsin. For a breakdown of where the Wisconsin DOC has integrated COMPAS, see the section "COMPAS—Potential Decision Points (County Adult)." State of Wisconsin, *Electronic Case Reference Manual*.

trained to evaluate COMPAS-produced data. Whatever biases COMPAS may possess within its training data, the tool does not operate in a vacuum, but interacts with various human agents, such as probation officers, judges, and lawyers, who themselves are constrained in their actions by local laws and policies, as well as conscious or unconscious biases of their own.

A 2012 webinar summarizing the lifecycle executive flowchart and the early deployment of COMPAS in Wisconsin preceding Loomis's arrest confirmed the deep integration of COMPAS in the criminal justice system. Jared Hoy, Reentry Director of Wisconsin DOC, acknowledged that behind each of the decision points on the chart are "reams of business process for each classification or each staff person that says the who, what, where, and why" for how to handle the offender.[57] Neal Goodloe, an implementation consultant at Northpointe, demonstrated the capacity of COMPAS to chart the offender's record through the byzantine corrections system. COMPAS is more than a stand-alone set of algorithms, he explained, it is a software package designed to incorporate its evidence-based analysis into the Department of Corrections record-keeping system.[58] COMPAS logs each assessment conducted by an agent and makes it available for editing or updating. It functions, thus, as a platform that simultaneously preserves *and* informs an offender's criminal record. In short, we ought to locate COMPAS's historical agency not at the level of an algorithmic software tool, but as a complete *system*, marked by the combination of algorithms, data, software, and officers using the software to track offenders through the Wisconsin corrections system.

Aware of the many points of interpretation along the process, the Wisconsin Supreme Court wavered on how much agency algorithmic data should possess compared with the professional analysis of corrections officers, at one point quoting the *Case Reference Manual* (which quotes the *Practitioner's Guide*) that "staff are predicted to disagree with... [COMPAS] in about 10% of the cases due to mitigating or aggravating circumstances to which the assessment is not sensitive."[59] Statements such as these were intended as reassurance that the actuarial tool had not overtaken the human decision-making process. Nevertheless, the court recommended circumscribing the use of a COMPAS risk assessment in future sentencing. PSI reports, the court ruled, were to include the following warning of COMPAS's accuracy:

---

[57] Jared Hoy, Neal Goodloe, and Bob May, "JISP Beacon Webinar: The Wisconsin Unified Corrections Coalition—a Project of the Wisconsin Department of Corrections" (Washington, DC: National Criminal Justice Association, 2012), https://vimeo.com/60187317.new_apevi_u009.docx.

[58] Ibid.

[59] *State v. Loomis.*

> [S]ome studies of COMPAS risk assessment scores have raised questions
> about whether they disproportionately classify minority offenders as having
> a higher risk of recidivism. ... Risk assessment tools must be constantly
> monitored and re-normed for accuracy due to changing populations and
> subpopulations.[60]

The cautionary note struck by the court is the direct product of the black
box effect, a call for reform prompted by the realization that critical evidence
for evaluating COMPAS remains unattainable and that the evidentiary
grounds will constantly shift the more the tool is employed within "changing
populations."

CONCLUSIONS

This case study chronicled efforts by state authorities to evaluate an AI
system and its influence on real-world outcomes. Those investigating COM-
PAS encountered an epistemic obstruction in the form of an algorithmic
black box. The defendant questioned the algorithmic process that measured
his criminal record against a data set of unknown records. Was his score
derived from some unforeseen bias, and, if so, what among the criminogenic
factors compelled COMPAS to interpret his behavior as "high risk" to his
community? Would knowing COMPAS's training data sets and the formula
for weighting criminogenic needs have allowed him to contest his sentencing? How did the corrections officer's engagement with COMPAS recidivism
risk and criminogenic need scores affect the overall investigatory process?

Historians will encounter similar epistemic challenges to those observed here when unraveling causal or agential impact that an AI system
has on a given event, policy, or long-term development. They will likely
never obtain, for instance, the proprietary algorithms driving Amazon's
recommendation system, Facebook's News Feed, or ChatGPT's text outputs.
These gaps will force historians to adapt or develop new historicizing
methods, in the process reevaluating the impact AI systems have on historiography.[61] Developing methods to compensate for a lack of evidence about
the system's operations, however, only takes us so far in understanding
AI's deep social, political, and cultural integration. As we saw when the
lens was broadened to include the corrections officers assigned to apply
COMPAS in their assessments, just as important in the historicizing process

---

[60] Ibid.
[61] Marnie Hughes-Warrington, "Toward the Recognition of Artificial History Makers," *History and Theory*
61, no. 4 (2022): 107–18.

will be consideration of how human and nonhuman agents contextualize and recontextualize evidence in absentia. The black box effect itself becomes a class of evidence worthy of historical analysis.

History has always been dependent on an incomplete evidentiary record. Studying the age of artificial intelligence, in some respects will be no different. Just as archives and libraries steward only a small percentage of what has survived through the ages due to natural and human causes, what will survive of our AI systems will be a sliver of their data and outputs, represented predominantly in second-hand traces. At the end of the day, historians will want to probe what human and nonhuman agents knew at a defined moment in time and how that knowledge affected outcomes. A historical method for contextualizing AI systems must hold two seemingly contradictory truths simultaneously: On the one hand AI systems think, behave, and experience the world differently from humans. At the same time, those fundamental differences stem from human decisions and contexts such as the selection of training data, the type of machine learning employed by the system, or how developers tweak the system to accomplish certain goals. If this microhistory offers a suggestion as to how historians should deal with what is in store for the future historical study of the twenty-first century, it would be that historians should confront the catalytic force of an algorithmic system's black box effect as evidence, to reveal the relational depth among human and algorithmic agents.

BIBLIOGRAPHY

Ananny, M., and K. Crawford. "Seeing without Knowing: Limitations of the Transparency Ideal and Its Application to Algorithmic Accountability." *New Media & Society* 20, no. 3 (2018): 973–89.

Angwin, J., J. Larson, S. Mattu, and L. Kirchner. "Machine Bias." *ProPublica.* (May 23, 2016). https://www.propublica.org/article/machine-bias-risk-assessments-in-criminal-sentencing.

Bao, M., A. Zhou, S. Zottola, B. Brubach, S. Desmarals, A. Horowitz, K. Lum, and S. Venkatasubramanian. "It's COMPASlicated: The Messy Relationship between RAI Datasets and Algorithmic Fairness Benchmarks." *arXiv preprint arXiv:2106.05498*, last modified April 28, 2022, https://doi.org/10.48550/arXiv.2106.05498.

Benjamin, R. *Race after Technology: Abolitionist Tools for the New Jim Code.* Cambridge, UK: Polity Press, 2019.

Brennan, T., W. Dieterich, and B. Ehret. "Evaluating the Predictive Validity of the COMPAS Risk and Needs Assessment System." *Criminal Justice and Behavior* 36, no. 1 (2009): 21–40.

Bucher, T. "Neither Black Nor Box: Ways of Knowing Algorithms." In *Innovative Methods in Media and Communication Research*, edited by S. Kubitschko and A. Kaun, 81–98. Cham, Switzerland: Springer International Publishing, 2016.

Campolo, A., and K. Crawford. "Enchanted Determinism: Power without Responsibility in Artificial Intelligence." *Engaging Science, Technology, and Society* 6 (2020): 1–19.

Carabantes, M. "Black-Box Artificial Intelligence: An Epistemological and Critical Analysis." *AI & Society* 35, no. 2 (2020): 309–17.

Casey, P. M., R. K. Warren, and J. K. Elek. *Using Offender Risk and Needs Assessment Information at Sentencing: Guidance for Courts from a National Working Group*. Williamsburg, VA: National Center for State Courts and Center for Sentencing Initiatives, 2021. https://www.ncsc.org/__data/assets/pdf_file/0019/25174/rna-guide-final.pdf.

Center for Sentencing Initiatives. "NCSC Fact Sheet: Evidence-Based Sentencing." 2014. https://www.ncsc.org/__data/assets/pdf_file/0018/25290/ebs-fact-sheet-8-27-14.pdf.

Crawford, K. *The Atlas of AI: Power, Politics, and the Planetary Costs of Artificial Intelligence*. New Haven, CT: Yale University Press, 2021.

D'Ignazio, C., and L. F. Klein. *Data Feminism*. Cambridge, MA: MIT Press, 2020.

Eaglin, J. M. "Constructing Recidivism Risk." *Emory Law Journal* 67, no. 1 (2017): 59–122.

Eckhouse, L., K. Lum, C. Conti-Cook, and J. Ciccolini. "Layers of Bias: A Unified Approach for Understanding Problems with Risk Assessment." *Criminal Justice and Behavior* 46, no. 2 (2019): 185–209.

Gebru, Timnit, J. Morgenstern, B. Vecchione, J. Wortman Vaughan, H. Wallach, H. Daumé III, and K. Crawford. "Datasheets for Datasets." *Communications of the ACM* 64, no. 12 (2021): 86–92.

Gillespie, T. "The Relevance of Algorithms." *Media Technologies: Essays on Communication, Materiality, and Society*. (2014): 167–93.

Ginzburg, C., and A. Davin. "Morelli, Freud and Sherlock Holmes: Clues and Scientific Method." *History Workshop* 9 (1980): 5–36.

Hoy, J., N. Goodloe, and B. May. "JISP Beacon Webinar: The Wisconsin Unified Corrections Coalition—A Project of the Wisconsin Department of Corrections." Washington, DC: National Criminal Justice Association, 2012. https://vimeo.com/60187317.

Hughes-Warrington, M. "Toward the Recognition of Artificial History Makers." *History and Theory* 61, no. 4 (2022).

Iliadis, A., and F. Russo. "Critical Data Studies: An Introduction." *Big Data & Society* 3, no. 2 (2016): 1–7.

Introna, L. D. "The Enframing of Code: Agency, Originality and the Plagiarist." *Theory, Culture & Society* 28, no. 6 (2011): 113–41.

Jones-Imhotep, E. "The Ghost Factories: Histories of Automata and Artificial Life." *History and Technology* 36, no. 1 (2020): 3–29.

Klingele, C. "The Promises and Perils of Evidence-Based Corrections." *Notre Dame Law Review* 91 (2015): 537.

Knorr-Cetina, K. *Epistemic Cultures: How the Sciences Make Knowledge.* Cambridge, MA: Harvard University Press, 1999.

Latour, B. "Technology Is Society Made Durable." *The Sociological Review* 38, no. 1_Suppl. (1990): 103–31.

———. *Reassembling the Social: An Introduction to Actor-Network-Theory.* Oxford: Oxford University Press, 2008.

Leistert, O. "Social Bots as Algorithmic Pirates and Messengers of Techno-Environmental Agency." In *Algorithmic Cultures: Essays on Meaning, Performance and New Technologies*, 158–72. London: Routledge, Taylor & Francis, 2016.

Lipton, Z. C. "The Mythos of Model Interpretability." *arXiv preprint arXiv: 160603490.* (2016). https://doi.org/10.48550/arXiv.1606.03490.

Lynch, C. "Stewardship in the 'Age of Algorithms.'" *First Monday* 22, no. 12 (2017). http://dx.doi.org/10.5210/fm.v22i112.8097.

Mackenzie, A. "The Production of Prediction: What Does Machine Learning Want?" *European Journal of Cultural Studies* 18, nos. 4–5 (2015): 429–45.

Marcus, G. "Deep Learning: A Critical Appraisal." *arXiv preprint arXiv:1801.00631.* (2018). https://doi.org/10.48550/arXiv.1801.00631.

McQuillan, D. "Data Science as Machinic Neoplatonism." *Philosophy & Technology* 31, no. 2 (2018): 253–72.

Noble, S. U. *Algorithms of Oppression: How Search Engines Reinforce Racism.* New York: NYU Press, 2018.

Northpointe Inc. *Practitioner's Guide to COMPAS Core.* 2015. http://www.northpointeinc.com/downloads/compas/Practitioners-Guide-COMPAS-Core-_031915.pdf.

Rauer, v. "Drones." In *Algorithmic Cultures: Essays on Meaning, Performance and New Technologies*, 140–57. London: Routledge, Taylor & Francis, 2016.

Roberge, J., and M. Castelle (2020). "Toward an End-to-End Sociology of 21st-Century Machine Learning." In *The Cultural Life of Machine Learning: An Incursion Into Critical AI Studies*, edited by J. Roberge and M. Castelle, 1–30. Cham, Switzerland: Palgrave Macmillan, 2020.

Scheuerman, M., K. Wade, C. Lustig, and J. R. Brubaker. "How We've Taught Algorithms to See Identity: Constructing Race and Gender in

Image Databases for Facial Analysis." *Proceedings of the ACM on Human-Computer Interaction* 4, no. CSCW1 (2020): 1–35.

Schmidt, S., R. Heffernan, and T. Ward. "Why We Cannot Explain Cross-Cultural Differences in Risk Assessment." *Aggression and Violent Behavior* 50 (2020).

Seaver, N. "Knowing Algorithms." In *digitalSTS: A Field Guide for Science & Technology Studies*, edited by J. Vertesi and D. Ribes, 412–22. Princeton, NJ: Princeton University Press, 2019.

Seyfert, R., and J. Roberge. "What Are Algorithmic Cultures?" In *Algorithmic Cultures: Essays on Meaning, Performance and New Technologies*, edited by R. Seyfert and J. Roberge, 1–25. London: Routledge, Taylor & Francis Group, 2016.

Shaw, R. "Big Data and Reality." *Big Data & Society* 2, no. 2 (2015): 1–4.

Skeem, J. L., and J. E. Louden. "Assessment of Evidence on the Quality of the Correctional Offender Management Profiling for Alternative Sanctions (COMPAS)." 2007. https://webfiles.uci.edu/skeem/Downloads.html.

Starr, S. B. "Evidence-Based Sentencing and the Scientific Rationalization of Discrimination." *Stanford Law Review* 66, no. 4 (2014): 842.

State of Wisconsin. *Electronic Case Reference Manual*. Madison, WI: Department of Corrections, 2020. https://doc.wi.gov/GuidanceDocuments V2/Reentry/OOS_Electronic%20Case%20Reference%20Manual.pdf.

———. "Presentence Investigations." In *Electronic Case Reference Manual*, 157–76. Madison, WI: Department of Corrections, 2020. https://doc.wi.gov/GuidanceDocumentsV2/Reentry/OOS_Electronic%20Case%20Reference%20Manual.pdf.

———. "Offender Life Cycle." In *Electronic Case Reference Manual*. Madison, WI: Department of Corrections, 2010. https://doc.wi.gov/Documents/AboutDOC/Reentry/offenderlifecycle.pdf.

Striphas, T. "Algorithmic Culture." *European Journal of Cultural Studies* 18, nos. 4–5 (2015): 395–412.

Wisconsin State Public Defender's Office. "Pre-Sentence Investigation." 2014. Accessed July 14, 2021. http://www.wispd.org/attachments/article/272/COMPAS%20PSI%20Presentation%20by%20DOC.pdf.

Chapter 10

When Voices Become Data: Reading Data Documenting Contemporary Reading

Jennifer Burek Pierce

In 1976, Italian historian Carlo Ginzburg published *The Cheese and the Worms: The Cosmos of a Sixteenth-Century Miller*. This widely translated work has been described as "an archeology of knowledge," a "study of popular culture," a "ground-breaking work of microhistory," and evidence of the lives of those on the margins of society and "'subalterns.'"[1] Researchers in the entwined fields of print culture, book history, and the history of readers and reading consider a further aspect of Ginzburg's account of Menocchio, a sixteenth-century miller accused of heresy. For us, the Inquisition's administrative records of Menocchio's trials document what happened when a lone reader consumed any book he could get his hands on, meditating and musing aloud about how he understood those works; these records of his own voice, which now represents a sort of gold standard for scholars interested in how readers make meaning from books, provided the evidence used to condemn him. This landmark study focuses on an individual, allowing us to understand what he read, how he made sense of it, and how others responded to the ideas that emerged from his reading.

---

[1] Carlo Ginzburg, *The Cheese and the Worms: The Cosmos of a Sixteenth-Century Miller*, trans. John and Anne C. Tedeschi (Baltimore: Johns Hopkins University Press, 2013), https://jhupbooks.press.jhu.edu/title/cheese-and-worms; Samuel Cohn, *The Journal of Interdisciplinary History* 12, no. 3 (1982): 523–25, doi:10.2307/203274; "A Peasant Versus the Inquisition: Cheese, Worms, and the Birth of Microhistory" *CBC Radio* (20 Aug. 2018), https://www.cbc.ca/radio/ideas/a-peasant-vs-the-inquisition-cheese-worms-and-the-birth-of-micro-history-1.4034196; Michael S. Kimmel, *Theory and Society* 11, no. 4 (July 1982): 555–58; Christiano Zanetti, *Sixteenth Century Journal* 44, no. (2014): 186–87.

The distinctive nature of the evidence of readerly activity is almost beside the point of most evaluations of this book, focusing instead on this unusual story of passion for the written word gone awry. As the *Catholic Historical Review* observed, Menocchio "insisted repeatedly that he had developed his ideas from the books he read, including Boccaccio, Mandeville's *Travels*, the *Fioretto della Bibbia*, and possibly the Koran."[2] The data comprising church records showed both what Menocchio read and how the Roman Catholic Church read Menocchio's words in turn.

If his reading began as a pathway to a wider world of ideas, it was one where he went tragically astray. Rather than finding himself part of a community of readers, Menocchio's interpretations of the motley lot of books available to him put him at odds with others, most significant the Roman Catholic Church, whose officials eventually condemned Menocchio to death for his opinions about what he had read.[3] The vividness of Ginzburg's construction of Menocchio's ill-fated passion for books led one reviewer to conclude that "the reader who has followed Dr. Ginzburg in his wanderings through the labyrinthine mind of the miller of the Friuli will take leave of this strange and quirky old man with genuine regret."[4] This history of a flawed yet determined reader, reliant on Menocchio's own voice, allows us to understand reading in a previous era as an act of turbulent, emotional, and provocative dimensions. It reminds us that being a committed reader, a book enthusiast, is not necessarily an indication that a reader's time with books results in affirming or valued interpretations; being a reader can put one at odds with a larger community and its ideas of what books can mean.

Almost forty-five years have passed since *The Cheese and the Worms* was first published; increasingly, in the intervening years, much scholarly attention has turned from studying the lone reader to considering many

---

[2] H. C. Erik Midelfort, "Review of *The Cheese and the Worms*," *The Catholic Historical Review* 68, no. 3 (1982): 513–14.

[3] Although its concerns arose from misgivings about political leanings and mob rule rather than fidelity to Church dogma, early seventeenth-century Britain was the site of similar concerns about the implications of misreading. Adrian Johns notes that one William Gilbert complained about "the common herd and fellows without a spark of talent are made intoxicated, crazy, puffed up" with the idea that reading certain books meant they could "'profess themselves philosophers ... while contemning men of learning.'" See Adrian Jones, *The Nature of the Book: Print and Knowledge in the Making* (Chicago: University of Chicago Press, 1998): 184–85.

[4] "Reviews," Johns Hopkins University Press, (n.d.), https://jhupbooks.press.jhu.edu/title/cheese-and-worms/reviews.

readers.[5] Although single-reader studies and those focusing on small numbers of readers have not vanished, there is now a more pronounced interest
in "reading as a social activity," in "the reading public," and in the ways
that even "individual acts of reading are always embedded ... in reading
communities."[6] These studies sometimes nod to the *Annales* school of
book history's quantitative methods, yet they draw on or create textual
records. We are able to obtain these records in part because some committed
book discussants have taken their conversations to the Internet, with docu-
mentable activity of this sort taking place since the mid-1990s.[7] When,
as now, communities of readers form and engage across digital platforms,
we contend with what Joshua Sternfeld has referred to as an "abundance of
evidence," in contrast with the limited documents that remain to reconstruct
Menocchio's story. Thousands, or even millions, of testimonials to people's
interest in bookish subjects might accrue on one social media site or be
distributed across several platforms.[8] These studies of reading communities
now extend into a terrain that sees researchers turn the practices associated
with "distant reading" and "big data" from the analysis of literary creation
to its consumption.[9] Instead of responding to a single and singular voice,
and the emotions it might reflect or provoke, we see scholars increasingly
turning to large, quantitative sets of data for evidence of how and what
people read.

Even so, they do not leave Menocchio entirely behind. Scholars like
Micah Bateman and Melanie Walsh, who interpret large amounts of digital
data to make sense of people's quotation of and allusions to literary works,

---

[5] Representative studies include Christine Pawley, *Reading on the Middle Border: The Culture of Print in Late-Nineteenth-Century Osage, Iowa* (Amherst: University of Massachusetts Press, 2010); Frank Felsenstein and James J. Connolly, *What Middletown Read: Print Culture in an American Small City* (Amherst: University of Massachusetts Press, 2015); Collette Drouillard, "Growing up with Harry Potter: What Motivated Youth to Read" (Ph.D. dissertation, Florida State University, 2009); Elizabeth McHenry, *Forgotten Readers: Recovering the Lost History of African American Literary Societies* (Durham, NC: Duke University Press, 2002); and Jonathan Rose, *The Intellectual Life of the British Working Classes* (New Haven, CT: Yale University Press, 2001).

[6] Janice Radway, *Reading the Romance: Women, the Patriarchy, and Popular Literature*, rev. ed. (Chapel Hill: University of Carolina Press, 1991): 1, 4; Thomas Augst, "Introduction," in *Institutions of Reading* (Amherst: University of Massachusetts Press, 2007): 2; Christine Pawley, "Seeking Significance: Actual Readers, Specific Reading Communities," *Book History* 5 (2002): 157.

[7] Peter Boot, "The Voice of the Reader: The Landscape of Online Book Discussion in the Netherlands, 1997–2016," *Edinburgh History of Reading: Common Readers*, ed. Jonathon Rose (Edinburgh: Edinburgh University Press, 2020): 258–79.

[8] Joshua Sternfeld, "Historical Understanding in the Quantum Age," *Journal of Digital Humanities* 3, no. 2 (2014), http://journalofdigitalhumanities.org/3-2/historical-understanding-in-the-quantum-age/.

[9] For a brief overview of Moretti's distant reading online, see Kathryn Schulz, "What Is Distant Reading?" *New York Times* (June 24, 2011), https://www.nytimes.com/2011/06/26/books/review/the-mechanic-muse-what-is-distant-reading.html; *distant reading* is also defined as "using computers to analyze large corpora" (410) by Kirschenbaum and Werner, "State of the Discipline: Digital Scholarship and Digital Studies," *Book History* 17 (2014): 406–58.

observe apparent misreadings of that source matter, such as misattribution of quotes to a prominent literary figure or words wrested out of context in support of a nascent social cause or political moment.[10] Other researchers point out that "the social media landscape" may be "dangerous," a "perilous" and "sometimes malevolent place" because of bullying and other threatening behaviors.[11] Bookish domains are no exception to this at-times threatening rule, if reflective of different sorts of vulnerabilities. Scholarship that examines traces of reading online, then, continues to attend to themes evoked by Ginzburg while simultaneously thinking about the reader differently.

A key difference between a study of one historical reader and an analysis of contemporary readers via sites like the Amazon-owned Goodreads; the niche but popular #bookstagram, a subset of Instagram posts dedicated to both reading and books as objects; BookTube, the unaffiliated collective of YouTubers who make videos about books and reading on this platform; and BookTok, a popular hashtag on the micro-video platform TikTok, which together form subsets of activity on general social media platforms, is what we might know about the reader.[12] When we study larger communities of readers, the way we regard and represent the individuals who comprise the collective necessarily shifts. Menocchio was an individual whose identity could be discerned from persistent records. His birth and death dates, his occupations and avocations, and his family members allow us to see him as a real person, to fix him in relation to social and political structures. He stands out in these contexts in part because his literacy was relatively unusual, as well as the ideas he derived from it. Our contemporary studies of readers in online communities shift from intricate attention to an individual's mindset and feelings to what an aggregate can tell us.[13]

---

[10] Micah Bateman, "Tweeting (in) 'Dark Times': Brecht's Second Svendbord 'Motto' Post-Trump," *ecibs: Communications of the International Brecht Society* 1 (2020), https://e-cibs.org/issue-2020-1/#bateman; Melanie Walsh, "Tweets of a Native Son: The Quotation and Recirculation of James Baldwin from Black Power to Black Lives Matter," *American Quarterly* 70, no. 3 (September 2018): 531–59.

[11] Kirschenbaum and Werner, "State of the Discipline," 407, 408.

[12] For a study of a book-specific social media platform, see Melanie Walsh and Maria Antoniak, "The Goodreads 'Classics': A Computational Study of Readers, Amazon, and Crowd-Sourced Amateur Criticism," *Post 45 x A Journal of Cultural Criticism*, 7 (21 April 2021), https://post45.org/2021/04/the-goodreads-classics-a-computational-study-of-readers-amazon-and-crowdsourced-amateur-criticism/. To date, the only peer-reviewed study of #booktok is by Margaret K. Merga, "How Can BookTok on TikTok Inform Readers Advisory Services for Young Readers?" *Library and Information Science Research*, 43, no. 2 (April 2021), https://doi.org/10.1016/j.lisr.2021.101091. Both articles consider the popularity of books on their respective platforms as evidence of taste and appeal.

[13] Admittedly, there are historical studies of print culture that rely on large, quantitative data to represent, at least in part, the nature of reading; these works might include everything from Richard D. Altick, *The English Common Reader: A Social History of the Mass Reading Public, 1800–1900*, 2nd ed. (Columbus: Ohio State University Press, 1998) to William St. Clair, *The Reading Nation in the Romantic Period* (Cambridge, UK: Cambridge University Press, 2007).

Instead of being interesting because of their singular nature, the resulting data sets are interesting because there are so many of these readers.

Further differences should call our attention to the fact that although we may know about more readers, there are limits to what we may know about them and how we can construct their lives as readers. Unlike Menocchio, their identities may be hinted at or obscured by usernames and avatars that fail to locate actual identities and geographical contexts that might have factored in their reading choices. Further, public education and other factors mean literacy is something we expect in Anglophone nations, rather than something that itself is worthy of attention. What we observe about contemporary, digitally rendered readers, then, often derives from publicly available information, whether presented by the individual or inferred from other sources, like government literacy statistics or foundation figures that represent the average number of books read annually.[14] There are ways that Ginzburg's study of Menocchio and our present-day studies of contemporary readers diverge, then, in both number and kind, at the same time that researchers who want to understand the people Christine Pawley has called "individual readers" see themselves as part of the same field, as engaged in the same kinds of inquiry.

When documented reading acquires these curious aspects, it suggests additional questions for our study of people who love books and literature and share their interests in more public settings, thereby creating data that we can assess. This change from a focus on one to a focus on many readers means we must consider what we understand as evidence of reading and as evidence of who is reading. We must think about what allows us to make sense of many records, what forms the basis for determining a focal point in the large data sets that result from online documentation of reading. What do we make of the documentation of reading that is now put forward in online reviews, reading lists, or photographs of books acquired from stores, libraries, or publisher give-aways? What do these digital testimonials, when gathered computationally, explain, if they are no longer significant just because they indicate literacy or dissent from the dominant paradigm? How do we understand the choices these readers make in construing literary quotations as commentary on contemporary events? How, even though their fates may be less dire, do we treat these large groups of readers with the sort of sensitivity and humanity that Ginzburg accorded the singular

---

[14] It should be noted, however, that there are historical, though not always digitized, studies of large numbers of readers. Key studies in this vein are Christine Pawley, *Reading on the Middle Border: The Culture of Print in Late-Nineteenth Century Osage, Iowa* (Amherst: University of Massachusetts Press, 2001) and Frank Felsenstein and James Connolly, *What Middletown Read: Print Culture in an American Small City* (Amherst: University of Massachusetts Press, 2015).

Menocchio? Some of these questions figure in the work of Bateman and Walsh, and in my book, *Narratives, Nerdfighters, and New Media*; some, however, emerge from the juxtaposition of our more recent studies with landmark work like Ginzburg's that has shaped our sense of what it means to understand what readers mean when they talk about books. This juxtaposition involves both comparison and contrast, directing our attention to how these scholarly projects differ fundamentally from microhistory while, I would argue, revealing ways of rendering readers as human beings with distinctive voices, rather than impersonal, quantitative data.

These questions about how we regard the people whose voices make up our data are important both as an aspect of research ethics and how it leads us to perceive the resulting evidence. Although tens of thousands of reader responses comprise a data set that can be searched and mined with multiple computer programs, a focus on these readers' voices can tell us something different about reading than numbers alone might lead us to believe. Although data describe the existence of large numbers of readers, thereby asserting that reading continues and flourishes in a digital age, attention to what readers actually say could suggest further ways of understanding what it means to read. Their voices can tell us things we would not have known to search for in data sets, things that might not even be readily searchable, regardless of the software available for such purposes.[15] It is one thing to have data, for example, showing that 402 of 420 members of a rural community visited their local library, demonstrating what many librarians would regard as an enviable level of usage and engagement with their library. At the same time, we lack indications of how those library users felt about what they found on the shelves.[16] In other words, it is all too easy to use data to confirm the existence of readers and their commitment to books; we must also consider how these voices might tell us something different from our presumptions. In a sense, we must offer an equivocal answer to a question that Matthew Kirschenbaum has asked recently: "Can we close read numbers?"[17]

In some instances, it is possible to analyze more than the metric trends that can be identified in data sets. A data set built from readers'

---

[15] The challenges of searching a digital resource for information are established aspects of the library and information science literature, including considerations in training users to run their own searches. Experts in online information retrieval often describe the fundamental problem of searching databases by noting that we search with words but want to know about concepts. See, for example, Suzanne S. Bell, *The Librarian's Guide to Online Searching* (Westport, CT: Libraries Unlimited), 106.

[16] Carol Ueland and Ludmilla A. Trigos, "F. F. Pavlenkov's Literacy Project: Popular Serials and Reading Rooms for the Russian Masses," *The Edinburgh History of Reading: Common Readers*, ed. Jonathan Rose (Edinburgh: Edinburgh University Press, 2020), 173.

[17] Matthew G. Kirschenbaum, "Can We Close Read Numbers? Serious Question," Twitter (18 June 2021), @mkirschenbaum.

comments about reading may contain anxieties, joys, kindness, and other, sometimes surprising, words. Besides affirming the existence of sizable numbers of readers, their voices can enable us to think about what it means to see their words as extending a continuum of readers' testimonials that have accrued since Menocchio was compelled to testify about his thoughts about books.

NERDFIGHTERS AS A COMMUNITY OF READERS

One contemporary reading community that asks us to consider these matters can be found within Nerdfighteria, the geographically dispersed yet allied individuals united by their interest in media created by novelist John Green and his brother Hank. In 2007, the Green brothers created a YouTube channel, *Vlogbrothers*, which saw a dramatic mid-year gain in popularity after Hank's video about waiting to read the last *Harry Potter* novel was featured on the platform's home page.[18] Today, their YouTube channel has more than three million subscribers. Nerdfighteria has been seen as having its origins in the audience for these videos, but its development is relatively complex and owes much to books and reading. With the motto "Don't forget to be awesome" that expresses the imperative to be kind, sincere, and otherwise one's best self, the community has both on- and off- line elements. Beyond its shared passion for books and stories, the community articulates an ethos of giving and respect as a means of governing both its internal actions and its attitude to the larger world. Nerdfighters' willingness to describe their reading stems from the combination of these community norms, which create an environment of openness and sharing, and from their deep connections to books and stories. Nerdfighteria is a group, then, that can tell us about twenty-first-century reading. Its members also reveal fundamental tensions in online community, ones that could encourage us to wonder whether their thousands of responses document individual acts of reading or a community of readers. Their differences, I argue, do not detract from the overall basis for community.

Given Nerdfighters' reliance on books, YouTube videos, and other social media interactions, they form what Ursula Franklin has called a "vernacular reality" based on "shared experience carried out in private."[19] There is research that demonstrates that communities like Nerdfighteria,

---

[18] Hank Green, "Accio Deathly Hallows," *Vlogbrothers*, YouTube video (18 July 18, 2007).

[19] Ursula M. Franklin, *The Real World of Technology*, rev. ed. (Toronto: House of Anansi Press, 2004), 39, 40.

which are characterized by "connection to large, mostly anonymous groups," are "important for the fulfillment of psychological needs and a sense of psychological well-being."[20] The communications of Nerdfighteria, this sense of belonging it generates, foster the community's willingness to divulge their feelings and ideas about what they read, even if their reception is fragmented by time, place, and sometimes language.

The evidence of their sense of community and shared belief in reading derives from evidence found in the Nerdfighteria Census. Since 2014, *Vlogbrothers* has conducted this annual survey, which asks numerous questions, among them, "What are you reading right now?" and "Who is your favorite author?" The responses generate qualitative, unstructured data describing a vast and varied culture of reading in the twenty-first century. For example, after the release of John Green's *The Fault in Our Stars* as a movie, the 2014 questionnaire netted more than 149,000 responses, each one motivated by some sort of attachment to the stories the Greens tell. I had intended to read these remarks about reading as I would an archival folder, moving through each entry as though it were a hand-written page to be turned, but the scale of responses year after year made plain the advantages that would result from computational sorting to tally favorite titles and to readily identify the comments where readers did more than list a title or two.[21] Still, my first forays into the data set, this qualitative reading of data, informed and shaped the creation of computational queries.

This two-fold approach to learning what the data set could say about reading reflects an applied instance of a conversation playing out in the scholarly literature about how we can best interpret large amounts of data. Sternfeld, for one, calls attention to the theoretical challenges of this project, the need to "'discover technically and theoretically how to negotiate between distant and close reading.'"[22] At risk of oversimplification, then, an iterative process that allows us to gain a sense of what is being said by respondents before generating computational queries forms a critical step in examining data sets.[23] Although there are many possible ways of undertaking the

---

[20] Shira Gabriel et al., "The Psychological Importance of Collective Assembly: Development and Validation of the Tendency for Effervescent Assembly Measure (TEAM)," *Psychological Assessment* 29, no. 11. (2017): 1349–62.

[21] A full discussion of research methods occurs in *Narratives, Nerdfighters, and New Media* (Iowa City: University of Iowa Press, 2020); see especially the Introduction and Appendices B and C, as well as the concluding Bibliographic Essay.

[22] Sternfeld, "Historical Understanding in the Quantum Age."

[23] This kind of mixed-methods study, in which a survey of a population producing large amounts of data based on individual experience was preceded by qualitative focus groups to determine the language and the issues that should be surveyed is described by Anthony Stamatoplos and Robert Mackoy, "Assessment of User Response to IUPUI University Library: 1999–2003 Studies," August 2003, https://scholarworks. iupui.edu/bitstream/handle/1805/415/UserResponseReport.pdf?sequence=1&isAllowed=y.

negotiation Sternfeld describes, the effect of using close and distant reading sequentially and even repeatedly, as stages that use one mode to inform the other, reduces the likelihood of simply counting what readers do and comes closer to permitting us to read words rather than allowing numbers to define trends or patterns in the data as preferred by the computational distant reading methods intended to determine the "true scope and nature of" the ideas in a digital data set.[24]

In addition to describing contemporary reading then, these data speak to contemporary questions about how and why we read data. A tendency in studies of the massive data that can be gleaned when computational studies intersect with book studies is to represent what we know in terms of numbers. In addition to the studies I have already mentioned, we might consider a work like Andrew Piper's *Enumerations*, a study that explores questions like "What happens when we look at 3,388,230 punctuation marks, 1.4 billion words, or 650,000 fictional characters?"[25] Here he illustrates that one of the ways we assert the significance and the merit of these more recent studies is through the tallies of records that point to massive communities, to representations of almost incomprehensible numbers of people who put their ideas into words. Their significance, in other words, arises from their fundamental difference from Menocchio's story as told by Ginzburg, but our research thus far has attended to the quantitative aspects of this difference, rather than cultural ones. The latter, however, allows us to account for variations within a community of readers, which should inevitably manifest in larger assessments.

The number of Nerdfighters who answer the annual survey by providing information about their reading habits and preferences could lead us to see them as an undifferentiated group of eager readers. The average number of books they read might be understood as evidence of a readerly diaspora who embody Joe Queenan's account of his own inclinations in *One for the Books*: "There is nothing I would rather do than read books. ... I have read somewhere between six thousand and seven thousand books. ... Seven thousand books is a lot of reading, but the mysteries, the beach reading, and the out-and-out trash really puff up the numbers."[26] Lest we be overawed by his tally, Queenan reminds us that "Winston Churchill supposedly read a book every day of his life, even while he was saving Western Civilization from the Nazis."[27] Nerdfighters who complete the

---

[24] Sternfeld, "Historical Understanding in the Quantum Age,"para. 4.

[25] See the author's description of his research at http://piperlab.mcgill.ca/enumerations.html.

[26] Joe Queenan, *One for the Books* (New York: Viking, 2012), 3, 5.

[27] Queenan, *One for the Books*, 5.

Nerdfighteria Census year after year would seem to suggest that neither Queenan nor Churchill are isolated as examples of what it means to be a dedicated reader, that we should not idealize readership based on numbers of books consumed.

Yet what do these metrics mean? Why accept what "big data" studies might tell us about reading and interest in books? Simone Murray argues that "we need to guard against naively taking reader accounts at face value," and Bateman has uncovered indications, for example, of Russian bots that tweet and recirculate quotes attributed to certain literary figures.[28] Elsewhere, he has written about the outpourings of a purposeful online reading community.[29] His research, then, points us to the value of a data set that reflects the ideals of a motivated community that has spent years developing its norms and ethos.

Numerous patterns in Nerdfighters' response suggest fellow feeling, common interests, and shared values.[30] To think about these patterns means recognizing titles and authors whose names appear frequently in Nerdfighters' accounts of their reading lives: John Green and his books are among the most frequently mentioned interests. Prior to 2021, other frequently mentioned books include *You're Never Weird on the Internet (Almost)* by Felicia Day, volumes in the *Harry Potter* series, many classics, Roxane Gay's essays, and more.[31] They note their enjoyment of "poetry by W. H. Auden (whom I discovered through *Looking for Alaska*, thanks John!").[32] Responding to this survey the same year that British fantasy author and satirist Terry Pratchett died, a number of them mentioned their incipient "nostalgia" for the years marked by their anticipation of a forthcoming novel in his Discworld series. One described the feeling of loss, writing that "Discworld is over forever, and we'll never have a Thieves' Guild book or know what happens to any of the characters." Nerdfighters' responses to this survey reveal their connections and their shared enjoyment of particular titles, depicting reading a recommended book as a way of connecting with the community members they may never meet in real life. These patterns, however, do not mean uniformity.

Menocchio's problems with the Inquisition arose because of his passion for books; his inability to understand their words the way the community

---

[28] Simone Murray, "State of the Discipline: Reading Online," *Book History* 21 (2018): 379; Micah Bateman, Guest lecture in "History of Readers and Reading" (lecture, University of Iowa, Iowa City, March 4, 2020).

[29] Jennifer Burek Pierce and Micah Bateman, "Song of 2,000 Whitman Lovers," *Chronicle of Higher Education* 61, no. 17 (5 Jan. 2015): B20.

[30] For the sake of convenience and brevity, and having read and written about the Nerdfighteria Census responses more fully in *Narratives, Nerdfighters, and New Media*, I draw on the relatively compact 2015 Census responses here.

[31] "What are you reading right now?" multiple years, Nerdfighteria Census Dataset.

[32] "What are you reading right now?" 2015 Nerdfighteria Census Dataset in the author's possession.

of readers comprised by the Catholic Church did, producing heterodox interpretations; and his insatiable need to tell others about what he was reading and thinking. He was, demonstrably, a reader with eagerness and failures to comprehend what he saw on the page in equal measure. All these years later, survey responses collected by *Vlogbrothers* show Nerdfighters to be people who want to share what they're reading and what they think of it. Although the consequences belong to different worlds, Nerdfighters elucidate their shortcomings as readers and their concerns about how their reading might be regarded by others. Despite the presence of virtual Queenans or Churchills among them, there are others on less confident and comfortable footing when it comes to books.

For any number of reasons, reading isn't simply a trip down pleasant garden path or a leisurely escape. In addition to enthusing about writing that inspires and satisfies them, Nerdfighters tell us about barriers to reading enjoyment. One reader was in the midst of a "pretty terrible book that I'm reviewing" for a professional publication.[33] For another, a pile of well-regarded titles inspired procrastination: "I should be doing my summer reading (*Fast Food Nation*, *The Things They Carried*, and *The Glass Castle*) but instead I'm taking a survey at 10:22 p.m."[34] Still another acknowledged that their current reading list was comprised of "all the physical books I bought for grad school classes but did not read at the time due to time management."[35]Similarly, another was chagrinned to admit to having a pile of "books for graduate school that are too expensive and that I'm not really reading." Although John's books usually receive adulation, one reader confessed, "To be honest, I never finished *An Abundance of Katherines*, and I probably never will."[36] Another mentioned "trying to get through *Paper Towns*."[37] These remarks allow us to see that being a reader and a nerd isn't a homogeneous experience: reading as avoidance, avoidance of reading, and not being enthralled by some books, even those written by a favorite author, are all as much a part of a readerly life as beloved books and long lists of things read or to be read.

Their remarks sometimes suggest that in their circles, some kinds of reading carry a certain stigma. Mostly this arises when they opt for stories that they find comforting or amusing rather than intellectually rich or critically acclaimed. A devotee of fan fiction "[promised]" that the stories they read were "well written." A romance reader admitted to being in the midst of a "trashy" title, while another followed their list of titles by

---

[33] "What are you reading right now?" 2015 Nerdfighteria Census Dataset in the author's possession.
[34] "What are you reading right now?" 2015 Nerdfighteria Census Dataset in the author's possession.
[35] "What are you reading right now?" 2015 Nerdfighteria Census Dataset in the author's possession.
[36] "What are you reading right now?" 2015 Nerdfighteria Census Dataset in the author's possession.
[37] "What are you reading right now?" 2015 Nerdfighteria Census Dataset in the author's possession.

"[swearing] I don't read this much sex stuff this often." They wonder whether some genres and media, like comic books, count. Whether they share Chimamanda Ngozi Adichie's philosophy that "the premise of 'book as guilty pleasure' is that one should not enjoy some books that one does, and it is an idea rooted in the cult of literary snobbery" and should be replaced by the categories of "books that interest me and books that don't," it is clear that they sense others' disapproval of what they want to read.[38]

When we think about evidence of reading and large data sets, it is common to look for markers like the number of titles read; these numbers stand in for signals of enjoyment and determination to read, come what may. Not unlike the value of the data set, which has something to do with its affordance of a once unimaginable number of readers for analysis, these data sets encourage us to engage with the patterns that can be identified computationally, via queries that will produce numbers that suggest, per this internal logic, their significance.[39] What Nerdfighters tell us is that reading is not a homogeneous experience; not simply because they read different kinds of books, but because they put books down, they persist through titles they dislike, and they fail to diligently read things they're supposed to. The evidence this community offers us is that being a twenty-first century reader, whether a professional or passionate one, involves any number of secrets, shortcomings, and disappointments rather than a perfectly curated #bookstagram account or a diligently completed TBR (to be read) list on Goodreads.

CONCLUSIONS

The history of reading has, for many years, vacillated between evidence that reading is a widespread cultural phenomenon and that it is of most interest when we can examine the vivid details of a reader's intellectual and emotional encounter with books. Now that the number of readers whom we can find online is exponentially greater than those accounted for in the first quantitative studies of the so-called common reader, we must think about this dichotomy and its implications for how we think about data created by contemporary readers. Simone Murray has argued that when we engage large data sets, we must not forget the aims of humanities

[38] "By the Book: What the Novelist Chimamanda Ngozi Adichie Reads While She Works," *New York Times Book Review* (23 April 2020), https://www.nytimes.com/2020/04/23/books/review/chimamanda-ngozi-adichie-by-the-book-interview.html.
[39] See also Pawley's discussion of categories, the metrics that can be calculated based on them, and statistical assessment of those numbers in "Seeking Significance," 148–49.

research.[40] Sternfeld similarly acknowledges the tension between how historians have long worked with primary sources and how those materials are transformed by digital documentation.[41] I would argue that we must extend the logic of these contentions about our methods to our subject matter. For all that what many, many voices that tell us about their reading may be most readily understandable when they become data, if we attend to their words, they show us the individuality of their feelings for books and things we may not have expected prolific readers to say. To see the data sets of Nerdfighters' descriptions of their reading as humanistic evidence means looking beyond what a computer can tell us they say to what their words say. If we want to see what reading means in their lives, not just what they read, we must listen to their voices.[42] To do so is, necessarily, a complex undertaking.

The tandem considerations of how we recognize that individuals' words make up a data set and the mechanisms that studying them involves a commitment to mixed-methods studies. Further, this case study of a reading community indicates that mixed-methods studies are not linear, but iterative, in their workings.[43] Use of this intellectual strategy enables us to read data sets, rather than to mine them for particular, already anticipated, content. It acknowledges both differences from and continuity with the way readers have been understood before computers could capture the details of their approaches to books, so that it is not simply topic that unites a discipline expanded by new methodologies, but philosophy. It reflects a pronounced commitment to enhancing our collective, disciplinary thinking about the ways that what it means to read can alter with time and by place, rather than eliding changes with sporadic, token nods to change that fall away when we consider the larger picture.

Christine Pawley has argued that understanding the "reading choices" of "millions of ordinary readers who lived out their lives in anonymity" in earlier eras requires that we "imagine them in collective terms."[44] Today, myriads of ordinary readers leave traces of their reading interests online, and a variety of technologies allow us to access and assess their responses

---

[40] Murray, "State of the Discipline," 378–79.

[41] Sternfeld, "Historical Understanding in the Quantum Age."

[42] There are certain parallels between this statement of research aims and Wayne Wiegand's advocacy for understanding "the library in the life of the user" rather than emphasizing "the user in the life of the library;" see, for example, Wayne Wiegand, "Main Street Public Library," *American Libraries* 42, nos. 9–10 (2011): 46, https://americanlibrariesmagazine.org/2011/09/27/main-street-public-library/.

[43] A discussion of iterative research methods in the study of print culture can be found in Jennifer Burek Pierce, *What Adolescents Ought to Know: Sexual Health Texts in Early Twentieth-Century America* (Amherst: UMass Press, 2011): 6–14.

[44] Pawley, "Seeking Significance," 145.

to books. One example of how such numbers can be refined and made more manageable, Nerdfighters' voices can be found and collected from all the outpourings on the Internet because they belong to a community. Evidence may be difficult to parse because of the scale of these responses, in contrast with the older problem of archival scarcity, but we still construct perceptions of readers first by understanding them as a community, before turning to the utterances and images that characterize their relationships with books.[45]

Both John and Hank Green contend that it is possible to create communities only if we "imagine others complexly," seeing this premise as the basis for stronger relationships, mutual understanding, and work worth doing.[46] This philosophy urges us to augment the digital media and quantitative methods that allow us to identify the patterns in Nerdfighters' discussions, like favorite authors and numbers of books read annually; qualitative analysis reveals other sorts of stories about the experience of reading. Much as Walsh, in her study of how James Baldwin's words were tweeted in support of the Black Lives Matter movement, concluded that no matter how many times this eminent writer's words were recirculated, it did not reflect "a single reproduced Baldwin" nor a "single monolithic group of Twitter users," examining the qualitative responses to the Nerdfighteria Census tells us that a single kind of reading does not arise in this online community.[47] This is not to shrug off the possibility of knowledge and understanding but to insist on complexity, on the idea that multiple voices and differences are inherent in community. Community represents a gathering point, a locus of conversation, rather than uniformity.

Evidence of reading provided by Nerdfighteria tells us that engaging with books and media is full of ambiguities as well as the enjoyment often associated with leisure reading. Part of what unites Nerdfighteria as a community, then, is this willingness to speak honestly about their reading, to admit their imperfections as readers. For the most part, many of them live during a time and in places where literacy is widespread and misreading or disregard for a book is far from dangerous. Because of their freedom and their trust in the audience for their words, what they tell us when they talk about reading is a nuanced story that calls attention to the ways we

---

[45] Other studies of contemporary readers that collect data from communities are discussed in A. Lang, ed., *From Codex to Hypertext: Reading at the Turn of the Twenty-first Century* (Amherst: University of Massachusetts Press, 2012).

[46] Hank Green, "Changing Our Business a Bit," *Vlogbrothers*, YouTube video (7 Oct. 2016), https://www.youtube.com/watch?v=p0McA9BDHEU.

[47] Melanie Walsh, "Tweets of a Native Son: The Quotation and Recirculation of James Baldwin from Black Power to Black Lives Matter," *American Quarterly* 70, no. 3 (Sept. 2018): 534.

study large data sets. Instead of trusting that a computer can tell us what they are saying, we must involve them in the process.

Conclusion: About Evidence and the Use and Misuse of Data[1]

Robert M. Hauser

s Executive Officer of the American Philosophical Society, I was
asked to join the wrap-up panel of the July 2020 APS conference,
Evidence: The Use and Misuse of Data. My fellow panelist was the
eminent historian J. R. McNeill, and our discussion was moderated by
APS Librarian, Patrick Spero. Most of the presentations at the conference
focused on the use of evidence in historical research. As a sociologist,
demographer, and social statistician, I brought different perspectives and
issues to the discussion—issues that were neglected in the conference
presentations. For example, in the social and behavioral sciences there is
increasing pressure and, fortunately, practice, favoring the sharing of data,
code, and documentation as a means of establishing the validity of published
findings.[2] Also, I have mentioned new sources and forms of data that may
inform future historical research. Yet, in my reading of the chapters, and
in our closing conversation, I have been able to identify key themes and
issues that transcend academic disciplines.

It is fitting, I think, that the American Philosophical Society has
commissioned a book about the use and misuse of evidence at this time.
A large fraction of the American population is enmeshed in vacuous fanta-

---

[1] My thanks go to Linda Greenhouse, J. R. McNeill, and Patrick Spero for helpful comments on earlier
drafts of this text. Of course, I am responsible for all errors, omissions, and gaffes.
[2] National Research Council and Committee on National Statistics, *Sharing Research Data*, eds. Stephen
E. Fienberg, Margaret E. Martin, and Miron L. Straf (Washington, DC: National Academies Press, 1985);
National Research Council, Science,Technology, and Law Panel, Policy and Global Affairs Division, *Access
to Research Data in the 21st Century, An Ongoing Dialogue among Interested Parties: Report of a Workshop*,
Compass series (Washington, DC: National Academies Press, 2002); National Research Council, Panel on
Data Access for Research Purposes, and Committee on National Statistics, *Expanding Access to Research
Data: Reconciling Risks and Opportunities* (Washington, DC: National Academies Press, 2005), http://
www.nap.edu/books/0309100127/html/; Committee on Science Engineering and Public Policy et al., *Ensur-
ing the Integrity, Accessibility and Stewardship of Research Data in the Digital Age* (Washington, DC:
National Academies Press, 2009).

sies that deny medical and epidemiological science, climate change, electoral outcomes, and other elementary, readily observable, and repeatedly reproduced facts. And it is not merely among the general public that prevailing conceptions of evidence are in question. Thus, this book, I think, exemplifies the Society's mission of promoting useful knowledge.

In the opening, keynote session of the conference, Richard Shiffrin, Stephen M. Stigler, and Kathleen Hall Jamieson—all Members of the American Philosophical Society—were asked to offer a broad view of the assessment of evidence. As they explained there are, presently, both controversy and discourse about the quality of evidence and the methods by which it is assessed in every field of literature, art, and science. To make a long story short, whatever the issue and method, there is a common and indispensable role for dispassionate, informed, expert judgment. To that, my fellow discussant, J. R. McNeill, wisely added, persuasive evidence is often convergent evidence from divergent sources. In my opinion, those are two of five leading themes of the conference. A third is that, under some circumstances, evidence sufficient to support or disconfirm a query cannot be assembled, either because there is no known way to do that or because no such evidence exists. Worse yet, the creation of data is itself contingent on potentially fallible or biased human activity. The fourth theme is that reading—what is read, how it is read, who reads it, and the effects of that reading—significantly affects the creation, use, and effects of evidence. Last, but by no means least, is that, in many fields of research and scholarship, future knowledge will likely depend on new forms of evidence.

THE FUTURE OF EVIDENCE

The importance of new sources and forms of evidence was elaborated in the final session of the conference, a conversation among historians J. R. McNeill and Patrick Spero, and a nonhistorian—this writer. It was prompted by McNeill's erudite and provocative Presidential Address to the American Historical Association, "Peak Document and the Future of History."[3] Rather than relying mainly on documentary evidence, McNeill argued, historians of the future will increasingly depend on physical and biological evidence. As one example, he pointed to the LiDAR (light detection and ranging) technology, which has identified a vast array of previously unknown Mayan

---

[3] J. R. McNeill, "Peak Document and the Future of History," *The American Historical Review* 125, no. 1 (2020): 1–18.

structures and roadways in northern Guatemala—suggesting that the region was once populated by millions. Another surprising finding, based on analyses of mitochondrial DNA, has shown that the antecedents of the present-day population of Iceland were not primarily of Scandinavian origin, as suggested by Norse legend, but were primarily Irish and Scottish. Because mitochondrial DNA is passed on from mothers to daughters, the implication may be that "The social origins of Iceland now looked more likely to involve Viking slavers and abducted women."[4] Goldstein's genetic history of the Jews is an another example of such work.[5] Recently, genetic analysis has shown that skeletal remains at Roopkund, a remote location high in the Himalayas, are, mysteriously, of Mediterranean origin.[6]

Such findings, the questions they raise, and the likelihood of more to come, imply that both the training of historians and the conduct of historical research will change. To be sure, histories have long been informed by nondocumentary sources. McNeill notes that, "Africanists focused on periods prior to 1800 have for decades summoned considerable ingenuity to work with oral traditions, archaeology, historical linguistics, and other tools of their trade rarely needed by those of us who work in document-rich environments."[7] Gary Nash's masterful history of Philadelphia is built around the analysis of preserved physical artifacts, largely those of the upper and lower classes.[8] Archeological contributions to history have long rested on the recovery of preserved artifacts—including human remains.[9] However, scientific developments, like genetic analysis and laser-based surveillance, have vastly altered the way that histories are created.

As McNeill wrote, "Paleogenomicists, paleoclimatologists, paleopathologists, paleo-everything are flooding the scientific landscape with new information about the human past and other pasts that infringe upon the human."[10] Thus, beyond skill in the use of documentary evidence, would-be

---

[4] McNeill, "Peak Document and the Future of History," 2.

[5] David B. Goldstein, *Jacob's Legacy: A Genetic View of Jewish History* (New Haven, CT: Yale University Press, 2008).

[6] Éadaoin Harney et al., "Ancient DNA from the Skeletons of Roopkund Lake Reveals Mediterranean Migrants in India," *Nature Communications* 10, no. 1 (2019): 1–10.

[7] McNeill, "Peak Document and the Future of History," 5.

[8] Gary B. Nash, *First City: Philadelphia and the Forging of Historical Memory* (Philadelphia: University of Pennsylvania Press, 2002).

[9] For example, Fabio M. Guarino et al., "Recovery and Amplification of Ancient DNA from Herculaneum Victims Killed by the 79 AD Vesuvius Hot Surges," *Turkish Journal of Biology* 41, no. 4 (2017): 640–48; Estelle Lazer, *Resurrecting Pompeii* (New York: Routledge, 2009); Estelle Lazer et al., "Inside the Casts of the Pompeian Victims: Results from the First Season of the Pompeii Cast Project," *Papers of the British School at Rome* (2015): 1-36; Pierpaolo Petrone, "The Herculaneum Victims of the 79 AD Vesuvius Eruption: A Review," *Journal of Anthropological Sciences* 97 (2019): 69–89.

[10] McNeill, "Peak Document and the Future of History," 4.

historians will have to become at least conversant with scientific concepts, findings, and technologies. Their research projects—rather than remaining one-person operations—will increasingly be undertaken by multidisciplinary teams. Breadth in the training and practice of historians will remain important, especially because, as McNeill has noted, convergent evidence is a key to validity in historical accounts.

From my own disciplinary perspective, that of sociology and demography, I will add that the methods of these fields, applied to both documentary and nondocumentary evidence will—or at least should—inform historical analyses of the future. One of the many possibilities is the development of new data and analyses to feed the movement of "history from below," that is, history that is based on the life experiences of ordinary people, rather than the elites who have been most likely to create documentary records. For example, Song and Campbell have reviewed the use of genealogical databases to inform historical studies of social mobility and related phenomena.[11] More specific, bureaucratic records and population registers have added greatly to analyses of Chinese history.[12]

The likelihood that future research and scholarship will depend increasingly on new forms of evidence was exemplified in the chapters by Mark Turin and Joshua Sternfeld, which present contrasting accounts of evidentiary openness and invisibility in the age of big data. Turin describes and interprets the 20-year history of Digital Himalaya, a collaborative project to find, digitize, and distribute visual ethnography from the Himalayas (http://www.digitalhimalaya.com/). Turin and his colleagues faced questions about whether to focus on raw footage or edited documentaries—strongly preferring the former. They shared the digital holdings with the communities from which they came as well as Western scholars; they learned in that process that, over time, Himalayan natives were quite as able as their peers to access materials on the Web, while the latter often preferred the DVDs that were originally prepared for native consumers. In the end, Turin reports, the ethnographies were preserved in multiple sites,

---

[11] Xi Song and Cameron D. Campbell, "Genealogical Microdata and Their Significance for Social Science," *Annual Review of Sociology* 43 (2017): 75–99.

[12] James Z. Lee and Cameron D. Campbell, *Fate and Fortune in Rural China: Social Organization and Population Behavior in Liaoning 1774–1873*, vol. 31 (Cambridge, UK: Cambridge University Press, 2007); James Lee, Cameron Dougall Campbell, and Shuang Chen, "China Multi-generational Panel Dataset, Liaoning (cmgpd-ln) 1749–1909: User Guide" (Ann Arbor, MI: Inter-University Consortium for Political and Social Research, 2010); Xi Song, Cameron D. Campbell, and James Z. Lee, "Ancestry Matters: Patrilineage Growth and Extinction," *American Sociological Review* 80, no. 3 (2015): 574–602; Bijia Chen et al., "Big Data for the Study of Qing Officialdom: The China Government Employee Database-Qing (CGED-Q)," *Journal of Chinese History* 4, no. 2 (2020): 431–60; Cameron Campbell and James Z. Lee, "Kinship and the Long-Term Persistence of Inequality in Liaoning, China, 1749–2005," *Chinese Sociological Review* 44, no. 1 (2011): 71–103.

and access has become possible through applications other than the original project website. Thus, through the continuing development of storage and dissemination technologies, the project succeeded beyond the expectations of its creators, but in ways they could not have anticipated.

Sternfeld describes the ways and reasons why artificial intelligence (AI), that is, algorithmically based information applications, create "black boxes" that limit human understanding of how they were created, how they work, and their consequences – some of which cannot be understood by their creators, let alone those affected by them. To some degree, one might think that AI applications are no different from other exogenous influences, for example, pandemics, volcanic eruptions, or tornadoes. But what's different is that AI applications are human intellectual creations. Sternfeld's chapter offers a cautionary example of the widespread use and judicial acceptance of COMPAS, a proprietary application that purports to predict the likelihood that an arrestee will become a recidivist. The opaqueness of the AI application is multiplied by the tendency of its creators to treat the application as proprietary, thus hiding both the algorithms and the data they have been fed.

Examples of institutions and individuals creating new data sources abound and opportunities for new research questions spurred by these sets are only growing. The American Philosophical Society is actively participating in the creation of new forms of data from documentary records that were previously inaccessible or available only in narrative form. Completed digital projects now include the creation of a publicly accessible database of Benjamin Franklin's post-office records from the mid-eighteenth century, late eighteenth-century indentures in Philadelphia, and nine-teenth-century records from the Eastern State Penitentiary (https://www.am philsoc.org/center-digital-scholarship). Work is now underway to increase the temporal coverage of Franklin's postal records and to create a database of his business ledgers. It is notable that Franklin's records were not thought worthy of inclusion in the Yale project that has preserved, analyzed, and published his writings, yet they provide a wealth of information about ordinary lives, social networks, and social organization in Colonial America.

More recent data sources will also nourish future histories. There are many well-curated data archives. IPUMS (Integrated Public Use Microdata Series), at the University of Minnesota, now preserves and distributes linked Census records that cover America's history since the presidency of Washington (https://ipums.org/), along with many other historical statistical data. IPCSR (Interuniversity Consortium for Political and Social Research) at the University of Michigan is the largest repository of social surveys in the United States (https://www.icpsr.umich.edu/).

The National Opinion Research Center's General Social Survey has created a time series of cross-sectional surveys of the US population from the 1970s onward in which most items have been repeated over many years (https://www.norc.org/Research/Projects/Pages/general-social-survey .aspx). The Panel Study of Income Dynamics has continuously followed a panel of Americans (and their family members) since the 1960s (https:// psidonline.isr.umich.edu/). The National Longitudinal Studies of Youth (a cooperative activity of the Bureau of Labor Statistics, Ohio State University, and the University of Chicago) have carried out three long-term cohort studies since the late 1960s (https://www.bls.gov/nls/). The US Department of Education has carried out longitudinal studies of school children since the 1970s (https://nces.ed.gov/surveys/slsp/). The Health and Retirement Study (https://hrs.isr.umich.edu/) and the Wisconsin Longitudinal Study (https://www.ssc.wisc.edu/wlsresearch/) are longitudinal biosocial studies of the life course in representative cohorts of Americans.[13]

In each case—and these are just a few among many—these survey-based studies were initiated to address contemporary theoretical or policy issues, but their preservation, along with public access to them, has made them indispensable resources for future historians.

EVIDENCE FROM THE PAST

The following paragraphs assess the ways in which the preceding chapters exemplify other major themes of the conference. Given the dominance of history in public perceptions of the Society and its activities, these chapters focus mainly on the availability, use, and misuse of historical evidence. This is perhaps unfortunate, for there is a far broader array of disciplines, as Shiffrin, Stigler, and Jamieson have testified, in which the validity of evidence is now in question. Three chapters offer complementary takes on the availability and use of historical evidence. Angela G. Ray chronicles the Clionian Debating Society, an organization of free Black men in Charleston, South Carolina, that was active between 1847 and 1858. Ray emphasizes the difficulties of describing and assessing the role of this organization, despite its clear and complete records, in light of the fraught social context

---

[13] Robert M. Hauser and David Weir, "Recent Developments in Longitudinal Studies of Aging in the United States," *Demography* 47, no. 1 (2010): S11–S30; Robert M. Hauser and Robert J. Willis, "Survey Design and Methodology in the Health and Retirement Study and the Wisconsin Longitudinal Study," in *Aging, Health, and Public Policy: Demographic and Economic Perspectives*, ed. Linda J. Waite (New York: Population Council, 2005).

in which its members lived and the fragmentary evidence about its members and supporters that was created and has survived.

Andrew M. Schocket offers exemplars of the misuse, often deliberate misuse, of historical data. He offers examples of twisted, unethical, and controversial uses of historical materials and, thus, argues that historians lack recognized standards for the truth of their contentions and are especially vulnerable to confirmation bias. His first example, a publication by the American Civil Rights Union (ACRU),[14] blaming Democrats for Jim Crow and celebrating Republicans' contributions to its end, strikes me as weak. The ACRU makes a pretense of nonpartisanship, but it was in fact created in the Reagan era as an advocacy organization, a right-wing counterpart to the American Civil Liberties Union. One need to look no further than another of its publications, "The Truth about Gun Control, Racism, and Genocide," to learn that the ACRU is no purveyor of historical truths.[15] Schocket's second example is the notably discredited article and book by Michael Bellesiles,[16] which falsely claimed that guns were not in wide use in early America. That this patently defective work won the Bancroft Prize and was subsequently debunked, first by a lay person and only later by scholars, is almost as much an indictment of peer review as of its author.[17] The third case, "the Iroquois Influence Thesis," is an argument that the organization of the Haudenosaunee Six Nations, was a model for the federation of the colonies. That thesis appears to be in a state of constant scholarly litigation. In my judgment, there is a plausible case that historians lack standards of truth and an equally plausible case that the variety of contexts and sources of data with which they work make the creation of such standards unlikely. With respect to the latter supposition, I think it would be hard to validate the claim that confirmation bias is any more a threat to validity in history than in any other discipline— or in everyday life.

From these two chapters, I would draw three corollaries to the first major theme of the conference: that historical narratives are doubtful and, often, controversial, when evidence is thin; that they are subject to deliberate distortion and misuse by individuals or institutions with ulterior motives;

---

[14] American Civil Rights Union, "The Truth about Jim Crow," (2014), https://theacru.org/wp-content/uploads/The-Truth-About-Jim-Crow.pdf.

[15] American Civil Rights Union, "The Truth about Gun Control, Racism, and Genocide," (2015), https://theacru.org/the-truth-about-gun-control-racism-and-genocide/.

[16] Michael A. Bellesiles, "The Origins of Gun Culture in the United States, 1760–1865," *The Journal of American History* 83, no. 2 (1996): 425–55; Michael A. Bellesiles, *Arming America: The Origins of a National Gun Culture* (New York: Alfred A. Knopf, 2000).

[17] While *Arming America* was a trade book, the preceding article was peer reviewed, and the author credited advice from eight named individuals, plus anonymous reviewers.

and that they are sometimes plagued by sheer carelessness and incompetence. In each case, independent, expert judgment is part of the remedy.

Three chapters exemplify the absence or weakness of evidence. Jutta Schickore's history of blue milk, Gordon Fraser's exploration of the hypothesis that reading advances the democratic prospect, Lindsey Grubbs's analysis of Issac Ray's writings on insanity each depict a search for the cause of an effect. Blue milk, found in the middle of the nineteenth century to be the product of a bacterium, *Vibrio cyanogenus,* was the subject of dozens of investigations, beginning in late eighteenth-century Germany. Yet, for close to 75 years, the source of this form of spoilage remained opaque, largely because of the multiplicity of factors in the production and storage of milk and the absence of a conceptual framework that could guide its discovery. Thus, until Christian Joseph Fuchs and Christian Ehrenberg examined and identified biological specimens microscopically, any number of experiments failed to identify the source of the problem or to solve it.

Fraser's admirable account of a New England woman's reading habits in the early nineteenth century is consistent with the hypothesis that reading supports democracy, which he explains in terms of the unique ability of novels and—in some cases, biographies—to create an otherwise inaccessible understanding of other people. Moreover, popular reading grew in tandem with early American democracy. However, Fraser acknowledges that there is little systematic evidence about the effects of reading, and moreover, that serious readers have always been a small and select fraction of the population.

Issac Ray tried to explain insanity and most notably, moral insanity—"emotional rather than intellectual insanity"—through case studies.[18] The study of cases remains prominent in psychiatry, as in medicine generally, not just through the time of Freud, but up to the present day. However, Grubbs's close reading of Ray's writings demonstrates that many of his case studies were borrowed from the observations of others—rather than his own clinical work—and that they presented an odd mix of medical and fictional accounts of biography in which Shakespeare's mad characters, for example, Lear and Hamlet, played a leading role. Thus, Ray's "evidence" would not stand present-day scrutiny, and Grubbs's critique exemplifies an effect of reading that stands in stark contrast to that of Fraser. In short, neither anecdotes nor haphazard collections of anecdotes are evidence.

Jennifer Burek Pierce's chapter adds to the theme of reading as evidence, but also exemplifies new forms of evidence that depend on

---

[18] Issac Ray, *A Treatise on the Medical Jurisprudence of Insanity* (Boston: Little & Brown, 1838).

network computing. Burek Pierce contrasts what we can learn from Carlo Ginzburg's account of the life of a sixteenth-century Italian miller, Menocchio[19]—an unfortunate reader who was ultimately executed by the Inquisition—with the statistical and textual records of the Nerdfighteria, an online community of thousands of readers. Not only do those records offer a quantitative record of what has been read, but also what reading has been abandoned or avoided. Moreover, the textual reports of readers provide details that parallel those in Ginzburg's account of Menocchio's reading.

As Burek Pierce has shown, new technologies may validate (or invalidate) previous findings, a fact that ties together some common themes of this book. Not only do the sources and uses of evidence continue to evolve, but the need for expert judgment in the use of evidence remains constant. I hope that the preceding text has identified these and other themes. However, it would be better to read the ten chapters in full, as I have more than once, than to take my word for it.

BIBLIOGRAPHY

American Civil Rights Union. "The Truth About Gun Control, Racism, and Genocide." (2015). https://theacru.org/the-truth-about-gun-control-racism-and-genocide/.

———. "The Truth About Jim Crow." (2014). https://theacru.org/wp-content/uploads/The-Truth-About-Jim-Crow.pdf.

Bellesiles, Michael A. *Arming America: The Origins of a National Gun Culture.* New York: Alfred A. Knopf, 2000.

———. "The Origins of Gun Culture in the United States, 1760–1865." *The Journal of American History* 83, no. 2 (1996): 425–55.

Campbell, Cameron, and James Z. Lee. "Kinship and the Long-Term Persistence of Inequality in Liaoning, China, 1749–2005." *Chinese Sociological Review* 44, no. 1 (2011): 71–103.

Chen, Bijia, Cameron Campbell, Yuxue Ren, and James Lee. "Big Data for the Study of Qing Officialdom: The China Government Employee Database-Qing (Cged-Q)." *Journal of Chinese History* 4, no. 2 (2020): 431–60.

Committee on Science Engineering and Public Policy, National Academy of Sciences, Division of Policy and Global Affairs, and Institute of Medicine. *Ensuring the Integrity, Accessibility and Stewardship of Re-*

---

[19] Carlo Ginzburg, *The Cheese and the Worms: The Cosmos of a Sixteenth-Century Miller* (Baltimore: John Hopkins University Press, 2013).

search Data in the Digital Age. Washington, DC: National Academies Press, 2009.

Ginzburg, Carlo. *The Cheese and the Worms: The Cosmos of a Sixteenth-Century Miller.* Baltimore: Johns Hopkins University Press, 2013.

Goldstein, David B. *Jacob's Legacy: A Genetic View of Jewish History.* New Haven, CT: Yale University Press, 2008.

Guarino, Fabio M., Claudio Buccelli, Vincenzo Graziano, Pietro La Porta, Marcello Mezzasalma, Gaetano Odierna, Mariano Paternoster, and Pierpaolo Petrone. "Recovery and Amplification of Ancient DNA from Herculaneum Victims Killed by the 79 Ad Vesuvius Hot Surges." *Turkish Journal of Biology* 41, no. 4 (2017): 640–48.

Harney, Éadaoin, Ayushi Nayak, Nick Patterson, Pramod Joglekar, Veena Mushrif-Tripathy, Swapan Mallick, Nadin Rohland, et al. "Ancient DNA from the Skeletons of Roopkund Lake Reveals Mediterranean Migrants in India." *Nature Communications* 10, no. 1 (2019): 1–10.

Hauser, Robert M, and David Weir. "Recent Developments in Longitudinal Studies of Aging in the United States." *Demography* 47, no. 1 (2010): S111–S130.

Hauser, Robert M., and Robert J. Willis. "Survey Design and Methodology in the Health and Retirement Study and the Wisconsin Longitudinal Study." In *Aging, Health, and Public Policy: Demographic and Economic Perspectives*, edited by Linda J. Waite, 209–35. New York: Population Council, 2005.

Lazer, Estelle. *Resurrecting Pompeii.* New York: Routledge, 2009.

Lazer, Estelle, Kathryn Welch, Dzung Vu, Manh Vu, Alain Middleton, Roberto Canigliula, Stijn Luyck, Giovanni Babino, and Massimo Osanna. "Inside the Casts of the Pompeian Victins: Results from the First Season of the Pompeii Cast Project." *Papers of the British School at Rome* (2015): 1–36.

Lee, James, Cameron Dougall Campbell, and Shuang Chen. "China Multi-Generational Panel Dataset, Liaoning (Cmgpd-Ln) 1749–1909: User Guide." Ann Arbor, MI: Inter-University Consortium for Political and Social Research, 2010.

Lee, James Z., and Cameron D. Campbell. *Fate and Fortune in Rural China: Social Organization and Population Behavior in Liaoning 1774-1873.* Vol. 31. Cambridge, UK: Cambridge University Press, 2007.

McNeill, J. R. "Peak Document and the Future of History." *The American Historical Review* 125, no. 1 (2020): 1–18.

Nash, Gary B. *First City: Philadelphia and the Forging of Historical Memory.* Philadelphia: University of Pennsylvania Press, 2002.

National Research Council, and Committee on National Statistics. *In Sharing Research Data* edited by Stephen E. Fienberg, Margaret E. Martin, and Miron L. Straf. Washington, DC: National Academies Press, 1985.

National Research Council, Panel on Data Access for Research Purposes, and Committee on National Statistics. *Expanding Access to Research Data: Reconciling Risks and Opportunities*. Washington, DC: National Academies Press, 2005. http://www.nap.edu/books/0309100127/html/.

National Research Council, Science, Technology, and Law Panel, Policy and Global Affairs Division. *Access to Research Data in the 21st Century, an Ongoing Dialogue among Interested Parties: Report of a Workshop.* Compass Series. Washington, DC: National Academies Press, 2002.

Petrone, Pierpaolo. "The Herculaneum Victims of the 79 Ad Vesuvius Eruption: A Review." *Journal of Anthropological Sciences* 97 (2019): 69–89.

Ray, Issac. *A Treatise on the Medical Jurisprudence of Insanity*. Boston: Little & Brown, 1838.

Song, Xi, and Cameron D. Campbell. "Genealogical Microdata and Their Significance for Social Science." *Annual Review of Sociology* 43 (2017): 75–99.

Song, Xi, Cameron D. Campbell, and James Z. Lee. "Ancestry Matters: Patrilineage Growth and Extinction." *American Sociological Review* 80, no. 3 (2015): 574–602.

Index

Page numbers in *italics* refer to illustrations.